CW00551277

Carpworld's
The BIG Interviews
REVISITED
Volume One

ANGLING PUBLICATIONS

First published in 2012

British Library Cataloguing in Publication Data

The Big Interviews – Volume One
Carp Angling
Angling Publications Ltd.

ISBN: 978-1-871700-85-5

Designed and produced by Angling Publications Ltd.

Printed by Butler, Tanner & Dennis

Books by the Interviewees

The titles and year of publication of first editions of books written by the interviewees are shown below. Some have been reissued and some have been re-published, but as far as collectors are concerned it is the first edition of a book that is the real collector's item. Many of these titles are out of print and difficult to add to a collection. Some have been published as limited-edition leatherbounds.

Ian Chillcott
Tackling Carp, 2007
Light My Fire, 2008

Dave Lane
An Obsession With Carp, 1988
A Flick of the Tale, 2008

Rod Hutchinson
Rod Hutchinson's Carp Book, 1981
The Carp Strikes Back, 1983
Carp Now and Then, 1988
Carp Along the Way, Volume 1, 2008
Carp Along the Way, Volume 2, 2009
Carp Inspirations, 2011

Lee Jackson
Lee Jackson's Carp Clinic, 2001
Just For the Record, 2009

Pete Springate
Big Carp Legends: Pete Springate

Kevin Nash is currently completing his first book, which is due to be published later this year. Look out for the eagerly awaited "Memoirs of a Carp Fisher – the Demon Eye". . We believe that are further books by Ian Chillcott, Dave Lane and Pete Springate are in the process of being written or published.

Acknowledgments and Thanks

The Interviewees
Our thanks to the interviewees, Martin Locke, Dave
Lane, Rod Hutchinson, Lee Jackson, Bob Davis, Kevin
Nash, Pete Springate, Danny Fairbrass and Ian Chillcott
(and Lynn) for giving of their time for the interviewees,
providing the pictures and captions, and for the
cooperation and additional help they have given in arriving
at the final format and content of the interviews.

Original Idea
Thanks to Nigel Banks for the idea of converting the
Carpworld big interviewees into book format and
giving them a well-deserved permanent record.

The Interviewers
Thanks to Jim Foster and Tim Paisley for conducting
the interviews in the first place and for their
efforts in bringing the book to fruition.

Production
Thanks to Jemima Musson and Julie Davies for
their production and proof reading efforts.

Special thanks to Gary Hood and Andy 'Pete' Gascoyne
for their tireless and creative efforts in converting the
raw material into the book you have before you.

Photographic material
Our thanks to anyone who has supplied photographic
material for the interviews and whose work hasn't
been already acknowledged in the above lists!

Contents

6   Foreword by Jim Foster

8   Introduction by Tim Paisley

10   Martin Locke, Part One
           from Carpworld Issue 234, March 2010

28   Martin Locke, Part Two
           from Carpworld Issue 235, April 2010

50   Dave Lane
           from Carpworld Issue 254, November 2011

66   Rod Hutchinson, Part One
           from Carpworld Issue 251, August 2011

84   Rod Hutchinson, Part Two
           from Carpworld Issue 252, September 2011

104   Lee Jackson
           from Carpworld Issue 236, May 2010

126   Bob Davis
           from Carpworld Issue 243, December 2010

148   Kevin Nash, Part One
           from Carpworld Issue 238, July 2010

170   Kevin Nash, Part Two
           from Carpworld Issue 239, August 2010

188   Pete Springate
           from Carpworld Issue 242, November 2010

208   Danny Fairbrass, Part One
           from Carpworld Issue 244, January 2011

222   Danny Fairbrass, Part Two
           from Carpworld Issue 246, March 2011

244   Ian Chillcott
           from Carpworld Issue 233, February 2010

Foreword by Jim Foster

I remember the day well – it was a Saturday afternoon in late-November 2009 and I was at the Carp Society's annual show at Sandown Racecourse, catching up with a few old mates, looking at the latest tackle innovations and generally enjoying myself. I'd left the angling industry some 18 months earlier to work in publishing with Haymarket Media Group on titles as diverse as Classic & Sports Car, Autocar and Autosport and was now living locally; so when I spied Tim working hard on the Angling Publications stand – pushing his latest book releases – I thought I'd wander over and say hello.

There's something about Tim that commands respect. I have always felt that way, even when I was a competitive editor at the helm of Total Carp. Perhaps it was the fact that Tim would always find time to say 'hello' and express an interest in my life, despite the fact that I ran a rival title and was employed by the opposition. Or perhaps it was the fact that here was a man, pushing 70 years old, who possessed an incredible intellect, an analytical writing style unmatched in angling journalism, as well as a maintained passion for all things carp fishing that would see him travel across the Continent in pursuit of huge fish when most men his age would be more content to sit in their back garden, supping tea whilst tending to a flower bed. Not to mention his involvement in angling politics, helping support and grow the industry... Put bluntly, carp fishing as a sport would not be where it is now, were it not for the vision of Tim Paisley (or the 'Godfather', as my carping friends and I refer to him. Come to think of it, he is a kind of Yorkshire version of Marlon Brando's character, Vito Corleone, in Coppola's Godfather part 1 masterpiece)!

So, there I was, walking up to his stand, my eyes briefly distracted by his able and thoroughly beautiful lieutenants, Jemima and Pippa. He greeted me in his usual fashion, shook my hand and looked me straight in the eye with those piercing blue orbs he has; attired as usual in his trademark black tracksuit bottoms and a white top. The light glinted mischievously in his pupils as he contemplated what he was going to say next. I could sense his brain whirring. "Come over for a job?" he quipped in his northern accent. (Martin Ford had recently departed the editorship of Carpworld.) I laughed and said no, though I was definitely interested in some freelance work, if he had any, seeing as I was still in the publishing game but not working for any rival titles. We quickly got onto the subject of the Big Interview – and that was that, deal done, though I seem to remember I had to negotiate quite hard to get the rate I wanted (ever the businessman, our Tim). And so it was that I'd been commissioned to produce a series of Big Interviews, each one some 10,000 words long – a few longer! – to be published over the next couple of years in Carpworld.

I was delighted. I'd written in the past for Total Carp, Advanced Carp and was to add Carpworld to that list. And, I'd get to meet up with some of the legends of carp angling, most of whom I knew anyway, but all of whom I'd not seen for a while. I travelled around the country to interview them and accumulated many great memories in the process – Chris Ball at his home in Dorset, watching bullfinches in his back garden. Being ambushed in a dark alleyway at Dinton by Dave Lane and Paul Forward, who were hiding in bushes before catapulting me with rock-hard 18mm boilies (the sods). Seeing Chilly's unfeasibly large, yellow truck on the forecourt of his house in Aldershot and talking to him about his 18 years' service for our country in the Paras. Welcoming Terry Hearn to my house in Twickenham, before fishing with him in a secret swim on the tidal Thames: we didn't catch anything that evening, but fishing with Tel on the Thames must be the angling equivalent to playing football with the England team at Wembley. Visiting Lockey at his warehouse in Kent, listening, riveted, as he recounted the story of his Rainbow whacker – and how he almost lost his life after getting mown down by a car near Savay in the late-1980s. Seeing Lee Jackson's koi pond, drinking a bottle or three of wine with him before being sexually assaulted on my left leg by his dog, 'Ari!

All fabulous stories, and more, all reworked and collected in one place, in this book and in the volume to follow. It's been a pleasure putting the words together for the interviews I conducted. I hope you enjoy them. See you at a carp show soon!

BELOW
Jim with a mid-30 from his current syndicate water.

Introduction by Tim Paisley

When I was handed back the editorial reins to Carpworld after Martin Ford left us for pastures new at the back end of 2009, I was keen to have a regular series of big interviews in Carpworld. But big interviews are very time-consuming and I didn't know if I would be able to fit them into my already-stretched semi-retired life. Then a guardian angel appeared in the shape of one Jim Foster, former editor of Advanced Carp Fishing, and a friend dating back to the '80s. As he describes in the Foreword, he reintroduced himself to me at a carp show, explained that he was still involved in publishing – but in a non-angling sphere – and wondered if there were any freelance opportunities in connection with creation of Carpworld material. I thought for at least a nanosecond, and then asked him how he felt about taking on a series of interviews for Carpworld. We agreed a shopping list, and his remuneration, and a series of Big Interviews was commissioned. Some of those interviews form the basis of the chapters that appear in the pages that follow, while some of the interviews that appear here were put together by me. The selection in the pages that follow represents only a percentage of the interviews we have on file from the last few years, and the collection here has no element of 'Who's Best' about it. It is based purely on trying to achieve a balance between this volume and the next one.

For the sake of the book the format of the interviews has been changed, but not the content. We have followed the current popular media idiom of removing the questions and letting the text speak for itself. It is a contradiction but interviewers tend to be an intrusion in an interview! (If you watch the interviewers' egos at work in MTV interviews you will understand what I mean!) So the content that follows is based on the interviewees telling their own story in their own words based on questions asked by the interviewer. Most of the interviews are with anglers who have more to offer than an impressive list of carp captures, but they are all big men in carp circles, and outstanding achievers in one way or another. What follows is not a long list of carp-fishing results but a book of memories and reflections on the background to the achievements of a remarkable set of people.

I've had the job of converting the question and answer interviews to straight text, and a fascinating exercise it has been, too! I conducted some of the interviews, and, prior to publication in Carpworld, I read those Jim carried out on our behalf at least twice. But when I came to remove the questions and focus on the content I was amazed at some of the revelations the interviews contained. The background to much of our carp-fishing history is rewritten here. The readership barely needs reminding of the stunning carp-fishing results of Pete Springate, Dave Lane, Lockey, Lee, Chilly et al, but the memories of Bob Davis, going back to the start of the evolution of the Colne Valley as a prime carp area, his friendship with Lenny Middleton and

Kevin Maddocks, and his involvement with the start of the Carp Society merit the permanent record featured in Bob's interview. Likewise, the efforts that went into the evolvement of the successful companies run by Kevin Nash, Martin Locke, Danny Fairbrass and Rod Hutchinson down the years warrant the permanent record they are accorded here.

I have bookshelves full of biographies and autobiographies. People interest me, hence my own fascination with interviews. My collection of biographies and autobiographies reflects my interest in people, and the background to their achievements. Why are some people so much more successful than others? How did they arrive at the position they are in now? What makes them tick? What are their strongest memories looking back down the thorny, or rosy, path? Wanting to know the answers to those questions is the basis on which the Big Interview subjects are selected in the first place. The common denominator, of course, is that as achievers they have all been inspired by carp, as have the interviewers!

The interviews are by no means intended as definitive outlines of the interviewees' lives in angling and carp fishing. Some follow that format; some are merely a reflection of the latest adventures of the carp angler in the spotlight, and their reflections on some of the latest episodes in their lives. Some are writers whose work appears regularly in the media; others choose to be less high profile in print. For those readers who wish to become more familiar with some of our interview subjects we have included a list of their books in the introductory pages. (At the time of writing neither Martin Locke nor Kevin Nash had published a book, although both have eagerly-awaited books in the process of being written, or in production.)

What follows is a terrific read. The book was suggested by a member of our editorial team, Nigel Banks. The original material was supplied by yours truly, Jim Foster, and the interviewees, and has been converted into the book you have before you by the tireless Jemima Musson and the creative Gary Hood. Our thanks to them, and to Martin Locke, Dave Lane, Rod Hutchinson, Lee Jackson, Bob Davis, Kevin Nash, Pete Springate, Danny Fairbrass and Ian Chillcott (and Lynn) for making what follows possible. If you enjoy the book then look out for Volume Two!

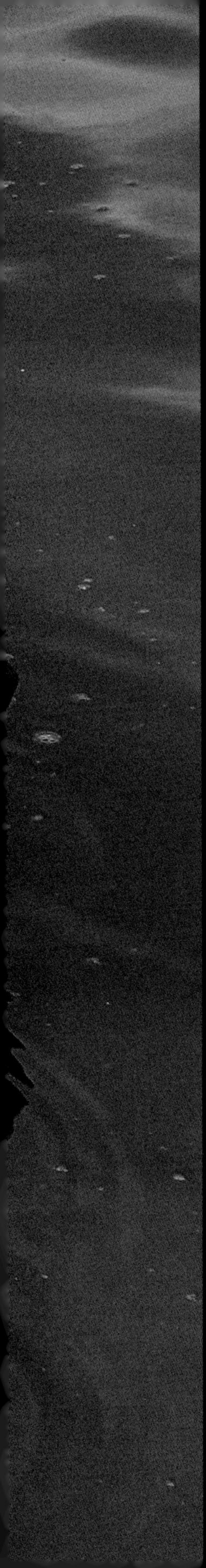

Carpworld's Big Interviews Revisited

Martin

Locke

Talking to Jim Foster • Part One

From Carpworld Issue 234

'Lockey' has always been a bit of a hero to me. Martin frequently caught the biggest carp in the lake he's fishing, whether that be Sally from Savay, Chop Dorsal from a Herts club water, Benson from Bluebell, or that jaw-dropping 94-pounder from Rainbow Lake. Lockey is larger than life but I have always been struck by his modesty and lack of self-importance. He's into carp fishing because he loves it, not because he wants to be in the magazines. Martin is still very much at the helm of the company he set up in the mid-1980s, Solar Tackle, and he's one of carp fishing's great innovators. We start with Martin reflecting on his Rainbow experiences and the capture of that incredible world record of 94lb.

M y world record carp came from Rainbow Lake (near Bordeaux). My first trip was just over five years previously in December 2006. A good friend of mine from Holland, Marco, put me onto the venue before it was getting too much publicity, because those 'in the know' realised it had some very special fish that were growing to huge sizes. Marco said he'd booked a swim for the first week of December and would I like to go? Of course I would! I later saw that Paul Hunt had caught a 74-pounder from the place, so I thought, 'There's something in this Rainbow Lake', and as the weeks ticked down I got more and more excited. It's a long journey down to the lake; it takes nine or 10 hours on the road. Usually we take the Eurotunnel to Calais on the Friday morning, then do the drive and get to Rainbow in the evening. We sleep on bedchairs for the night, then on Saturday morning meet the anglers who are leaving. You say hello to them, find out how they've done, and discover how the lake is fishing. There's always a really good camaraderie at Rainbow, a fantastic and unique atmosphere.

I hadn't seen many pictures of the lake before I went, but I had all sorts of images in my mind as to how it might be. I'd heard there were lots of islands and that it was very beautiful, but because it was December it was dark when we got there that first time, so I had to wait just that little bit longer to get a glimpse of it. When I arrived, I saw that there were a few pictures of the lake dotted around the clubhouse.

I said to the owner, Pascal, whilst looking at one of the photos, "What swim is THAT?" He replied that that particular photo was an image of Swim 19. The photo was just unreal, looking out through the islands over the lake on a really misty

PREVIOUS PAGE
Check out the width of these massive rainbow fish.

BELOW
Rainbow Lake from the air. Swim 12, where Lockey caught the world record carp is clearly marked.

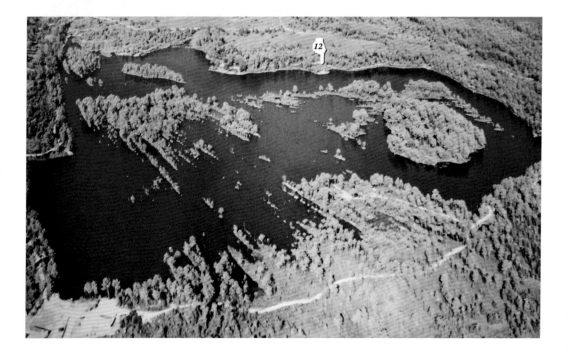

morning. Then, on the Saturday morning, it was time to see it for real. I still had this image in my mind – that the double swims wouldn't be very big, that there would hardly be enough space to peg the bivvies, that it would all be really tight. Then I saw Rainbow for the first time. That was when it hit me – I experienced one of the biggest 'wow factors' I have ever had. I was looking out from Swim 19, the one I'd seen in the clubhouse. I thought to myself, 'This place is unreal: I'm going to have to spend the rest of the week here!' Life isn't so bad when you have that view to wake up to in the morning. The water quality of Rainbow is perfect. There's the right balance of stock with predators, plus there are very few silver fish, so nearly all the introduced bait gets eaten by the carp at some stage. Perhaps it has something to do with the way Pascal runs it as a fishery. Once a year in February, he puts in about 10 tonnes of lime, or chalk powder, to make the pH

TOP
The rods raised in the left-hand side of Swim 19.

ABOVE
Fun for all the family! Martin with wife Wendy and baby daughter Charlotte posing with a big mirror caught from Swim 19.

of the lake absolutely optimum for the carp. I'm not a fishery scientist, so I don't know for sure what effect that would have, but I do know that Rainbow is just the perfect environment for carp.

It is peaceful, too. The silence on a still night is indescribable. When you hear your alarm going off in the middle of a quiet night, it's blood-curdling, it sends your pulse racing. I don't think there's anywhere you can fish that's more exciting, certainly in carp fishing. People think that because it's Rainbow you must get hassled by other anglers, and because it's booked so far in advance it must be busy. It's a common misconception that there are loads of people crammed in, fishing shoulder to shoulder. That's not the case, there are 13 swims (mostly doubles) in 100 or so acres. It's also broken up by literally hundreds of islands, some of which aren't more than little tufts of grass; others more than an acre. The topography of the lakebed is pretty savage. You go out in a boat with the echo sounder and it's mad. There are vertical drop-offs like cliff faces descending from 12in or so to well in excess of 20ft. There are bars, channels, humps – the lot. It's hard to describe. You wonder what they were thinking of when they excavated it. Anyway, the end result is a lake with loads of hiding places for the carp, and brain damage for any carp angler trying to suss them out! I think they stopped excavating around 1962 (the year I was born), so it's a well-established lake now. But on that first visit I wasn't worried about the history of the lake, I was thinking about the fish that were in it – I wanted to get on them and catch them. Sorry if I keep going on about it, but the tension in the air, the camaraderie between anglers, it's unlike anywhere else. For me, the only other lakes I've fished that felt anything like Rainbow were Brooklands in the '70s and Savay in the '80s, though for different reasons.

Rainbow is the kind of place I like fishing because of the challenges, the methods of fishing you have to employ – for instance, the Heath Robinson gadgets you need to make while you're angling to deal with certain situations. That sort of angling is perfect for me; I love that kind of stuff. All sorts of little problems might, or might not, happen while you're fishing Rainbow, which keeps you on your toes. Thinking of ways round problems is what I try to do wherever I am fishing. The place

BELOW
Looking out from the bivvy on a Swim 19 sunset.

BOTTOM
The use of a boat for baiting up, dropping rigs and playing fish is essential when fishing Rainbow. Here, Martin returns to the bank after getting the better of another Rainbow resident.

is definitely a bit of a one-off when it comes to the kind of tactics you have to employ. It's certainly different to anything I have experienced in England. For one, I hadn't used boats before that first trip. You turn up at Rainbow and you pretty much have to use boats. Every swim has a boat in it for you – they're good too, there's no need to take an inflatable with you. But using them is a different thing! I take an electric motor with me, complete with batteries. It's like driving a car, in that when you start learning how to manoeuvre it's a bit daunting, but after a while you can handle it easily. The better you can use a boat, the more you enjoy your fishing at Rainbow. There are swims where you can cast to showing fish, but for the most part you boat out your baits and have a look around with the echo sounder to help pick your spot. In some swims it's pretty obvious where to fish, in others, locating what you think will be the right spot takes a bit of sorting out.

You don't have to go out for the fish every time you hook one in every swim, but I prefer to get in the boat for two reasons – firstly, because I am confident in it, but also because of the bars. A lot of people, when they see Rainbow for the first time, are surprised at the lack of visible snags. But you use the boat when you hook a fish because of the bars – a lot of them run parallel to the bank and, as I said, some of them are only just below the surface before dropping down 20ft or so. This means I'd sooner get in the boat and get over the top of the fish, rather than chance it by playing it from the bank and pulling the fish over the bars. As long as the carp isn't snagged when you get in the boat, you're usually OK.

Because that first trip was in December we were a little unsure of whether we were going to catch anything. We knew we'd give it our best shot, but we were so excited to actually be there that catching was almost incidental. After the drive down you tend to be a bit knackered, which means that – from my point of view at least – you're not fishing at your best until Monday, or maybe even Tuesday. You put the rods out, cook up your particles, then by Saturday evening collapse into bed, almost hoping for a quiet night. Well, the carp didn't allow me that luxury. I caught my first Rainbow fish on the first night of that first trip! I woke up to find myself already holding a rod. Not only that, but I found myself slowly walking backwards up a slope, keeping the rod held high, all the time wondering where I was. Most carp anglers know what it's like when you're in a deep sleep and get a take. You react in automatic mode, but your body sometimes takes longer to fully wake up. I suddenly woke up attached to what turned out to be a 41-pounder. It was a great start. The next day I had a double, but then the next evening I was taught a valuable lesson. I hooked and lost a *really* big fish on the second evening. I was being clever with the rig – or I thought I was being clever. I had opened up the eye of the hook and put a small swivel in it before closing the eye back up again. I knew when I did it that I was making a mistake putting that rig out. I knew I didn't need to be fannying around with my presentation – I even looked at the rig before boating it out and saw that the thin wire on the swivel could get caught in the gap between the hook's eye and shank if I was unlucky. I didn't think too much of it, yet knew deep down it was wrong. I put it out there anyway – big mistake! After I'd had a take on that rod, I found myself attached to what was probably the biggest carp I had ever hooked. Then I suffered what I thought was a hook pull and I lost the fish. I wound in the end tackle and had a look at it, as you do. I hadn't had a hook pull – the swivel, with a mangled eye at one end, was still there, but the hook wasn't. Its eye had obviously been opened up by the swivel getting jammed! It cost me what was most likely a personal best. But it was a lesson learned. The next morning my mate Andy Wiggins had a take, got in the boat and landed a 50. He and I knew that the fish I had lost was probably bigger.

That evening I followed up Andy's fish with a 48 and the next morning I bagged

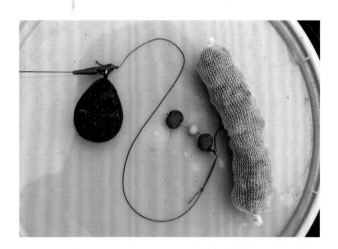

a 50 myself, at 52lb. So we'd been there three days and I'd had a 41, a 48, a 52 and lost a bigger one. Plus Andy had had his 50. And this was in December! I was thinking, 'This place is the bollocks…' Then it went quiet for three or four days before we caught a few more at the end of the week. And that was my baptism on Rainbow.

I learned from losing that big fish because after that the tactics I used to catch the world record definitely did not involve any 'fannying' about. We're talking a 12oz lead, a Size 1 hook and an 85lb hooklink. I always reckon that carp aren't the cleverest creatures in the world, but they're not stupid, either. So, on balance, and in my experience at Rainbow, I would rather sacrifice a degree of subtlety and fish with stronger gear to ensure that when I do hook a big fish, I get it in. I think that's one of the key points at Rainbow; the fish can be massive and you don't want to muck about. I reckon that fishing

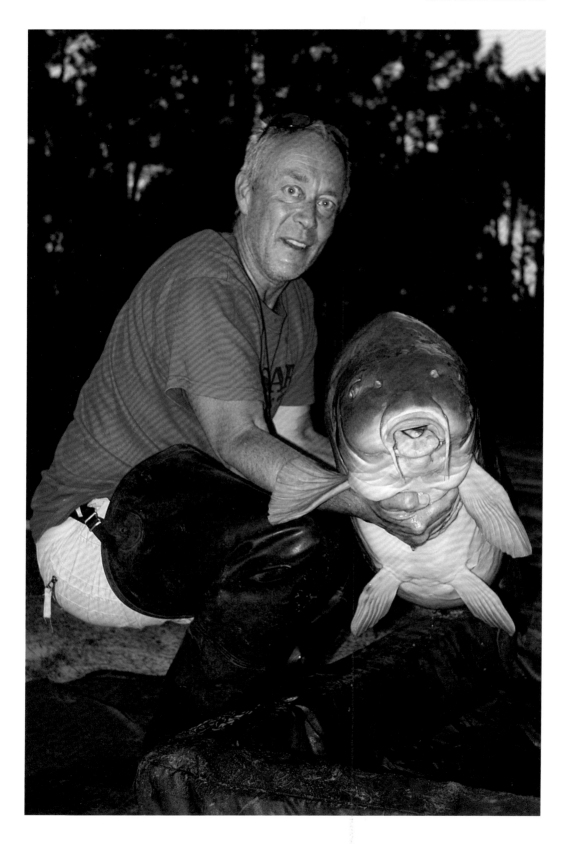

TOP
*Poised for action
as night falls
at Rainbow.*

ABOVE
*Daughter Charlotte
casting her spell
on the lake!*

heavy gear is better for the bigger fish, anyway. In my opinion, the smaller carp are, the more acutely they see things. It's the same as when kids pick up tiny grains of stuff off the carpet, stuff adults can't even see. The bigger fish don't always see the smaller details and are often more aggressive feeders. This all means that fishing heavy might mean fewer takes, but sometimes it can bring a bigger percentage of large fish. Most importantly, they will be landed. Behind the rig I use 10 metres of 85lb Ton-Up leader, which has brilliant abrasion-resistance and is great at dealing with the bars and snags. Hooklink is either 10in of the same 85lb Ton Up or our (Solar) 40lb Unleaded. Hooks I use are Size 1, maybe a Size 2, our 101 pattern. That's not big at Rainbow. And when you get some 85lb Ton-Up in your hand, it isn't as cumbersome as you might think. I've scratched my head before at Rainbow and thought, 'Shall I use a size 2 hook, or a 4? Or maybe a size 1?' But then you land a 30, 40 or 50lb fish and you can see that you were worrying about nothing – their mouths are about as big as carp mouths can get and a size 1 isn't big in comparison. In this country you change from a size 8 to a size 10 and think that makes a difference. Maybe it does, but it's whatever gives you confidence. You need to be cute about things, but you need to land your fish too, wherever you're angling. At Rainbow there's an obvious bit of physics that comes into play; I like to think that the bigger the hook and bait combination, the harder it is for the carp to get rid of. It's as simple as that. If your small hook is hanging there in a huge mouth and was streamlined going in, it's going to be streamlined on ejection as well.

We started by using 6oz leads, but when you get a bit of wind and some undertow they can move, especially because I use 34lb Dynon braided main line. Dynon is very good line; it acts a lot like mono in that it sinks down through the water, but not low into any snags, branches, or anything on the lakebed. But it is obviously a lot more sensitive than mono, thanks to its lack of stretch, so when you get a wind blowing, it can move a 6oz lead. When you hook a fish, the lead should come off the clip so you're in direct contact, then there's no lead hanging below the mouth; I'm sure that helps to keep hook pulls to a minimum. As you're getting into the boat, you'll also find that the fish won't go anywhere, as there's no pressure for it to run against, or from. Carp don't always run to snags, they run away from the pressure being exerted on them. You find that anywhere. So you need your lead to drop off on the take, and a heavy lead will do that every time. The leads are all coated, so there shouldn't be a problem with them being left in the water.

You're fishing locked-up to put the brakes on the fish. There's a cable-tie method I use for keeping the rods on the rests, because if you didn't do that, you would lose a rod on every take! It's like a javelin going into the lake... You need to fish properly locked-up to make sure that you go home with as many rods as you arrived with! So you get that sorted and stick the rod tips in the air – firstly, because it looks incredible when you get a take (!), but also for practical purposes. You fish four rods at Rainbow, each one on a single bankstick set-up. Two will be fished on one side of the swim, two on the other, with the lines high in the air and the boat sitting in the middle for ease of use: if you need to get to an outside rod you can do it pretty quickly and not have three other lines to negotiate. You also need to angle the rod tip in the same direction as the line; if you have the line going off at 45° you can kiss your rod, and fish, goodbye. The rod usually bangs straight over when you get a take – and you need to be on it fairly quickly. You don't get a good sleep most nights at Rainbow. You're on edge all the time!

On the record-breaking trip we travelled out on New Year's Day at 6.00 a.m. At one stage it looked like we weren't going to go, as there were issues at work I needed to sort out. So I only confirmed that I could go two days before the trip was due to start. Nigel Turner and I ended up in Swim 12, with Paul Brookes away to my left in 14 (there is no Swim 13). All the swims at Rainbow are booked in advance so you know where you'll be fishing before you get there. It's the way the system is at Rainbow. There are plenty of fish in the lake and there are loads of features in each swim. At some stage during the week, fish will be in your swim, probably in numbers. The biggest fish can be caught at any time, from any swim. People say there are good and bad swims at Rainbow, but to me they're all good swims. It wouldn't make a difference where I was fishing. The only preference I have is in the summer, when I take the family over. Then I need one of the swims that has room for my caravan, just so I can keep an eye on my two young daughters! And there are only a couple of swims that offer that. There are obviously some swims that people have a preference for. That's just the way it is, but when you fish the lake I think this system adds to the camaraderie because everyone is normally happy with the swim they are in, and make the best of it. There's loads of water, you have lots of features to go at wherever you're fishing and you're not staring into someone else's bivvy.

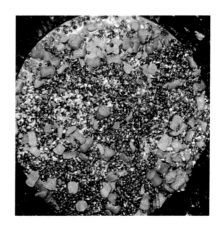

BELOW
*My Rainbow
groundbait mix.*

The islands obviously help to break it all up.

The previous two sessions I'd done in Swim 12 had seen me fish on the right-hand side. The two sides of this particular swim are like polar opposites; one's fishing at 9 o'clock, the other at 3 o'clock, so your neighbour doesn't come anywhere near your water. Anyway, in advance I had a hunch which side I'd go on, I phoned Mrs Wendy and mate Andy Wiggins and told them I fancied the left because I hadn't fished there for a couple of trips. Wendy said go left for sure and Andy said it was due to produce a big 'un, so that was my mind made up – I went on the left.

When I got in there I set everything up; the bivvy, the rods, then went out in the boat and had a good look round. The left side of Swim 12 is a little odd for Rainbow in that there isn't any one feature that really strikes you as being an obvious carp-holding area. Whatever swim I am in, if I can't find what I think are four good areas, then I won't put out four rods for the sake if it. I'll hang back and be patient until I get a feel for what's going on – you know, watching the water, seeing what's happening, getting in tune with it. This is the case even more in the winter, where you can have a long wait between takes. Sometimes, even in the best spot in the world, you can wait three or four days for a take, or even wait till the last day, so it's important to get it right and be happy with each spot. So I took my time, put out the markers in varying depths, from three metres up to five metres, at ranges of up to 150 yards out and then got the rods out. I was happy enough with them when I'd finished.

Bait-wise I always stick to what I know works. It's not rocket science. I like using Red Band aniseed-flavoured Pigeon Conditioner Seed Mix, to which I add some hemp in a 50/50 ratio. Boilie choice is the frozen Club Mix, which I air-dry before going out there. I also add Stimulin Amino Compound to some crushed boilies, just to boost attraction a little. Because the boilies are air-dried, I know they're going to stay on the Hair for days, so I have the confidence to leave them. To help concentrate some attraction around the hookbait, I fill a 4-6ins-long PVA 'sock' full of the crushed boilies. I hook it through the middle, then swing the rig over the side. I have a feeling that all the bait just lies there on top of the lead, but I've never had a tangle doing this, so I am confident to leave it out there. As long as those baits stay on the Hair, they can stay where they are. Talking to the lads who fish Rainbow, you find that a lot of the action doesn't come until the hookbaits have been in the water for 48 hours or more. You might be lucky and get a fish quicker, like I did on my first trip, but on those colder trips, if you put the baits out Saturday, I wouldn't usually expect anything until Monday at the earliest. As far as I am concerned, those rigs are now going to be staying there for the best part of the week, if necessary.

This business of leaving the baits in position for two or three days, or even longer, takes some getting used to. If you're fishing in England and you see a fish jump 30 or 40yds out, you think nothing of winding in a rod and recasting it to that fish. You'd expect to get a take, but on Rainbow, chasing the fish around just doesn't seem to work. It's almost like they are visiting the areas all the time and won't take the hookbait until they think it's safe. Perhaps that's one of the reasons why you don't tend to get a lot of action to start with; maybe the carp are polishing off the 'safer' baits that have been left in front of you from the guys who fished in the swim the week before you.

We've tried all sorts of ways of getting round this waiting period but nothing seems to work. The bait needs to be sitting at the bottom of the lake, in front of the carp, so they can see it. The longer the bait stays there, maybe the fish think the safer it is. That's the way we're thinking about it. I put the hookbaits out and from Monday onwards I feel confident. In fact, the more time that passes, the more confident I get. I put out three or four scoopfuls of bait in the winter, along with the PVA bag. This quantity changes to eight or ten scoops in the summer. The freebies go over the top of the hookbait and are also scattered in the general area, and that's it. I usually won't go out there again until I get a take.

For hookbaits I use what I call the Kebab Rig, which consists of two 14mm, air-dried Squid and Octopus Club Mix boilies at each end of a reasonably long Hair, with a plastic 8mm Everlasting 'bait' in the middle. The rubber in the middle of the two bottom baits grips the Hair tight. I like to have a gap of 5, 6 or 7mm between each of the baits, creating a kind of necklace effect. Rather than being three baits grouped together, the plastic helps keep them as three separate baits. If you put a mishmash of bait over the side, such as chops, and round and crushed boilies, having a presentation like this on the Hair means it blends in a bit better. The most important thing is to make sure the bait stays on the Hair. As such, I make sure that I use a long Hair loop and put the knot by the 'hook end' so I don't have to drag it through the boilies. Also, I use a thin 'maggot needle' to thread the baits onto the hair. Doing that means that less water gets into the bait, ensuring it lasts longer in the water.

Once the baits are in position I use what we call 'Line Biters'. Originally, these weren't designed to detect line bites, but as markers to let us know where our lines were when we were out in the boat and coming back to the swim. One of the worst things that can happen when you're fishing with a motor on your boat is to tangle your lines in the propeller, so to stop that happening we got some ping-pong balls, punched a hole in them, and glued an Abseiler backlead clip in them with some Araldite. We stuck on a bit of reflective tape from Halfords, so we could see the reflection in the torchlight and know where all the lines were at night. We'd thread the balls down the line and they'd hang there in mid air, up to 20ft from the rod tips. However, it turned out that they had another major benefit. When they were in place, every now and then you'd see one bounce around, indicating a line bite. We'd inadvertently created 20ft swing tips that really accentuated what was happening in the swim! The Line Biters showed us if fish were around, knocking into the line, that kind of thing. Sometimes a Line Biter can move around 12 or 15 times before you get a bleep or a take, it really is that sensitive. Nineteen times out of 20, if you get a line bite on your ping-pong ball, that's the rod that goes. It shows that the carp are mad for that area of food. You honestly can't believe how many times they move around with no sound coming from your alarm. I wouldn't be without them now, either in England or anywhere else.

I was getting line bites before I hooked the record fish. Nothing happened on the Sunday, then on the Monday one of the Line Biters started moving around a little bit. It wasn't subtle; it would jump up six or eight inches and then take a few seconds to settle down again. There was no doubt that it was a pull from a fish. So it was obvious that a few were mooching about – I just hoped they might be interested in feeding because it was really cold. The temperature was hovering a couple of degrees above freezing during the day, but it was much colder at night. It was a job to keep warm. There was a really sharp frost on the Tuesday night – far crisper and colder than we get in this country, maybe because there was no dampness in the air. We took the water temperature and the thermometer read 2.5 degrees !

Then, at 4.00 a.m. on Wednesday morning, things started to happen. I had a bleep, just one bleep. That might not sound like much to get excited about, but from experience at Rainbow I know that if you get a bleep and there's no wind , there's nothing else that can cause it except a carp, unless there are coypu around – which there weren't on this occasion. I knew then that there was definitely a customer investigating the bait! I was uneasy and tense! About an hour later, the same alarm bleeped once more. It was flat calm, so by now I really was on edge. Then, at 6.00 a.m., the moment I had been apprehensively waiting for happened – the indicator slowly pulled up tight to the rod.

I was straight into my boots, grabbed the life jacket and in a second was on the rod. I picked it up. There was no time to muck about putting on jackets and coats; all I had on was trakky bottoms, a T-shirt and the life jacket over the top of that! Everything was so tight it was a job to get the rod out of the rest. As I lifted into the fish, my swim mate Nigel had heard the alarm and was up and about too. Dealing with big carp at Rainbow is usually a two-man job – it's as exciting for one as it is for the other. There was then the problem getting into the boat and getting it launched. It was very slippery, so I had to take extra care to avoid slipping over. Also, it was secured via a short 2ft length of rope tied to a bank stick to stop it blowing away if the wind got up. It was so cold that the rope was frozen stiff, so we couldn't get any slack in it to release the boat. If that rope had been 20ft long, it would still have been stiff, it was that cold! So the boat had to be pulled up the bank a little to slacken the rope off, in order to get it off the bank stick. This was all done in a few seconds but at the time it seemed to take ages. Then I was into the boat and away. I shone the torch beam down the line and was off. It's usually the case that only one person goes out in a boat to net a fish. There are three main reasons why. Firstly, for balance, because another person moving around can make the boat move all over the place in the water. Secondly, you need someone on the bank for safety reasons, to raise the alarm if you get into any grief. Lastly, there's someone on the bank taking care of the other rods should they go off! (Not a problem in this instance, on this session!)

Everything needs to be right before anything happens; you have to think of every eventuality. Such as the rope attaching the boat to the shore is so short, because you don't want it hanging too deep over the side when you're playing a fish in case it decides to swim around the bow of the boat and catch on the loop. Another thing is the net in the boat has to be in the right position; the mesh can't be hanging over the side. If it is, then as you're motoring along the net can be dragged into the water and be gone! Everything has to be thought about in advance of the moment you hook a fish. Believe me, if it can go wrong, it will go wrong! The powerful headtorch that I mentioned is also very important. You need to see where your line is going and get your boat headed towards it straightaway. Without it, in the dark you're making things very difficult for yourself.

I remember it being so cold that I could hardly wind the handle of the reel as the grease was freezing up. The net was welded to the boat so badly with the frost that when I released it, there was a tearing sound that made me think I'd ripped the mesh! It felt like it was -10° with the gentle breeze that was now picking up . Anyway, I soon got out over the top of the fish and saw the reel line going directly below the boat, into a snag. I thought, 'Oh no, this is all I need.' I was in autopilot mode and bounced the tip a few times to try to get the line to ping out of the snag. Just as I was thinking I might have to resort to some drastic tactics, it came free, and before I knew it some of the 10-metre leader wasn't just off the rod tip, it was on the reel.

With that advantage, I started leaning into the fish properly. It was lethargic in the cold and wasn't doing much, but it was obvious that I'd got a very, very big carp on the end. Some reports in the non-angling newspapers quoted me as saying it was like hitting into a 'big, fossilised lump of carbon tree trunk'! Actually, it was like being locked up in a massive weedbed that will only move at that critical moment before your line gives way. I looked up at the rod bent over and saw the silhouette against the trees on the skyline – it was more than bent double. I was lifting, lifting, lifting and then lifting some more, thinking: "For f***'s sake, what is this?" It felt like the veins were popping out of my neck.

I was waiting for the rod tip to start nodding, same as playing most big fish. It was painstaking; I was moving the fish literally half an inch at a time, then whenever I got it moving I heaved even harder. I wanted to keep the momentum going. This probably went on for a minute or two, me heaving, making very slow progress. Then, suddenly, there it was, lying on the surface 4ft in front of me...

Martin pauses at this point as he thinks about what he saw at that moment. There in front of him, rolling on the surface of the lake, was a carp bigger than any other caught before (not that he knew that at the time). As he recounts the story and thinks about it, I can see him reliving that very moment through every sense in his body.

I thought, 'Oh – My – God. LOOK at the size of that!' It emerged out of the blackness into the torchlight like a massive, ghostly grey-white shape. I could see it was an absolute beast, but obviously at that moment I didn't know the significance of exactly how big it would turn out to be. I was kneeling in the bottom of the boat and from that angle, it looked like the fish was as deep as it was long. Somehow I had to get this monster into my normally perfectly adequate – but at this moment rather inadequate – landing net. I knew that the netting procedure was going to be tricky, owing to the fact that the mesh was as stiff as a board with frost, and possibly with a hole in it! I went into autopilot again and thought about what I had to do, not easy when this HUGE carp was lying in front of me. You sometimes need to think quickly at Rainbow or risk losing the fish and of all the carp I've ever landed, I certainly didn't want to lose this one! I had to react fast and it was obvious I couldn't net the fish in the conventional way. The only way was to get the fish's head 10 or 12ins in front of the spreader block and in the same movement, drop the rod, grab the net handle with two hands, poke his nose in there, then in one swoop move the net back round and bundle the tail in as well! It's hard to describe how I did it, but thankfully it went in first time – and there was no hole! I didn't have time to think about it; I just did it. Looking back on it I can best describe the moment as trying to land a hippo on a tennis racquet!! I shouted to Nigel on the bank that it was an absolute monster.

All the way back in I was thinking, 'This is ridiculous. This fish is absolutely huge.' But I wasn't bricking it – it wasn't like that. What I did think, the moment the fish was safely in the net, was how cold I felt. Adrenaline had kept the cold out until that moment. I was now freezing, shivering. So I took off the net's handle, folded the arms and positioned the fish so its nose was pointing towards the bow of the boat. Holding the net alongside, I started slowly motoring back to the bank, constantly making sure the fish was alright. In fact, I couldn't take my eyes off it. The five-minute boat ride back seemed like half an hour, but I got back eventually and gave the net to Nigel, who by now had his waders on. I jumped out, went to put on a fleece and jacket and in a few moments was back with Nigel and the fish. Then we realised that there was another problem. It was f*****g massive!! There are obviously massive responsibilities that come with handling a fish of that size, especially in the freezing conditions. We put the mat in the water to melt the ice that had formed, and then between us managed to very carefully lift the net, put the fish on the mat whilst it was in the water, taking great care that the mesh didn't give way! We then pulled the mat a small way up the bank, and an ice rink formed behind the mat as we did this! Then we zeroed the scales. Usually I'd have put the fish into one of our slings, but not this one; it was too big. It would have been like trying to wrap a pig in cling film! Nigel told me to lift up the fish to get the net out of the way, but I couldn't move it. We had to do it between us! Eventually the pair of us got it up onto the scales. Round the dial the needle went and Nigel was the first one to see it settle on 94lb.

He said: "This is a world record; it's 94lb."

"Shut up, Nigel," I replied, "It's what?"!!

At that shocking moment reality kicked in.

BELOW
"Oh. My. God. Look at the size of that!" The early January world record fish at 94lb.

"Ninety-four pounds Nige, ninety-four pounds? Do you know what you're saying?"

The camera was ready to take a quick snap of the scales and that's what I did, before getting the fish back in the water in the recovery sling. It was still dark. There's a Rainbow tradition where any fish over 25kg means a swig of this special Cognac, at whatever time – so we had a little tot each and both kept an eye on the fish until it got light. I was in a bit of a daze, no... I was in a complete daze! But at the same time I wasn't jumping up and down, punching the air. I wasn't going to *really* celebrate until I knew that the fish was OK and had swum off all right after the photos had been taken. Within a few minutes, the floats on the recovery sling were bouncing round as the fish was getting its energy back, so I knew everything was tickety-boo, which was a great moment. The significance of the capture, of it being a world record, still hasn't sunk in, and I'm not sure it ever will. It's nice to be top of the tree for a while, but it was the fact it was a carp of 94lb that really amazed me. A carp of 94lb!

At 7.00 a.m. English time I called Wendy, my mum, Andy Wigg and the lads at work and told them. Then Nigel went to get Pascal and Brooksey. Alijn Danau and Toni Schriever also came down from Swim 11. In all there were six of us there to see it photographed. We put the recovery sling on the mat in the water and dragged the mat up the bank a small way, unzipped both sides and revealed the fish. That moment was

BELOW
Thankfully, I managed to hold it long enough to get a photo or two! The other side of the world record fish.

absolutely breathtaking. No one said a word; we just looked at each other, smiling! It was just a real 'WOW' moment. Just to try to give you some idea of its size it was about 16ins across the back, not far off 2ft deep, and 45-46 inches long. The pecs were at least as big as table-tennis bats, while the front ray of the dorsal was as thick as my thumb. The dorsal fin itself was six inches high. You couldn't really hold it safely on the bank, because the second that mat was dragged up the bank, the water that was on it turned to ice. That was too dangerous, so we went back one step and put the mat in the edge of the margin. I tried to lift it there for the photos. Bear in mind it was still around -3°, with wind chill, and you'll realise it was f***ing chilly. I tried to lift it, couldn't, tried again, couldn't, then managed to get the old clean-and-jerk on it, like a weightlifter. Thankfully, the fish wasn't thrashing about and I managed to hold it long enough to get a photo or two. Seeing the fish swim off strongly was by far the best moment of the whole capture. That was the 'hands-in-the-air' moment. The other thing that amazed me was the fact it was January, when most of England was covered in snow and people couldn't get out of their front doors. Catching any carp would have been good enough, but catching one at that weight in January was just incredible.

The news of the capture spread like wildfire. It was nice sitting there a few hours later with the rods out as normal, while the rest of the world seemed to be buzzing around on the newswires talking about what had happened. It was off the scale. I was on the phone texting and talking to people constantly for the rest of the week. Kylie Minogue tweeted about it and apparently congratulated me. The fish weighed the same as her, supposedly! The Sun newspaper was on the phone, as was the Telegraph: all the fishing magazines were, and so on. One of the lads at the lake, 'Gooey', had a laptop with an internet connection, so Nigel uploaded the photos and emailed them out while we were on the bank – a bit different to how it was in the old days. Within hours of me catching the fish, people around the world knew about it; mates in California, India, Mexico, Australia... all heard about it that same day. It really was a buzz that went all over the globe, literally within hours. Apparently it got loads of hits on the search engines. I was interviewed on TV when I got back, on BBC local news. You know they have that 'and finally' kind of tongue-in-cheek feature at the end? That's what they used it for. So yes, it all caused quite a stir!

For anyone who is interested there is a video of the fish, taken by Alijn Danau, that can be seen on the Solar website. Check it out on www.solartackle.co.uk

TOP
"Yeeeeessss!"

ABOVE
Toasting the big fish with lake owner Pascal.

Carpworld's Big Interviews Revisited

Martin

———

Locke

———

Talking to Jim Foster • Part Two

From Carpworld Issue 235

In the second part of Martin's revealing interview he talks about his beginnings in fishing (in pursuit of lobsters in Scotland!); talks about the start of his carp fishing journey on his local waters in Kent; explains how he graduated to the big fish circuit waters, and then to the overseas fisheries in pursuit of monsters; admits that he would love to have been a DJ; describes his two brushes with death in the Colne Valley and his developing love of Formula One racing; and describes his iconic capture of Savay Lake's Sally, an image which is now the Solar logo.

PREVIOUS PAGES
*Lockey with Chop-
Dorsal at 50lb+
from the no-publicity
Hertfordshire
club water.*

The world record apart there are several captures from the past that are special to me. Obviously, the record fish, being the most recent, is receiving the most attention. But once the dust has settled, it would have to be Sally (the legendary Savay common) that sits at the top of my list. She's the fish on the Solar Tackle logo. If I had to identify the one capture that tops everything, it would be her. It's hard to believe that I caught her over 25 years ago. Savay was the water to be on back then: it was hallowed ground. I'd learned my trade on Brooklands and Darenth, and all the Darent Valley waters before moving on to places such as Fox Pool (Longfield). The more challenging the venue, the more determined I am to catch 'em. The challenge was one of the reasons I went to Savay. But to understand more about my fishing mentality I have to go right back to when I was a kid. I've been fishing since I was four years old. I first got into it as a youngster in Eyemouth, a small fishing village on the Borders in Scotland, where my nanna and grandpa, uncles, aunts and cousins live. I'm half Scottish, despite my London accent! The village was one of those places where everyone knew everyone else. I used go up there in the summer holidays and sit on the promenade with my grandpa and the local old boys in their flat caps, listening to their stories of their times on the seas, which was great. It was a lovely place to grow up and spend time as a kid.

I got my first fishing rod at the age of four. My nan gave it to me. It was a green, white-handled fibreglass job, about 4½ft long. At high tide I'd fish with it in the local harbour to catch juvenile coalies (podlies), flatties, and eels. Also, I was shown how to set minnow traps using big polybags on the River Eye, which progressed to fishing for the prized wild brown trout that lived there. I would go out boat fishing on the sea when the opportunity arose, then, when the tides were low, I'd venture out to the rock pools and explore. I soon discovered that the spring tide lows were the time to be in these pools as this was when the water retreated the furthest, uncovering creatures that normally live in much deeper water. What I didn't realise then was that exploring those rock pools formed the blueprint in me for wanting to catch things other people found difficult to get to grips with. Even at the age of six I wanted to bite off more than I could chew, a trait that's stayed with me to this day. I would fish every day for six weeks solid in those early years, so you could say I was a full-time angler from the age of four!

When the tide was out as far as it would go it would reveal some thick kelp beds. To be honest, it was quite dangerous for a kid to be out there, but through listening to the 'old boys', I had their experience and caution on my young shoulders. I knew where the boundaries were and spent a lot of time looking at the kelp beds in the distance before I actually went out to explore them. Looking at those kelp beds taught me a lot. I knew I had to be careful, that if I got it wrong I could have been surrounded and caught out by the rapidly incoming tide. It was a progressive thing. I'd venture a little further out each time. I'd start by catching shore crabs in the rock pools, then I wanted to catch the bigger, edible crabs. To do that, I had to slowly make my way further out, learning about the environment as I went. The old boys told me that I would be very lucky to find a lobster; even they had never heard of one being found out there. So as soon as they said that, a lobster became my target. I wanted to find one and prove to them that I could! As I said, even as a kid I wanted to bite off more than I could chew.

The lobster quest was an obsession that went on for two or three summers and started to get under my skin a little. Eventually there was a day when the tide was so far out, I thought, 'This is my opportunity.' So I went further out than before, peering into the depths of the kelp beds, lifting up huge rocks. Then I lifted a particular rock to see a pair of eyes staring back at me, plus claws. There it was; my lobster! I knew he wasn't going anywhere, so I was quite calm. I just thought, 'This is it then; I've got you,' and a huge shiver ran through me. I stuck my hand in and lifted him out!

I could have gone to the fishmongers and got a lobster there, or I could have gone out in a boat and got one in a pot. But that wasn't good enough. I wanted my own wild lobster from the kelp beds. It took three or four years but finally there I was – I'd done it!

Unfortunately I didn't manage to get a picture of him. In those days, cameras were a bit of a luxury – this was 1969 after all! I got him out of the water, put him in a rockpool closer to the shore and watched the way he wandered around. I kept him for half an hour before letting him go. I tipped my hat to him out of respect and that was that. It was a turning point in my life, although I didn't realise that at the time. I had pushed myself and ultimately achieved something that gave me the confidence to go on and fish for anything.

I was living in Belvedere at the time and used to keep on at my mum to take me out fishing. We didn't have a car, so I'm not sure how she found it, but one day we found ourselves in Dartford Park on the banks of the River Darent. I was seven now and my fishing gear was in Scotland, so a minnow net was my only weapon! I'd read some books about English crayfish, how they were rare and difficult to find, and that they only lived in some chalk streams – so of course that appealed to me and I wanted to find one. To catch the crayfish I had to look under rocks, in dark areas. Then one day I saw this tunnel-like bridge at the far end of the park. The river ran under it, and I thought, 'There has to be one under there somewhere!' So I wandered up to the bridge, despite probably being told not to by my mum had she seen me, and disappeared under it. But it was worth the trouble I got into, because, sure enough, I caught a crayfish, so I was chuffed to bits.

Then, quite literally, I noticed this light at the end of the tunnel. Being an inquisitive kid I waded towards it and emerged on the other side to find my Utopia – better known as Brooklands Lake. In the week or two that followed, I knew I wanted to fish there, but I didn't have anything in the way of tackle, so I made up some balsa wood floats and coloured them up with Airfix paint. I got a bamboo stick for a rod, cut it in half, got a ferrule from the local tackle shop, glued it on and made some line guides with safety pins – whipping them on with button thread. I wanted to go fishing, so if I couldn't afford to buy something I'd just go out and make it. That was how it worked in those days, bit like now I suppose! The lake was about a mile and a half from Dartford station, so I soon found myself on the bank angling. And that was me, just sitting there, happy as Larry, with my mum, a tartan rug and a picnic! Then an old fella walked round with his dog and asked me if I had caught anything. I said I hadn't, but that I liked it because it was nice and quiet. He retorted by saying it would be quiet, because the fishing season didn't start until the following week! That really summed up how much I knew about it then. I didn't even know there was a close season.

We're going back to when I was seven or eight. Mum got a bit worried that we might get in trouble, so she said we'd better pack up. I tried protesting by pointing out that I was only little and that the authorities wouldn't care about me, plus my float was just starting to get knocked about! But mum wasn't having any of it and off we went. When the season proper started I went back to the lake and properly began the next chapter of my angling apprenticeship: float fishing to start with, progressing through the ranks. If I needed any kit I'd make it myself, whether it was a seat box, floats, a rod rest, or whatever. It's not the same now. Back then – we're talking late 1960's-early '70s – I quickly learned how to catch tench on the float, bream on the leger, and so on. I was catching enough to keep up my interest, then I started to notice these men who sat underneath green umbrellas. These guys were a league apart. They weren't interested in what I was doing and sat on their own, in their green boiler suits. They were intimidating, fishing all night and not saying anything to anyone. It was very secretive. Mind you, I was a kid and they were all grown men, so why should they have talked to me?

I found out later that it was all happening down there. You had the likes of Jack Hilton and Fred Wilton (of HNV bait fame) fishing at Brooklands, as well as Paul Atu, Glenn Smith and Bobby Penfold, who were three of the very first carpers I met. I looked up to them so much it was unbelievable, so it's amazing to think they are still friends of mine to this day. By now, I had teamed up with Postman Pete. We met Glenn when we first started carp fishing, but there were other anglers on the banks of Brooklands whom you'd never dream of approaching. These were guys fishing the swims well out of the way. You wouldn't go near them in case you upset them. They never seemed to catch much during the days, but every now and then you'd see one of them playing a fish. This great big net would come out and the angler would walk back up the bank with his catch before weighing it and holding it for a photo. I thought, 'Cor, I'd love to see that close up.' Then one day I ended up being too close for comfort to this bloke as he caught one – and I couldn't help myself, I had to look. It turned out to be a 14-pounder, it was absolutely massive. It was then that I knew I had to have a piece of the action. So I got two paper rounds to pay for tackle and, together with the old faithful bamboo rod, saved enough to buy a fibreglass SS6 North Western blank as well as some cheap rings and a strip of leather that they used on tennis racquet handles (very trendy at the time!) to put round a reel fitting. (I still had the bamboo stick as my 2nd rod!) Then I got some Heron buzzers (that were soon modified) along with reels and various other bits and pieces. I slowly started to feel I belonged, that I had joined the ranks of the carp brigade.

ABOVE
Martin progressed from Brooklands to Darenth Big Lake.

It took me over a year to catch my first fish! It's funny – people say there weren't many carp anglers in those days, but that wasn't true about Brooklands. Saturday night could be banged out with people. The 'Tilley lamp brigade' would turn up and the 'proper' carp boys would be there – you could get 50 to 60 anglers fishing almost shoulder-to-shoulder. My first fish, a mirror, came on freelined luncheon meat and weighed 14lb 8oz. I caught it from under a tree in a corner on the A2 Bank. That was a great moment. I felt like I'd arrived when we weighed it on the old Avon scales. I was chuffed to bits! I made myself available for the rest of the day, hoping for as many of 'the boys' as possible to ask me if I'd had any last night!

That first fish was the hardest. After that I did start catching a few. We had to work at it to be successful, though. I would basically fish for the whole of the summer holiday, every week from Sunday to Friday. Then I'd spend the weekend at home before going back down there again on the Sunday afternoon. So I did do a decent amount of time in the summer, surviving on Happy Shopper Cola and ginger nuts. Yuk! A special evening would see me enjoy a bag of chips. To save money I was also using the cheapest luncheon meat I could find for bait, but that might have worked in my favour because it was the smelliest and lumpiest. If I remember rightly, I was using Tudor Queen meat, which was just as well, because if I'd bought Ye Olde Oak (a brand that is still going strong today I believe) I would have ended up eating it!

I was 14, 15 and 16 years old now. I'd go there on the train and walk to the lake from Dartford station, lugging all my gear on my back because there were no trolleys or barrows in those days. It's a very public lake and drunks and dog walkers were constantly passing by at all hours of the day and night. We weren't at all bothered and thankfully no harm came to any of us. Looking at it from today's point of view, with the media coverage making us aware of all the nasty things that go on in society, I'm sure those same things happened in those days, but we were never aware of it. In fact, I would be more worried about fishing there now than I was then. (Having said that, there are plenty of lads fishing there now with no problems, so perhaps I should pop down there for old time's sake!)

I fished Brooklands for years, whenever I could, whatever the weather, through winter and summer. I'd fish in the week during the holidays and at weekends during school terms. In the winter I'd often get to the lake to find it was frozen. When that happened I'd trudge back to Dartford station and go home on the last train, totally devastated. I learned an awful lot at Brooklands. And all the time I was learning, and didn't have much of a desire to move on. For example, there was a lot happening when it came to particles. A good lesson I learned (and something that has stood me in good stead right to this day) was witnessing what could happen when you put the right bait in front of the fish. While I was catching one or two a week, the top boys on the lake were emptying the place on peanuts. Two guys really stood out – Dickie Caldwell and Paul Gummer. They were the top two, along with several others. Their results were devastating! And because I was down there all the time, they took me under their wing. Even though I can't remember exactly how or when I was told (I certainly wasn't handed the information on a plate) I did find out what they were using!!! So I started using them and went from catching one or two fish a week to catching 25. It was ridiculous. It seemed that a different new particle would catch each year. Time and again it taught me what could be achieved if you got the right bait going in and applied it well. A couple of years later, a nut called tigers appeared. Brooklands was

BELOW
A winter-time Darenth Big Lake capture for Martin.

one of the first, if not the first, places that tigers were ever used. I didn't realise this at the time, but my mates and I were among anglers at the cutting edge of that area of carp fishing.

In 1980 I met a fella called Melvyn Streeter, who used to arrive on his moped and do day sessions in the winter. By now, I had teamed up with Mick Murray (Postman Pete had turned into a Teddy Boy/Rockabilly rebel by then!). Mick and I were young and keen through summer and winter at that time. As well as particles, we were using soft skinned boilies, with the hook buried in the middle, meaning you had to strike hard to pull the hook back through the paste in order to get a hookhold! Melvyn helped us out immensely and, like Dickie and Paul, he took us under his wing. He showed us these small, hard baits that he had flavoured with something called Amyl Acetate. They were the first rock-hard boilies we had seen. He told us the recipe for them and how to make them, so we were as keen as mustard and went out there and made some that week. And as if that wasn't enough, Melvyn also showed us tight-line fishing, using matchsticks taped to the rods as line clips. His results and methods showed us the way forward. I had asked my chemistry teacher at school if we could have some 'flavour' (amyl acetate). Not surprisingly he said no, so I helped myself anyway and nicked a few millilitres in a bottle from the lab. We were told it was the stuff used to flavour peardrop sweets. Melvyn said to go easy with it and only put a drop or two per egg into the mix. So that was what we did. The next thing was ethyl butyrate, the flavour in pineapple chunks, and this worked just as well as the amyl acetate. In my humble opinion, that's why pineapple-flavoured baits work so well. It's isn't the ethyl butyrate that makes pineapple flavours so effective. Also, it's thinner than water, more viscous and therefore always leaks out of the baits effectively, creating a scent trail, however low the water temperature may be.

ABOVE
Martin with a Darenth Big Lake mirror, caught in the snow.

It was also Melvyn who told us about the Hair Rig. I'll come to that in a bit, but before that he showed us how to fish a side-hooked bait. I'll always remember it: he told us there was another little trick to go with the clips and hard baits. He was good to us as he knew we would keep his secrets to ourselves. I can't tell you the difference that made; it was unbelievable. The takes went from twitches to rod wrenchers, even in the middle of winter! You couldn't miss the takes because the hooks were bare and would easily find a hold in the mouth, it was, quite simply, a revelation. When we were told all this, we kept it well quiet. We couldn't tell anyone about it, even close mates; that was the deal. For the first time I was starting to be a bit secretive myself. That winter there would be lots of people (summer anglers!) walking round Brooklands, and they would all ask why our lines were so tight. We would just play it down and say it was to help us see the twitches more easily, at the same time praying that one wouldn't go of with them in the swim!

Melvyn's brother Joe was fishing on Darenth at the time, which, unbeknown to me, was where Kevin Maddocks, Lenny Middleton and so on were using the Hair Rig. They were emptying the place, make no mistake. But, despite the secrecy surrounding it, somehow Joe got hold of the Hair and told Melvyn. To this day it's a mystery to me how he did this. Then one day, over a cup of tea at Brooklands, Melvyn made sure the coast was clear before showing Mick and me this new wonder rig – the Hair. There it was, in the palm of his hand, totally different to anything we had seen before. The bait was two or three inches away from the hook! The thing was we were doing so well on side-hooking that it was a job pulling off that and moving onto the Hair. So we decided to experiment and fish one rod on the Hair and one with a side-hooked bait. We actually found that the Hair didn't make a jot of difference to our catch rates.

Fishing with an exposed hook was the key. That was what *really* made the difference. I mean, look at modern day rigs. On most of today's presentations the boilie is often positioned slap bang against the shank of the hook, more like the old side-hooked method than the original Hair. How many modern rigs have a bait fished two or three inches from the hook tied with 1-2 lb mono? Not many! Today, baits are attached to 'D' rings, knotless knots, rings sliding up the hook's shank, all sorts of contraptions. But the one thing all these rigs have in common is the fact that the hook is exposed. That's what made the big difference then, and it's why today's rigs work so well, in my humble opinion.

We're jumping forward a few years now to the day I was invited by my good friend Kerry Barringer (of 'Roger and Kerry' fame) to go onto The Cons club waters in the Colne Valley as his guest. Guests were only allowed to do days, so I turned up at the Fisheries pub the night before to see the boys and have a bit of a social before fishing the next day. I arrived an hour before closing time – then it was decided that everyone would go down the Indian and have a curry. Because I hadn't had a drink, everyone said I should drive, but there wasn't room in my car because my gear was in it. But as it turned out, there *was* room in the car because it had been broken into and all my tackle had been stolen! My trusty Efgeeco seat box had gone, as well as my rod bag. Obviously I was very upset. However, at the time I was working as an apprentice engineer, so I thought I may as well make some replacement bits and pieces from the scrap metal that otherwise would have been thrown away. So that's what I

BELOW
An early range of Solar stainless products.

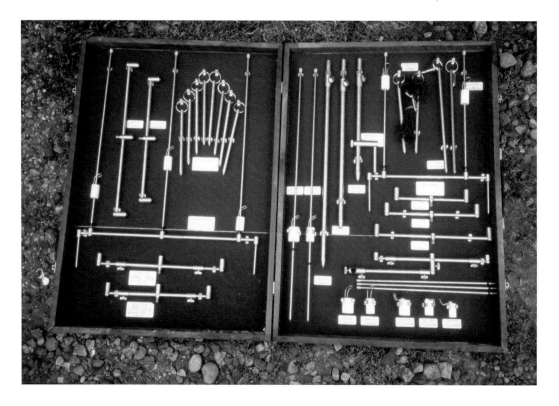

did, making stainless banksticks and
monkey climbers. I must have stood
out like a sore thumb with my new
kit on the bank, but the all boys liked
it because I was soon asked to make
more sets for them. I'm a great believer
that everything happens for a reason,
but Solar didn't start at that moment.
When I first started making stainless
I was making it for Rod Hutchinson.
He said, "Make all you can and I'll sell
it for you." So I'd make it and take a
carload up to him at his factory, with

ABOVE
*I must have stood
out like a sore thumb
with my new kit
on the bank, but
all the boys liked
it and I was soon
asked to make more
sets for them.*

his stickers on the product and sell it into the shops. This went on for a short time,
but then Rod's business went a bit pear-shaped, which forced me to rethink things. I
started selling it myself, so that's the moment Solar Tackle started.

I'm not sure about the year. It was in the '80s, maybe 1984 or 1985. And I also
have Maggie Thatcher to thank for Solar starting up, in a way! The Conservative
government had a scheme called the *Enterprise Allowance*, where they gave £40 a
week to someone with an idea to help them launch their own business. To get this
allowance, I had to have a bank account and a company name. I remember asking Tob
O'Brien (now of Les Quis fame) what I should call the company. My workshop was
a tiny garage (in the bottom floor of my mum's house) with no windows, and I was
putting in all the hours I could. To help pass the time I'd play the radio and the only
channel I listened to was a pirate station called Solar Radio. So that was it, the name
stuck. Looking back, it was a case of right place, right time really – I wasn't trying to
create a brand, just make a living. I was lucky because carp fishing started to become
fashionable just as I started Solar, which was a nice coincidence. The company didn't
grow as fast as it could have, because I wasn't that worried about money. I was more
worried about going fishing and having just enough money to do that.

It was around then that I started fishing Savay, I think. I had also fished the old
Fox Pool (Longfield) where I'd caught a few. But Savay was the next really big jump for
me, in terms of size, methods, the character of the place, the anglers and, of course, the
huge fish that live there. I was now angling for big fish with the big boys, who I'd only
seen in the magazines before then. It was daunting, to say the least! But Dave Whibley
and I just got our coats off and had a go! Like I said earlier, I've always been one to bite
off more than I can chew, so Savay was definitely the next logical step to take in my
fishing career. Catching at Fox Pool gave me the confidence to go there. It was one of
the first big pits to get properly carp-fished in England. Even now there aren't many
70-acre venues around with enough fish in to attract the anglers that it did then, and
still does. It was awesome because it made me think about my fishing, in the same way

ABOVE
*Martin returns an
early Savay capture.*

that Rainbow Lake does these days and Brooklands had in the formative years.

Like Rainbow now, Savay was the kind of lake that would always throw problems up, leaving you to sort out the solutions, and it suited me perfectly. These were problems you had to overcome if you were to catch anything at all, let alone consistently, problems that would make you think. It was just the sort of challenge that I relished. It was nice to be in the mix of all the things that were happening there, from the tackle developments (Savay was one of the first waters where distance fishing was being pioneered) through to the new bait ingredients that were being used. There was a period when every session would see someone on the syndicate bring a new flavour, attractor or tackle along to test. For example, Kerry came up with indicators hanging from a cord when the rest of the world used monkey climbers. I'm sure it was because he was too lazy to carry the monkey setup, but it certainly caught on. It would be fair to say that the three carp lakes which have played the most significant roles in my carp fishing have been Brooklands, Savay, and Rainbow, in that order, chronologically. Redmire was good, too, because you were fishing on hallowed ground, real history territory, although there wasn't so much tackle and bait development going on there when I was there, like there had been in Dick Walker's time. So while I really enjoyed Redmire it wasn't for the reasons that the other three lakes are mentioned. Redmire was somewhere I learned lots about carp behaviour, but the old 'give them what they want to eat' adage was true. On my first trip I had nine fish by piling in 24mm baits, but that's another story!

Savay played a key part in the development of the bait side of the business. I used to make my boilies on the bank there because there was no time to do it at home. It made more sense that way, because I'd be spending 18 or 20 hours a day working at 100mph to make sure we had enough stock to fulfil orders that would come in. My mum used to man the phone in the early days of Solar. She used to say to me, "Get the stock sorted then you can go fishing."

So I would work my butt off, making the stock until we had enough to meet potential orders, just so I could go fishing for the full rota week (Sunday till Sunday). I'd take 15kg of base mix with me in a wine brewing bucket, onto the lid of which I'd written the words 'Carp Food', which would later become the name of the bait brand. I'd go to the café on the way to the lake, have breakfast, get two dozen eggs, get to the lake, choose a swim and crack the eggs in a bowl and make my bait. The baits I would roll would depend on the swim I was in – if I was in a long-range swim, I'd make them bigger.

I was using birdfood bases, the original yellow and red Savay Seed Mixes in fact. People would say to me, "It's OK for you, you get your bait for nothing." Of course, that was ridiculous, I had to pay for the ingredients, and they weren't cheap. I would actually spend more money on bait than anything else. I always saw bait as the most important aspect of carp fishing, based on the lessons I learned initially at Brooklands. I still feel that way. You can have all the gadgetry in the world – the nicest rods and reels, the comfiest bivvy and bed, the best bite alarms – but what it always comes down to is whether your

BELOW
*Kerry Barringer
with Sally's Mate.*

ABOVE
Martin's mate Dave Whibley with a Savay 30. Although they knew they were angling with 'the big boys' they got on with it – and caught!

hookbait is going to get picked up by a carp. It's as simple as that. I think some anglers today spend too much money on their tackle and not enough on their bait.

I started manufacturing bait in addition to making stainless. I got an 8ft by 8ft shed built in mum's garden and bought a cement mixer. I got the stickers printed, some bottles for the flavours, and a bottling machine, and went from there. To start with I made the two Savay Seed Mixes and maybe six or seven flavours. Discovering a decent new flavour is always down to trial and error. You open the lid on some flavours and you just know whether they will or won't work. Then you try them out in boilies, at different levels in different mixes, and see for yourself if the carp like it. Of all the flavours I've used Squid and Octopus is probably my favourite product. We put as much precision and thought into our baits as we do into things like stainless and rig gear. I would choose Squid and Octopus, because of the ridiculous amount of huge carp that it has caught. It puts more smiles on more people's faces than anything else I have ever come up with. There are a few legendary flavours over the years: Richworth's Tutti-Frutti is up there; Hutchy's Scopex was just phenomenal, as was his Chocolate Malt. There are a few baits that will catch fish wherever they go and it's nice to have come up with the Squid/Octopus that is up there with the best of them.

When you're running a business and it's going well, it's great. When it's going bad, it's awful. There are few things in life as stressful as a business that isn't working out – and that's basically what happened with the Solartronics bite alarms. I take great pride in my job and what I do. Obviously there are bills to pay and you have to make money, but I hope readers realise by now that making money is not the priority for me. It never has been. As long as I have enough money to go fishing and look after my family with a reasonable lifestyle, then that's me sorted. What really inspires me is the sense of pride I get when people say how much they rate Solar products. That's the icing on the cake, along with the knowledge that you are making something that is of excellent quality that helps people catch carp and enjoy their fishing more. I think it's fair to say that I like to be in control of everything I do at business level. That way, if something goes wrong, customers can come to me. The bite alarms were a good idea in principle, but involved some quite complex electronics which I knew nothing about, so I suddenly found myself putting my trust in a company I didn't know. I got involved with them because they were suggested to us on recommendation.

To cut a very long story short, Solartronics was a separate company to Solar Tackle and it ended up with me having to divert a lot of money from Solar into the bite alarm business to keep it afloat. It was really scary. I nearly lost my house over it, everything in fact. I could easily have lost it all. That's why I stopped doing the alarms and decided to stick to things I know. I don't mind making mistakes, but that was a big one. I had to jump in with both feet to get the project to market and I almost paid for it with everything I had. You have to learn from these things. As I said, everything happens for a reason, though in this case I am yet to find out just what that reason was! I just kept going. It wasn't our (Solar's) fault that the bite alarm venture failed. For instance, at one stage there was a problem with the alarms in that they would short out. The effect of this was that they could go off at full tilt when you were fishing, making it seem like you'd had a screaming run when you hadn't. There aren't many things as frustrating as that in carp fishing. The cause of this problem revolved around the reed switch in the alarm. (A reed switch, put very basically, is an electrical switch inside the bite alarm that is operated by a magnetic field and completes an electric

ABOVE
A Savay 34 pounder.

circuit.) The company we were working with knew very well that if they soldered the reed switch off-centre, it could then cause arcing, which could make the alarm go off when it wasn't supposed to. To get round that problem, all you had to do was solder the switch straight up. That gets round all of it. You would've thought they would realise we knew what we were talking about, that they would accept the money they were getting and crack on. But they would still come up with more problems. Every time I thought we'd got round a problem, they would come up with something else. But it wasn't their reputation on the line, their brand printed on the box – it was mine.

We fulfilled our end of the bargain. We made sure all the parts were sorted and delivered, that the instruction booklets in four languages were correct, that the packaging and the marketing was good – and so on. The features on the alarms were our idea and worked well. But this company kept telling me that there were electronic and mechanical issues. We even ended up with our staff on their production line. The way I saw it, they kept making big problems out of what were, in reality, little or no problems at all. There was one instance when they called me to say, "We've ironed it all out now, you'll be getting 1,200 units a week," yet a couple of days later they'd ring up and say there was a new problem – the soldering wouldn't work, or this wouldn't work, or that wouldn't work. In other words they were pushing the boundaries all the time and we were only getting 100 units a week. We were promising shops that their orders would be in soon, and then they weren't. All of a sudden we were letting people down. And that's not me at all. When it was happening I did regret it because it was damaging my 'baby', the Solar Brand. It should have been so simple, but I had to draw a line under it before it was too late. I still have a set of Solartronics that works perfectly. But every time I look at them it reminds me of a very stressful time in my life, so I don't use them. And that's that.

Solar is fine now. We have an excellent team, which helps. They're all anglers, so they know what they're on about when they are talking to customers, as well as coming up with ideas and tweaks to keep the product development rolling along nicely. I take such a pride in making the gear we market. It might not be the cheapest, but it won't let you down and in the long run buying Solar kit will hopefully work out as a decent investment, because you'll still be using the same banksticks in 15 years' time. You'll catch fish instantly on the baits, too, and so on. I take it personally if any Solar kit lets people down, so we try to design products with that in mind

My private life has changed over the years. There is less clubbing now, because I have a family. But throughout my 20s and 30s I was fishing, clubbing, going to football matches and Grand Prix all over the world. Also I've always had an interest in music, and when house music and DJ-ing came along, I was mad for it. I bought some decks and put them in the front room. I never played out in public; I was too nervous I guess! My heroes were – still are – Sasha and John Digweed. I had immense respect for them because they never sold themselves down the commercial music road; they just stuck to what they know. In a way I look at Solar in the same way, and we leave the bottom end of the market to those who know it best. Contrary to rumour I never had a studio, but I did once record a track with a couple of mates who did have their own studio. We called the track 'Do It All Night' and it was Kiss FM record of the week! I did loads of CDs for my mates, and for me, so I could listen to the latest tunes in the car! Some of it is still going around now. When I first got into it, all I wanted was a sound-proof room where I could play music as loudly as I wanted. I had this vision of creating my own little nightclub with a sound system and lasers, all that kind of thing. This was just after I'd had my accident at Savay, so I knew I had some insurance money coming in that would help me put my dream into reality. That money would be enough to put an extension on the house I had my eye on, so I could build my own little nightclub. And that's what happened! The 'club' held around 20 people, so party times went into overdrive! It turned out to be worse than properly going clubbing, because there'd be nobody to tell you when to stop. I'd put one tune on, then another, then another and before I knew it, it was 3 or 4 o'clock in the morning and I'd have work the next day. I've got a great collection of records, around 8,000 -10,000. They were good times, but clubbing is completely opposite to fishing, in that fishing is done in almost complete silence, whereas going clubbing is about as noisy as you can get. There are similarities between the two, though. In both, you enter your own little world. While you're fishing there's often no one to talk to, and in a club the music is too loud to be able to talk to anyone!

As I mentioned earlier, the other thing I was really into was Formula One. That all started when I broke my leg after being run over at Savay. There have been a lot of turning points in life. Getting run over was a big one. It was serious. I was set up in the North Bay one evening. It was well documented that we used to go down the Horse and Barge most nights – there were two socialising 'shifts'. One we would call the 'early-earlies', the other the 'late-lates'. The 'early-earlies' used to go down the pub at 5.00 p.m. and would be fishing again by 9.00 p.m. The 'late-lates' would go down at 8.00 p.m. or 9.00 p.m. and stay until closing. You'd often get 50 or 60 anglers in the pub from Harefield and Savay and all the waters around there, so there'd be some banter going on. Everyone had a good idea and you'd learn a lot from each other. That afternoon Albert Romp said to me, "Do an 'early-early' with me son, you can be back angling by 9.00." I told him no to start with, because I was a 'late-late'. I knew what would happen – the 'early-early' session would turn into an 'early-late' as the other boys came into the pub later on. It's hard to say no to Albert though; he can be very persuasive, so he got me and, unusually for me, I went with him at around 5.00 p.m. At 9.00 p.m., just as we were leaving, the Harefield boys arrived – so I stayed until closing and had a few drinks with them. I knew I would; I didn't take much persuading, and I'd done many a 'pub cast' before, so another couple wouldn't make any difference. To justify it to myself I thought a few more hours 'swim resting' would only help!

Anyway, I came out of the pub at closing time to see Les Bamford and his mate doing a little fireworks show. I think he was letting them off from between the cheeks of his backside. He'd bend over, have a circle of cardboard with a hole in it that acted like a heat shield, plug a rocket in his arse through the hole and let it off !! The show went on for half an hour and when it stopped there was a big round of applause from the watching crowd, then off we went. The next thing I know was I was lying on the tarmac with Mr Dougal above me.

"What's happened Dougal?" I asked.

"You've been hit by a car," he said, "so keep still; the ambulance is on its way."

I didn't believe him at first.

"Do me a favour," I said, "I'm on the fish, so I'm going back to my swim now."

At that point I wasn't really in pain. Apparently I was 40 or 50ft from where the impact had happened, but at that stage I still didn't realise I had even been hit. The car had

BELOW
Nigel Mansell.

ABOVE
*Martin took the
opportunity to watch
a lot of Formula
One from the pits
after his accident.*

come over the humpback bridge, an old Peugeot 405. The accident investigators afterwards measured the skid marks and estimated it was doing 70 or 80mph in a 30mph limit. It had hit the other kerb first, then come across the road and hit the kerb I was on. It mounted the kerb, hit me and came to rest on a lamppost.

I asked Dougal, "Is it bad?" and he said, "Yes it is bad."

"Oh well, I'd better lie here then," was my reply!

I didn't know it was serious until I got to the A & E department in the hospital. The ambulance arrived and there were six or seven people waiting for me when I was pushed in. But I still couldn't feel much in the way of pain. To be honest, I've felt more pain by stubbing my little toe on the bottom of a door! They filled me full of sedatives, which obviously helped, but as well as smashing my leg I'd cut the back of my head and my elbow. I lost a lot of blood from the head wound. Straight after the accident, one of the lads had taken off his T-shirt to prop up my head. When I was taken away, it was soaked in blood, so much so that he had to wring it out.

A few days later the doctor said, "We're going to have to have a look at your leg now." It was badly broken and they told me they would need to operate the following day. So I went in for the operation, then when I came out I noticed the scar. It ran from my kneecap right down to my ankle. The doctor showed me the X-rays they had done before the operation – he described my fibula and tibia, the two main bones in your lower leg, as being like 'a packet of broken cornflakes'. The doc didn't want to tell me how bad it was before the operation. It was a similar injury to that one Barry Sheen got when he smashed himself up. There are 12 or 13 titanium bolts in my leg now!

When I was on the crutches, a friend of mine at the time came over to see me, John Townsend, who was a freelance F1 Grand Prix photographer, Nigel Mansell's personal photographer. One thing led to another and he sorted me out a trip to the Canadian Grand Prix... and in the middle of the Montreal track is a lake full of fish! So after that, whenever I went on an F1 trip, I'd fit in some fishing, too.

Ayrton Senna was a hero of mine, one of the few people I'd really look up to. To meet Ayrton was great. It tore me up when he died – which was on the same day as the Savay drowning tragedy. Both he and Nigel Mansell were just ordinary people, not arrogant or full of themselves, as the press would have you believe. I could just talk to them as normal, which is probably why I got on with them so well. This was the year that Nigel won the world championship. When he (Nigel) went out to the States to do the Indy series, I went to see him race loads of times. John got me passes to get on the grid for most races. There was me, walking up and down with the cars, the pop stars, models and VIPs and the buzz that goes with a Grand Prix just minutes before the start of a race, thinking, "How the hell did I get here? All I do is make a few bank sticks! Oh well, best I crack on taking some pictures to at least make it look like I should be here."

ABOVE
Ayrton Senna (then of McLaren Honda) and Nigel Mansell (Williams Renault) after the 1991 Monaco GP. Senna took the chequered flag and remains one of Lockey's all-time heroes. "Both Ayrton and Nigel were ordinary blokes to speak to, not at all poncy," he says.

Picture courtesy of latphoto.co.uk, part of the Haymarket Media Group.

I had the best and worst experiences of my life at Savay. What used to happen was, during the close season, Pete Broxup organised work parties that the syndicate members would go on. His wife would organise a picnic at lunchtime on the island. On this particular occasion there were 15 or 16 of us, doing the usual lunchtime routine, eating a pork pie, some sandwiches, orange squash or drinking a bottle of beer, then back to work. We were the last ones off the island after lunch. There was me, Don Hipkin, Clive Rigby, and Keith Selleck. We jumped in and Keith was steering. It was the same boat – a punt, in fact – that we'd used many times for ferrying gravel up and down the lake to make the paths. There was nothing untoward when we set off from the island: it was a flat-calm day and there had been no problems with the previous people who had been ferried back to shore. It wasn't even a long distance to go. From the island to the shore was maybe 70yds. We came to about the halfway point when suddenly water started coming in over the front corners of the boat. It just started pouring in. I don't know the reason why and to this day I don't know how it happened, but it was coming in ever so quickly and the boat started sinking.

Clive said to me, "I can't swim."

So I told him, "You're going to have to now, Clive, you're going to have to."

I hadn't swum since I was 15 or 16 when I was at school. And then the boat went down. It was a surreal experience. When you're in the water, just with your head sticking out, everything is at the same level. I knew the Secret Swim was the nearest point, so that was what I decided to aim for. I grabbed hold of Clive to try to help him. I hadn't done lifesaving or anything like that. It would be easy to look back now and say that, if I had, I could have saved him, but I can't look at it that way. I tried my best. I'm quite calm in any situation, so I remember taking off my jumper because I knew wearing it wouldn't help. I decided to go easy and just try and doggy-paddle my way out.

I held Clive three or four times. I told him to paddle his legs; that he had to do it – he had to. He got a certain distance, but I wasn't a very good swimmer myself, so I was shouting while we were in the water for other people to come and get us. It was probably more frustrating for them seeing what was happening without being able to do anything about it. Keith was slowing up. He got to within 10 or 15yds of the bank, then disappeared. I don't know if he got cramps because of the cold water. Don managed to scramble out on shore, then I climbed out, but Clive was still trying to paddle. Then Clive Williams jumped in to try and rescue Keith. The rest is a bit of a haze. Before we knew it we were in the middle of a major situation. There were helicopters, fire engines, police and divers all over the place. When I eventually left the lake, I was told to drive out of the gate and not stop. This was because the media was there; reporters and television news crews. When I got home I rang everyone I knew to tell them the whole story so they could hear it from the horse's mouth, not third-hand. Tragically both Clive Rigby and Keith Selleck passed away that day. Then someone told me that there had also been an accident at the Imola Grand Prix, that Ayrton had crashed badly and was in hospital; and that it wasn't looking good. He, of course, passed away, too. From that moment to this, I know that we tried our best for the boys who lost their lives on Savay that day, Clive and Keith. God rest their souls, wherever they may be. May 1ˢᵗ 1994, was a very very sad day.

I haven't been able to go on Savay since then, really. Then, since Pete Broxup died... I had my ticket from 1985 and dropped out only recently. I had the best of the fishing there with the best of the anglers, with all the things that were happening there with the tackle and bait. I kept thinking I would go back, but too many things happened to me on there. I had the best of it, and the worst of it. I draw a line under it now.

One of the best times was catching Sally; 'Sally, Pride of the Valley!' That's how she was known. Before I got my ticket on there, Sally was the first fish Roger Smith caught each season for three years on the trot! Generally speaking though, I think it's fair to point out that Sally was not particularly fond of having her picture taken. She came out maybe once a year; in fact, at one time I'm sure there was a three-year gap between captures. Roger Smith was the biggest influence on my fishing, for sure. He's Mr Logical, and is still as keen as ever today.

At that time Savay held about 100 fish in 70 acres. So by no means was it a pushover to catch anything. Traditionally at the start of the season the Canal Bank was the place to be, whereas the Colne Bank didn't really do much, not to start with, anyway. The season I caught Sally I actually bagged one on the first morning – on 16ᵗʰ June – which was a 19-pounder. Two or three days in and we hadn't seen anything else, so I went for a walk around the Colne Bank. Rob Maylin walked round with me. Anyway, we were having a stroll around, looking for bubblers, as you do. Sure enough, one fish jumped out in front of a swim we called The Hump. So I said, "That will do for me, I'm getting my gear." Rob said he was coming round as well, so I told him I was going in The Hump and that was that!

I think bait was the key at Savay, as it is on many of the big pits. I put more emphasis on bait than anything else. At 70 acres it was a big old lake and you had to carry your gear around with you because there were no barrows. No one had thought of making carp barrows at that time. The walk from the swim I was fishing to where I was going was near enough half a mile, so in order to get there quickly and in one trip, I took all the tea-making gear out of my seat box, along with other bits and pieces I didn't need and left it in Roger's bivvy, and filled it up with bait I'd made the day before. Then it was the long walk round to The Hump Swim.

ABOVE
Roger Smith:
"You'll never catch
Sally from the
Colne Bank..."

I suppose the hot spot there was a 70 or 80yd cast. You aimed at a dip in the trees on the far bank. Funnily enough, even though there were clips on the reels back then, we never used them. We just used to know when the rigs had landed on the right spots – you just knew when you'd gone the right distance. So when all the gear was set up and ready to go, I didn't cast out. Instead I was off to Wembley Arena because three of us had tickets to see Tina Turner! Wembley was only 20 minutes down the road, so leaving our gear, off we went – the three of us – to see this gig. We arrived back after 11.00 p.m. and it was absolutely throwing it down with rain; in fact it was monsoonal!

Most nights on Savay in those days, we'd say, "I hope someone catches Sally tonight." This particular night, we agreed that one of us definitely deserved to catch her, as the weather was so bad.

Roger said, "Well you're not going to catch her on the Colne Bank, because she doesn't live round the Colne, and she's never been caught round the Colne."

"But what if she's on her holidays," I replied!

The Hump wasn't really a proper swim; it was just a steep slope down to the water's edge, so it wasn't the safest. You'd worry about dealing with a fish if and when you hooked one. It was just getting light at about 4.30 a.m. when I woke up to a dropback. Invariably a drop back, turns out to be a tench, and I got out of bed bursting for a tiddle. I looked down at the rod, realised I'd have to deal with a tench on the slope – which didn't appeal – so I had said wee first!

When I got round to picking up the rod, the angle of the line had gone from 1 o'clock to 9 o'clock. I wound in the slack and all of a sudden connected with the fish. I thought, "F*** me, there is no way this is a tench. I hope it hasn't gone under Rob's lines…" because I couldn't see him to tell him not to strike if he got a false run from it. But thankfully the fish was under his lines.

The next problem was getting me and the net down the steep slope without slipping into 12ft of water. But I managed it and I remember the fish coming across the front of me from left to right, and that was the moment I saw her – Sally!!! To say my heart all but jumped out of my chest would be an understatement.

The usual type 'big-fish fight' ensued with a lot of plodding about before 'bosh', she was in the net. I didn't shout out when she was in the net because there was a problem getting both her and me back up the slope. Eventually I managed it, and then when Sally was secured in a safe margin spot I went to get Rob and John Yeatman (aka Fred Flintstone). We did the do, weighed her at 39lb and took photos. That was when we did the customary shouting of "SALLLLYYYY!!!!" as loud as we could across the lake.

And that was the last time she was caught, 19th June 1989… There were some floods, and rumour had it she disappeared up the river or canal. Who knows? She was never seen again, which was nice in a way, as she remains immortal to this day. When I remember all the catches I have made, there is no fish I was happier to catch than her. A fitting tribute is that she is the most printed carp there has ever been, because she is on our logo. Yes, Sally is the one for me, but the World Record fish is a VERY close second!!!

Dave Lane

Talking to Jim Foster

From Carpworld Issue 254

With five UK 50s to his name at the time of the interview, Dave Lane ranks as one of the most successful big-carp anglers ever to have wet a line. The fish he has caught at 50lb+ include The Eye from Sonning, Mary from Wraysbury, Two-Tone from Conningbrook, the legendary Black Mirror and The Fat Lady from St. Ives. He's written two books, and was one of two men behind the design of the ultra-effective 360 Rig.

I turned 50 recently and we had a big old party to celebrate. All the family and friends were there. It was awesome, we were in fancy dress and I went as a character from *Thunderbirds* – I think there's a video of me dancing like a puppet somewhere, doing a *Thunderbirds* impression. (Dave gets up and demonstrates the kind of dance he was doing, dressed as Scott Tracy from the 1960s kids' TV show, *Thunderbirds*. I have to be honest – if he was ever on '*Strictly*', he'd probably be voted off in the first week!) Obviously, I have responsibilities, so I never fish at weekends. Things are very different for me these days, certainly compared to five years ago. I've got married and between us my wife, Dee, and I have a combined total of five kids! Conor, my eldest boy, is 13! And into music in a big way – he's a very promising guitarist. Conor isn't even my eldest. My daughter Amy is 19 now...

I usually angle for two nights every week, on a Monday and Tuesday down here on Black Swan, with 'F' (Paul Forward). I'm doing OK here. The season kicked off on June 16th, so we're three months in, and I haven't blanked yet. I think I've had around 30 fish or so, the biggest 36lb. My biggest last year was 37 – along with a decent number of mid-30s and lots of 20s. There are a few reasons why I'm targeting Black Swan. Firstly, because the fish in here are stunning; loads of zip linears and fully-scaled mirrors. Collectively, you're unlikely to catch better-looking carp almost anywhere else in the country. They're gorgeous! Also, only a third of the stock has ever been caught, so you don't know what you're going to hook next. Although the lake has been here for donkey's years, this syndicate has only been in place four years, which means there should still be some mysteries in here... and maybe a very big uncaught fish, which is

PREVIOUS PAGE
Back to my younger days with a fish called Moonscale.

BELOW
What a motley crew. My 50th.

ABOVE
*Celebrating my
marriage to wife Dee.*

really what excites me. All you can take on board are the pictures Simon, the bailiff, shows you of the 44 that he had before it was opened as a syndicate, or the 41 – and they are stunning fish. The 41 was just like Shoulders out of Horton; it's an absolutely incredible-looking carp, but it's not been seen since. Up to now I haven't seen any big ones, so it is a question of 'how long do I give it, pursuing something that might be no more than a wild goose chase?'

The lake is clogged with weed. Full of it, which means we need to fish fairly heavy. So for me it's braided main line and lead clips that ensure your leads are free to drop off as soon as you hook a carp. Another key is carefully finding spots and accurately placing hookbaits, which isn't always easy. I don't see why so many fisheries don't like braided line. The safest way of dealing with a fish is to get it on the bank, unhook it and put it back. Now, if you're using mono in these savage conditions, you lose a lot of tackle. You can't help it. But with 20lb braided main line, you don't – it's easy. There are a number of good braids available and choice depends largely on what you want to achieve from it. If you want it to sink, then Nash Bullet is excellent. The trouble is, a sinking braid doesn't cast very well and (usually) a casting braid doesn't sink very well! So you need to weigh up which facet of your braid would suit you best. On Black Swan, you don't really need a sinking braid because in most swims the weed is up to within a foot of the surface. So maybe a casting-type braid would be better. I have recently tried the Fox braid, Graviton Pro, and I've found this to be a very good blend of both. One of the main criticisms of braid is that you risk damaging a fish during the fight so I use a 3ft polyurethane leader, which is soft. It sinks nicely

and is totally smooth on the carp's flank. When you are using braid leaders are more appropriate than tubing as well, because tubing can fly back up the main line during a fight, leaving the fish's flank exposed to the braid. Better to use a looped leader, tied to the main line, with the lead on a clip so it can come off easily. You have to make sure the lead can come off easily, that's incredibly important, again to avoid endangering the fish should the worst come to the worst and you lose it. A lot of the rules about not using braid are born of ignorance – not wishing to be rude, but that is the case. Suffice to say that, in my opinion, normal mono fished at range is more dangerous to fish than braid, because you're going to lose more gear – especially in weed. How do you break 20lb braid? You can't.

And of course, there is always the added benefit of vastly improved bite detection with braid, although you need a good clutch on your reel, that's for sure! I remember a bite I had recently on Black Swan. I was fishing a fairly slack clutch, or I thought it was slack, at any rate. I was in the bivvy and heard one beep from the buzzer, so I didn't pay too much attention. Then, suddenly, I heard a '*zzzzzzzzzzzzz*' as line was being ripped violently from a reel. I looked round and saw I'd had a bite which had torn the rod off the rests – but luckily the butt became stuck on the rear rest, with the rod bouncing around in mid-air as the fish tore off across the lake.

I started writing in about 1991. Rob Maylin rang me up and asked if I wanted to write about my capture of Jack from Horton. I hadn't written anything in my life before then – nothing at all – but I did it anyway. When I had finished the piece, I read it back and thought, 'Yeah, that's actually not bad', so I started to write some more. And I enjoyed it, too. When I went on Horton I wasn't sponsored by anyone, or fishing for anyone. And I didn't have a deal with any bait company. I was fishing for myself and was a self-employed Artexer in my home life. I'd work until Tuesday lunchtime, then take the rest of the week off to go angling! The aim was to earn £250 cash as soon as possible: I could survive on £250 for two weeks. It was enough to get me on the bank until the money ran out. When the cash disappeared, I'd do some more Artexing, and the cycle would start again.

The good thing about Horton was that when we started on there no one else knew anything about it. Of course, we knew about the fish that were in there, as most of them had come from Longfield – but it was a new syndicate, so it wasn't like moving onto a venue that had been fished for years and years. All the members started on a level playing field, which was pretty cool, and suited me down to the ground. A bloke called Jack Ashford used to run Leisure Sport, which controlled Horton back then. A lot of anglers, the old school, were upset that the fish had been moved from Longfield. Over the years since many reasons have come to light why the fish were moved, but I don't want to go into that because it's nothing to do with me! At the time I just thought, 'I have the chance to get a ticket for a syndicate on a new lake, with a lot of fish in it'. To be honest, I would have liked to have caught them from Longfield, but I couldn't fish for them in Longfield, because obviously they weren't in there any more.

So I joined Horton and stayed a member there for three seasons.

As it happens that first year wasn't spectacular. I caught nine or 10 in all; I can't remember exactly how many, off the top of my head. The main tactic was finding the fish and moving where they were: simple, really. It was the second Horton season when things really started to take off, just after I had got together with Mainline during the close season. We formed a little baiting team and decided to properly fill it in during the weeks before the season started – I mean, really fill it in with bait – and that was a move that paid off when 16th June came around. This was in the days before the Grange bait came on the scene. We'd wanted our own type of bait, so Kev Knight, (Mainline boss) made us some up. We caught rakes of fish that second season – I probably had half the biggies in the lake. Because we'd done so well in a baiting team that second year, other anglers on the syndicate got together and did a similar thing the following season, with their own baits. We stayed on the Mainline gear and kept putting it into the lake in large quantities, but we changed tactics while we were actually fishing. Instead of angling over big beds of bait, we fished single hookbaits. It worked a treat; I had 21 fish that season just by moving round and round and round the lake, casting a single hookbait at anything I saw moving. I had loads like that.

BELOW
Trying to guess which one is the restaurant!

BOTTOM
Explaining the finer points of a reel-fitting in Korea, in -22°!

I had all of the big fish from Horton: Jack, Shoulders, The Parrot, CP's, Heart Tail, Moonscale, The Peach... all of them! I suppose the capture that really stands out for me was Moonscale. I had her at 38lb when she hadn't been out for a long time. I think the time before when she had been caught, she was a mid-20, so it was a memorable capture. When I refer to singles I was just using the bait we were putting in, except on its own, not over a bed of freebies. Like I said, we were all still introducing bait to the lake in quantity – except for the most part, we weren't fishing over it. Another little edge that seemed to work was this: at the end of every week, I would save about 30 hookbaits and put them in a knotted, plastic bag so that they would sweat. They would then be my hookbaits the following week. During the intervening few days or so, the sugars in the boilies would come out and the boilies would go tacky, like tiger nuts do. I'm not talking about the white coating freezer baits get on them when you leave them for a while. They get like that if you leave them open to the air. That isn't so good. Leave them in sealed plastic bags and they get tacky – so sticky that if you put your hand in the bag of bait, the boilies will stick to it. They work really well in that state, possibly because they have started to break down, releasing sugars, enzymes and other attractants. That's what the fish seem to be attracted to. It's a confidence thing as well. Once you've caught a carp on any tactic, you know it works, so you stick to it.

It's worth mentioning that I was using 1½oz running leads at the time as well, with 18in hooklinks and long Hairs; really long Hairs, 2ins in length. I'd fish in thick weed, flicking the rig out underarm and leaving it where it landed. If you let it fall through the water, the lead would slide back up the line a bit, which meant you would, in practice, be fishing a 4ft hooklink.

It would be fair to say that I don't like to overcomplicate things. A bit of nylon and a hook are all you need to catch carp most of the time, although it does depend on the lake you're fishing, as some of the venues I've been spending time on in the last year are savage in terms of weed growth. This season I've been on Monks Pit (in Cambridgeshire) and here on Black Swan (Dinton) and both lakes have really bad weed. So I use coated braid hooklinks here, because I wouldn't really want to be attached to a carp on a mono hooklink in weed as thick as the stuff I have been fishing in recently.

Contrary to rumours I was never banned from Horton! On the contrary – by the time I stopped fishing Horton I'd been given a free Gold Card (the most sought-after Leisure Sport card, giving permission to fish all their waters – including prestigious venues such as the Yateley complex) because I was giving them publicity and getting them in the papers so much. They were selling loads of tickets, hand-over-fist, so I think it was their way of saying thank you, which was good of them. On the subject of bans you are probably thinking of Conningbrook, where I was banned for a while. In fact, it was you who got me banned, Jim! You'd come down to do a photoshoot and someone had had a bite, but the fish got stuck in the weed. So I took a boat out to try to free it. Trouble was, boats weren't allowed and you took pictures and then published one of them, showing me in the boat. Chris Logsdon, who ran Mid-Kent Fisheries then, saw this and banned me instantly! You knew about it at the time because I remember you writing Chris Logsdon a letter explaining what had happened, and apologising.

BELOW
The beauty of an African sunset.

Given all the fish I was catching back then, it was almost inevitable I would get an offer from a tackle company to work for them full-time and eventually I started working in the carp-angling industry. I don't know when it was: dates and such – or even years – aren't my strong point. I do remember I was still Artexing, being sent bits and pieces to test for tackle companies. Then I got a firm consultancy offer from Fox, so I started working for them. That lasted two years before I left. Soon after, Jeff from JRC offered me a few grand a year, again, just to be a consultant. I was with JRC for a little while before Jeff asked me if I wanted to work full-time for them – giving me a free hand on creating a high-end range of kit bearing my name, and on the existing JRC range. The trouble was that the job was in an office! It wasn't me at all: last time I'd been in an office was when I'd been caught smoking at school. Suddenly I had an office of my own and I was a manager of something. I did explain that I needed time out for fishing, that it was part of what they were paying me for and who I am. I didn't even have a budget. It was a case of, "Do the best rods you can, the best bivvy you can."

Looking back, I think half his plan was to get me on board and then sell the company with me involved in it, because I think I was used as a sweetener. That was OK though; I didn't mind because he was paying me good money. But then he sold JRC to Shakespeare, which was part of the K2 group that owns all sorts of different companies. That gave me a number of opportunities to do another of the things I really love in life – travel. They sent me to China, and then to South Korea to

develop a range of rods in the mountains, in -22° temperatures! It was freezing. They'd built this range of rods for me to test and took me to this frozen lake that had 2ft of ice on it, just so I could cast them and let them know what I thought. I broke a couple of them – because of the cold the carbon wasn't behaving properly and they shattered. But that didn't matter too much because I'd give them my feedback, then overnight while we were out eating and drinking, the factory would roll up a new blank. And then the next day we'd test the next batch. This went on for a week and was a massive experience.

What a different culture the Koreans live in from us; I can't even begin to explain how different it is to here. Most of the time when people go away on holiday, they go to somewhere that isn't much more than Little Britain, where people speak English, but not in Korea. It's real over there. The weirdest thing was, when I went to leave Korea, I got to passport control and they wouldn't let me out of the country. Because it was the first time I had done long haul travelling, I didn't know some of the little essential details you need to help things go smoothly, like getting a visa! I quickly

ABOVE
*The brothers
Forward and me
under an African sky.*

found out that whilst you didn't need a visa to get into South Korea, you needed one to get out... especially if you are going to China. So I was stuck. I had to go back to the people who'd been hosting me and get them to sort a visa! It took a couple of days, but eventually I got out.

Notwithstanding the visa problems I loved Korea! I went up into the mountains to these weird restaurants and ate some really strange dishes, like snake. Snake was quite nice. When I got there for the first night I was with this other English guy and he wanted to eat in the hotel, but I said no, we had to go out and explore the town. Bear in mind that nobody there speaks English and all the signs are in Korean... Anyway, we ended up at this restaurant, and to order food I just had to point at other dishes on other tables that other people were eating, saying "I want that!" I've travelled all my life and have loved it, ever since I was 17 or 18. So for someone to give me a well-paid job and send me to Korea, China, Switzerland, Holland, Denmark, etc. – it was great. At least, it was for the first year or two. After that, going away for a month here and two weeks there would get difficult, because I'd be spending time away from the family and, of course, fishing.

Then there was Africa! We (F, F's brother, his mate, Steve, and Dave) got asked to go out there to film a DVD and get some web footage for the African Carp Society. It was a golden opportunity, all expenses paid. This guy Steve was a guide out there and he was brilliant. The first place we went to was six hours north of Jo'burg and was called Durrandrai; it was a massive lake in a huge, private game reserve. There's a night fishing zone as soon as you drive into the park, but we weren't going there because we'd got permission to fish in water that hadn't had a line cast into it for a long time, if ever. It was a mile long this place, so we drove down into the park, halfway along the lake, and pulled in through these woods and bushes. It was nearly dark when we got there, but we could still see the mountains on the far bank. What an awesome place

it was! Then, when it got dark... you should have seen the sky! You've never seen a sky like it, the number of stars – it was like the heavens were wrapped around you. The most amazing place I've ever seen.

The only problem was that I was in a mess because I'd done my back in and could hardly walk, but we set up camp and got the barbecue going anyhow. Initially, I decided not to fish until the morning, but after a couple of glasses of wine you think a bit differently, so I wandered down to the margins and put a couple of rods out before collapsing into bed for the night. The tents we were staying in were made from heavy canvas, in a kind of army-style but looking like something out of *It Ain't Half Hot Mum,* or an old Carry-On film. The African Carp Society bloke said we had to row our baits out some 400-500yds. He'd advised to do this and do that... but I took one look at the lake and thought, 'No...' There were carp launching themselves out, and I mean *launching* themselves out of the water. They were everywhere, some at casting range, some at 150yds, so we rowed out, put in a line of markers and baited with a load of tiger nuts. We mullered it; we caned them, catching 20 fish a day to over 40lb. It was frenetic! There are pictures of the four of us lined up, all holding fish; we'd had three at once. And the condition of these carp was something else – I took photos of their mouths, close-ups, because they had never seen a hook. The lips on those fish! Some of them were like inner tubes; big, huge South African lips that were absolutely mint.

My back problem was getting progressively worse, though. On the second morning I got a one-noter and, while getting to the rod, which was some 50yds from the bivvy, I realised I was in trouble because I couldn't walk. I had to grab the poo shovel to help me make my way back to the tent while F wound in the fish. I was in agony! F landed the fish and had put it back before I got back to the tent. Then someone had the idea that if it was heat that helped my back, we could get a rock, warm it on the fire and put it in my bed with me resting it against my back. They wrapped it in 'F's bath towel – but it was so hot it burned a hole in the towel! It cooled slightly after that and relaxed my back a little bit, enough for us to fish on for a couple of days, by which time we'd had enough of that lake and wanted another adventure. So the South Africans decided to take us to this other place further north, which was right up in the mountains. It was a lake called Tzaneen, a big reservoir with sunken trees, all that kind of stuff.

We got there and, after seeing the spot we were fishing, F and I had a bit of a 'to-do' about who took which swim… we both wanted the swim at the end of this point, and we almost came to fisticuffs about it! In the end I threw my toys out of the pram and said, "Ah damn it, you have it, I'll go around the corner and fish in the forest of stumps!" As it turned out, the bit I went to was the bollocks, because all the carp were holed up in the sunken forest. I fished at 30yds, spodded out a load of tigers and caned it. I got run after run and nobody else had anything until we moved. They weren't big fish, up to mid-20s, but they were animals; commons and scattered-scaled mirrors.

About three nights in we were all sitting inside this big tent with a 'braai', which is basically a big, round barbecue with a lid on it, in the middle. They do this dish that looks like a big, big sausage – a South African delicacy that looks like a huge elephant turd. If you unravelled it, it would be about 20ft long! Anyway, we had tunes blasting on the iPod player, and we were all chilling out, when all of a sudden Steve heard something. He sat bolt upright and – as he did so – one of my alarms beeped! I said to him, "F****** hell, you're good, you can predict bites." I got up to run out of the tent but as I did so, Steve – who's 6ft 5ins – grabbed the back of my collar and held me back. I was so eager to hit the bite I was running on the spot for a moment as Steve stopped me going outside, like something out of a cartoon.

"Hold on, hold on," he was saying, as he knew something wasn't quite right. "It's a hippo. They're the biggest killers in Africa."

He'd heard them and he was right, because by then all three of my rods were going off. We gave it a few seconds then all ran towards the rods anyway, because we wanted to see what was going on. It was pitch-black and the run towards the rods was like a slow-moving whirlwind of men, because whoever was at the front realised they were at the front and slowed down so they ended up at the back… just in case, you know? I was fishing 30 or so yards out and these hippos were walking along the bottom of the lake – you can't see them – so I assume the lines came off their feet. Then, as they got around the corner, F's brother, Nick – who was using braid – hooked one of them properly, and his rod just screamed off. We were talking about using braid and how good it is, but it's no good when you've got a hippo on the end, because a 10-ton hippo is always going to win! Going for a poo in the bushes at night was an experience. You'd go in there, dig your hole, do your thing then switch on your headtorch – and all these eyes would be looking at you, glowing in the light! Just staring at you; and you had no idea what they were.

All the lions and leopards, all that sort of stuff, are in game reserves that have fences around them. There's one main park the size of Wales, the Kruger National

Park, and that's where most of the wildlife lives. You pay to go in there in your own vehicle, and then you're on your own. If you get out of your car, the chances are you will get killed and eaten. We went there for the day to try to get photos of the big five game animals, which, if I remember rightly, are lion, buffalo, leopard, elephant and rhino. I managed to get some top photos. At one point we were by this river and a hippo came up and did a big yawn, showing its teeth, so I got the pic. A leopard came so close to the van the others were screaming, "Shut the door, shut the door, get back in the van – these things kill you!" But I wanted to get some good, close-up photos.

At the end of the day, we ran out of time and were late trying to get out of the park, so we were speeding along this dust track, went round a corner and had to brake hard because there was this absolutely huge male lion lying on the road in front of us. When everyone's gone, all the animals lie on the road to absorb the heat, so he wasn't expecting to see us! I'd hired this proper zoom lens, so I managed to get some great shots as he was looking straight at me. I've been into photography almost as long as I have been fishing, since I was 16 or 17. Everything on cameras was manual back then; there was no such thing as a green square (auto) setting, you had to make the light readings yourself and work out the shutter speeds and exposures. Actually, I have just bought a new camera, a Canon D60 – it is the perfect carp camera. It's an SLR-quality camera, but has a turnaround screen and automatic self-focus, so you can do brilliant self-take shots. I'm highly impressed with it.

One of my current target waters is Monks Pit in Cambridgeshire. I've had some success there on Zig rigs, including a 46lb common during the February just gone. Success with Zigs is about finding the fish's comfort zone and presenting a bait there. Carp are used to eating food up in the water – hatching insects, etc. – and, until we came along with Zigs, all that food was safe to eat. But I don't think that's why carp take Zigs so readily. I actually think they work better in cold water, and that they are a brilliant winter tactic because, physically, the fish are more comfortable up in the water than they are on the lake bed. If you look at traditional winter bite times when fishing on the bottom, they only usually last half an hour or so because that will be the only time the carp will feel comfortable going down. That could be because of temperature, air pressure – whatever it is, they are physically uncomfortable visiting the lake bed for most of any given 24-hour period. The rest of the time they spend at a certain level below the surface.

I think the key is how far below the surface the fish might be, not how high off the bottom they are. I was fishing in about 15ft of water, 7ft or so under the surface – pretty much in midwater. Generally, if I am not entirely sure where the fish are, I'll split the depth of the lake into three and fish the middle third. So in 15ft I'll be fishing between 5ft and 10ft down – or up, depending on how you look at it. I think it will work anywhere, if you get it right. The best time for Zig fishing is late-winter and early-spring – February and March are awesome Zig months. You can use four rods on Monks at that time of year and I'll use all four on Zigs at all times, I won't even bother

fishing on the bottom. Hookbaits are tiny bits of foam, the same size as the filters you get for roll-up cigarettes. My mate Ian Brown made me up some really nice flies that imitated real insects to try. I caught nothing at all on them! Every carp I have caught has been on a tiny bit of black or yellow foam. I think flavouring the foam makes it less effective. With foam, they either take it or they don't. If it's flavoured, then it presents the fish with an extra decision it has to make. Fish it at the right depth, – the ideal place is one foot below the fish – and they will dip down and take it.

You have to work at it with Zigs; it's like a third dimension to carp fishing. Say, for example, you're fishing in midwater, it's 10.00 a.m. and you get two bites on Zigs. Then you stop getting bites. It doesn't mean the fish have gone, just that they could have moved up or down the water column. I've started getting bites again by lengthening the hooklink by 2 or 3ft, or shortening it. This means I'm casting all the time, trying different depths out in an effort to locate the carp. I'll fan out the four rods, trying different areas and depths until I get a bite. Then I will concentrate all the baits at that depth for a while and see what happens. The thing about Zigs is that they are instant. If I see a fish jump in winter, I'll stick three rods on it at different depths. Quite often, one of them will go off within a minute – it can be that quick. Come the end of April and early May, however, the fish are comfortable on the bottom – that's

when the bait really starts to work well. It all depends on the depth of water, too. On deep waters in late-winter and early-spring, Zig Rigs are devastating, awesome. They have totally and utterly changed my winter fishing.

The 46lb common I had from Monks was my UK personal best common, and was my first 40lb common from this country. It took me decades to get it and it was the fish I joined Monks to catch! It was a bit fortuitous really; I was out breaking ice the week before and went over an area that never gets fished, really. The hot spot in the swim I had the common from is like 110 yards out, but I was breaking the ice just 20 yards out so I could fish. And I saw a little common, about halfway down, which I drifted over. Then I saw a couple of others, definitely carp... so I tried Zigs for them. I caught nothing that session, but returned the following week and went straight into the same swim, fishing all four rods on Zigs at different levels. I caught one straightaway, within minutes. Bear in mind that there had been only one fish caught in three months – I had seven that day, biggest being the 46lb common. I got everything right on that occasion, location, the depth, and it goes to show what can be done with Zig Rigs in the right circumstances.

I've always done pretty well in the winter months. I had Mary in February, but that week of February is duffers' week! There's always a period in February when everything wakes up. It usually happens some stage between the second week of February and the second week of March: it used to be in the last week of the season. In those days everyone wanted to fish on and wonder at the riches that were denied us – but now we do fish on, we've realised that it isn't the proper wake-up, it's like a break in hibernation. It gets to mid-February, the light levels change, things start crawling around on the lakebed and bang! The fish feed. I'd bet that if you looked at the catch reports from February over the years, you'd see some kind of increase in capture rates. Most of the big fish in the country get caught then, before they shut up shop again. It's not until mid-April that they get caught on the bottom. There's always that window of opportunity when the light levels change in late-February; it has happened too many times to me to be a coincidence.

My greatest winter capture has to be Mary, really, off Bryant's Point – it weighed 49lb 15oz and was probably the biggest fish in the country at the time. I've landed five UK 50s now but Mary in February was truly memorable, like the 46lb common was from Monks in February this year. Like I said, I have caught and been witness to loads of big-carp captures at that time of year. It is probably my favourite month. October isn't a patch on February! Generally, November, December and January are shite, but Zigs are levelling that out now. Maybe this will inspire a few more people to get out there and fish Zigs during the colder months. They may be pleasantly surprised.

OPPOSITE
*Mary in February
at 49lb 15oz.*

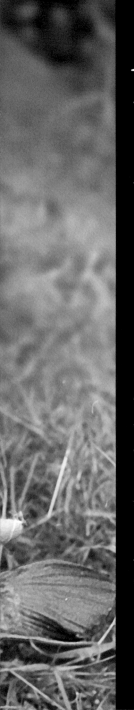

Hutchinson

Talking to Tim Paisley • Part One

From Carpworld Issue 251

Rod Hutchinson's third book, *Carp Now and Then*, was published the same year, 1988, as Carpworld One, which featured Rod on the cover. Although over the years Rod wrote for a number of publications, including *Carpworld* and his own catalogue/annual *Carp Scene*, it was 20 years before the publication of his next book, *Carp Along the Way, Volume One. Volume Two* and *Carp Inspirations* have also been published and Rod is working on the next volume of his memoirs, but in all honesty, the record of his iconic life in carp fishing has become somewhat fragmented. Here are some more fragments!

L ooking back I suppose it's amazing how many carp anglers who became influential household names I fished with in the '70s and '80s, people like Fred Wilton, Jim Gibbinson, Alan Smith, Lee Jackson, Lenny Middleton, Jack Hilton, Bill Quinlan, Chris Yates and so on. I just think that it was because there were so few carp lakes in those days and the carp enthusiasts all ended up at the same places. We heard whispers that there were big fish in these waters and that's where we all ended up. Carp fishing was a very small pond in those days and maybe at the beginning carp anglers could be counted in their hundreds, not their thousands. The keenest of the lot are often also the most inspirational, aren't they? The people who are there, and the people who catch regularly, you learn from them and I just think that we were the original keenies, in a position to find out things and pass on to others what we stumbled across. I just have to think back to when I was in Redmire in the early-'70s and Jack Hilton told me that he thought he knew of 10 carp waters in the country holding a 30-pounder. I said "Never!" I thought there were no more than six at the very maximum! There was so little carp fishing in our own areas that we were willing to travel to try to catch a big one, and that's how we came across all these fellow enthusiasts.

I have to admit that carp fishing did have me by the throat at that time, but knowing myself as an angler, looking back, my results at Redmire didn't mean as much as people might think. You look at the BCSG magazines from back then and whoever was in Redmire was the top rod of the time. There were only 10 anglers in

the syndicate, so you weren't exactly on a level playing field with the anglers who weren't in the syndicate. Bringing it up to date, it's almost like if you're fishing Les Graviers, Les Teillaits and Rainbow Lake; you're going to catch big fish, aren't you? It's a question of putting yourself in the right place and I always had the enthusiasm to make sure I got on those prime carp waters at the right time. Don't get me wrong; as you know I've played football all my life and fishing at Redmire was like playing at Wembley. It was the pinnacle of what you could achieve in carp fishing and at the time there was no suggestion that there was anywhere in the country to equal Redmire. You knew that you were in a privileged situation, and while you were in there you wanted to give it your best shot.

ABOVE
Jack Hilton at Redmire: he made a real impression on me and was a big influence.

Redmire was when I was first thrown together with Yatesy, because we joined at the same time, and were on the same rota. I think my strongest memory is that fishing there at that time taught me that there are more than two methods of catching carp. You have to realise that for me to get into Redmire in the first place was because I was a very successful angler at that time, and I was still young. I wouldn't say it was the arrogance of youth, but I knew I had a method which would catch carp from anywhere, using particles. I'd refined my methods at Pinetrees, which was a rock-hard water, and had gone on to have success everywhere I went with them. I had particles which worked, and I knew how to use them. And let's be honest, I probably used to put in 10 times as much bait as everyone else. Nowadays a 10kg bucket isn't a lot, but while other people were putting in a handful of bait, a few pieces of bread flake or half a pint of maggots, I was going in with a 10kg bucket of maples, tares and hemp!

I did some experimenting with particles but the fact is, I came up with the mix that worked best right at the beginning. Before I got to Redmire I'd started on maples at Pinetrees, and I'd got this mix together: quite honestly, to this day, I don't know whether I've ever come up with a better mix. I called it the Redmire Mix and it was three-parts maples, two-parts tares and one-part hemp. The idea was that when they were feeding hard you could get away with the bigger bait on the hook – the maples – but if they were a bit touchy you would maybe use the tares as hookbait; or if you were scratching, then you were on the hemp. It's a brilliant mix. Mally and I have just started on Rainbow and as far as I'm concerned we are absolute novices there.

But even after all these years you think, 'Well what do we go in with first?' We went there using the Redmire Mix as groundbait. We're still having to come to terms with catching fish from the lake but we knew from the off the mix we use would hold fish in an area and give us a chance of catching them – and we're talking about a mix I've been using for the thick end of 40 years!

The reason for me experimenting at Redmire was that you can't believe that you've hit the jackpot with the best bait at the first time of asking! You always have to keep trying out things to see if you can come up with something better, although whether we can ever come up with a better particle combination I don't know. The only way I could possibly improve the mix a bit would be to include some maize in it to make it a bit more visual. I experimented at Redmire with other particles, like cockles and prawns, and they caught a few fish, but the thing was that in those days, at Redmire, you could catch fish with some baits, but those baits were absolutely murdered by eels. We'd have run after run from eels, and that wasn't what we were fishing for!

Applying particles at Redmire wasn't much of a problem. You have to remember that this was Redmire where you could catapult some baits to the middle of the lake...

BELOW
Looking back, I suppose I spent a fair bit of my time at Redmire in my underpants, introducing bait or landing fish!

Well, my favourite swims were on the far bank rather than the car park side, Kefford's and up by the islands, and you could always wade out there for at least 10yds. So it was a question of going out in your shorts, or with nothing on, and baiting the centre channel, no problem. So 'catapulting' was actually a euphemism for wading out. I'd use a big bait apron and all the works and I'd go out and I'd pile it in. I would bait up the centre channel and then spread the bait around on my way back to leave a trail of bait out from the bank to the centre of the pool. It worked, and I would often catch fish very soon after wading out to bait up. Make no bones about it I did well at Redmire. On my first trip – which wasn't a week because I never had a week on Redmire; generally it was a three-day session – but that first trip I think Chris and I met up on the Tuesday, and I had 17 fish by the weekend. I'd never had that sort of result in Lincolnshire! Those tactics I'd developed were right for Redmire and I was in the right place at the right time. The difference was that I just wanted to catch carp, while in the eyes of other people only the big fish mattered. I go fishing and I love to catch carp, and I love to catch big 'uns, and I do get my share, but I've never had this focused, blinkered, one-eyed 'that's the fish I want' sort of approach. The buzzer sounding was always more important than the size of the fish on the other end of the line. Looking back to the Redmire days, compared to the current situation with the M62 and the M5, that was quite a journey to Redmire in an old banger. The motorways just weren't there! When I tell people that it used to take me seven hours to get there in an old Morris Traveller they can't believe it. And then of course the Traveller rarely made it home in one go; it invariably broke down at Shardlow near Nottingham on the way back!

I've got to hold my hand up to the fact that to some extent being in the Redmire syndicate affected my real life. Well, to be fair, we only have one life, don't we? No matter what I say you don't know what's coming up. You don't see what's coming. I was lucky because my mum and dad were together throughout my dad's life and nothing changed. When you are young you think that is how life is, or you did back then when divorce was a comparative rarity. I was fortunate in that I seemed to have a gift for catching carp and I had the chance to fish what was, at the time, the ultimate carp water. To be honest, I never expected ever to find anything like that again. I just thought that was a one-off shot in life and I had to go for it. At that time I never expected Savay to come up, and Cassien, and Orient and Chantecoq, and now Rainbow…

Redmire was exceptional, and over the years it has inspired so many people, and continues to do so. It's hard to imagine it now. Chris and I used to call it the Aquarium. It wasn't just the people you were fishing with, although that was great enough to fish with Chris, Jack Hilton, Bill Quinlan and so on, but you were also able to see how they went about catching carp. However good you think you are, you never stop learning, and you pick up all sorts of bits and pieces watching other top anglers in action. I remember some time ago someone made the comment to the effect that, "Well Jack Hilton would be no good today because carp fishing has moved on too far…" It hasn't! The rigs have been improved, as has the tackle, but anyone coming into carp fishing today has got access to all that anyway. But the big thing is, if you understand carp's behaviour and how carp react, then you are always going to be in with a shout. When he was at the top of his game Jack Hilton was a very focused, hugely successful angler, and people who make it to the top of the tree in any sport or pursuit would do whatever they had to do to make sure they were successful in any era. It's no coincidence that Jack was the first angler to catch three 30s. He set out to catch big fish and was successful. And the younger carp anglers may not understand that without Jack setting his mind on fishing at Redmire, the water might have been lost to carp fishing towards the end of the '60s. He was a very focused, determined man, Jack,

rang Jack about it. At that time, Jack had published that he'd seen this monster, which was fair enough. I didn't dispute it because you went to Redmire with those dreams in your head that those fish were there. I've never gone onto a water thinking that I want to catch **that** fish. I've never been a person who has targeted fish, but it's the unknown ones that are the exciting ones, and hopefully the biggest ones. Some carp anglers are realists and others are dreamers. Jack Hilton, and then Ritchie (McDonald) were the anglers who really targeted fish. Jack was very, very successful in the end, but he had that tunnel vision for one fish. He probably caught loads more fish from Redmire than he ever reported. He'd play a fish and unhook it in the water if it didn't measure up to what he was after. But I've never really been big-fish oriented, then this particular day came around, late-September or early-October; it was raining, and this common came up on the dam, and I couldn't believe what I was seeing. It was my last proper session and I'd had a good catch; I'd had three fish inside an hour and Bob Jones came down and took the pictures for me. That was the same day I saw this monster.

I rang Jack and said, "I think I believe your story!"

It was enormously long this fish; I thought it was at least 4ft long. You have to put things into perspective. Thousands of other carp anglers have now caught 40lb, 50lb and even 60lb carp, but very few, if any, of them are anything like that length!

Jack said, "I'm glad you've seen it because when I saw it I said 4ft long, but I thought 5ft!"

As good a time as I had at Redmire – and I had three really good years, including one incredible one, and the 'Night of the Beer Barrels' happened for John MacLeod and Billy Walkden, but there were so many carp in Redmire then – it is a fact that Jack was selling off the doubles – to be honest, I think we got it just past its peak, three or four years past its peak, maybe. There had been a population explosion and some of the commons were getting long and thin, nearly like river fish. So yes, I saw a 4ft long common, but I wouldn't like to attempt to put a weight on it. When Hilton saw the big fish people were very sceptical and suggested that a

BELOW
My biggest fish from Redmire at 32lb, although I'm sure I lost bigger fish.

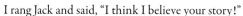

fish of that size would weigh in the region of 120lb, but I don't think it would have weighed anything like that. I saw it; others saw it; but it has never been caught so what it weighed is open to conjecture.

There seems to be some morbid curiosity concerning the circumstances in which I lost my Redmire place. It's not something I've ever talked about in depth because it's best forgotten really! Let's be right, I was on my fifth warning when I was thrown out, so I don't suppose it was any great surprise to those around me! First of all, I was complained about because my tackle was inadequate, and if it was true I think I've already explained the reason for that! You just didn't have four sets of tackle in those days because there was nowhere else you could use them however good a stroke-puller you were! The second warning was for parking on the dam! I was sorry about that, but I didn't know it was in the rules. I'd seen another member take his gear across the dam in his car and dump it by the stile at the far end, so I presumed it was permitted. The third warning, and this one really hurt, was for not cleaning out the toilet, which was not true at all. I only fished with two other people and we always cleaned it out.

In the list of captures in the book 'Redmire Pool' Bob Jones and I are jointly credited with a 27lb mirror which was caught on my rods, but apparently they couldn't wake me up to land it! That may sound extreme now, but in those days of unreliable buzzers you tended to fish yourself into a state of exhaustion trying to stay awake for days and nights on end in case it went off without the buzzer sounding. It was as simple as that. You used to fish your eyeballs out. It was very exhausting, and you just couldn't rely on most of the buzzers that were available then. And for me personally, mid-afternoon was the lowest ebb; that was when I ran out of steam and would crash out, and that's what happened on that occasion. But there was no warning in connection with that capture!

I don't really know what tipped the scales eventually. I truly don't know. I know the excuse was that I was supposed to have had an argument with the man who lived in one of the cottages, but that wasn't right. Chris and I knew the old boy and used to go and have a cup of tea with him. I don't know who had a row with him, but he wasn't in the same coloured car as me, and the bloke was much shorter than me and had jet-black hair. I guess my time had come. I'd had three good years on there. It hurt at the time, and for a while I even thought about giving up carp fishing, but life goes on and everything turns out for the best. It was a very special place and I have very special memories of it. I wouldn't have missed it for anything and I still feel very privileged to have had the opportunity of fishing Redmire at that time.

Looking back, the '70s were probably the most secretive period from my point of view. After coming out of Redmire you tried to find somewhere good again, and everyone was keeping their waters quiet! I fished around at a lot of different waters in the '70s and although Savay later turned out to be so special, Johnsons was the water that made a lot of things happen for me. This was when I started to make the switch from particles to 'specials', paste baits, which later became boilies. I would say that even started during the Redmire years. When I left, in addition to Kevin (Clifford) coming in, a number of Fred Wilton's friends, including Roy Johnson, got into the Redmire syndicate. So, having met Fred and talked to him about what he was doing, I knew that his baits would work on places like Redmire. Even going back to Jack Hilton, he started experimenting along the lines of 'specials'. I know on one session he turned up with something like Minced Morsels, or Purina, one of the originals of what were thought to be sinking cat food pellets. Jack came up to Redmire with two great big paper sacks of these things and I felt sure they had got to work, but he hadn't tried them in advance and it turned out they were full of air and just floated! In retrospect, I think the way we baited was almost as important as the bait itself. How we baited has now become almost a standard for groundbaiting and getting them feeding.

It's just a fact of life that some baits are more effective than others. I've been surprised at the reaction to my bait chapters in my book 'Carp Inspirations' to the point that some people want me to do another bait book. I tend to think that nowadays people just pick up the phone and order a sack of the going bait for the freezer, but there are still a lot of people out there looking for an edge in terms of coming up with their own bait. When I went down to fish in the Kent the scene was absolutely buzzing with bait talk and bait theories, and my bait discussions went back as far as Brooklands and Alan Smith. I talked about everything to do with carp fishing with Alan. To be fair, Alan's views on bait didn't seem to be a lot different to mine. Fred came up with this nutritional thing and after that it was a question of different

BELOW
Johnson's was the water that made a lot of things happen for me.

people's interpretations of how you provided that nutrition. And then you had fish HNVs for the first time as opposed to milk HNVs. Cat foods became a popular basis for baits. When you're talking about cat food, being born in Grimsby and working on Grimsby docks every day, there are thousands of tons of fish offal; half of it goes to the cat food factories and half of it goes to the fishmeal factories to be ground down. In the '70s a lot of people had the idea that the best bait would be the one that was the most convertible for carp, and even Fred said that should be carp. But it's more than just the protein: it's the vitamins and minerals; it's the oil content; it's the whole package.

After talking to Fred, while I believed in his nutritional ideas, I didn't necessarily share his views on the best ingredients. I've always said that. It's the same with percentages. I've gone higher with fish proteins than I ever have with milk protein, but I've never calculated actual percentages of the different ingredients. I was just happy to put together a bait that felt right, and in terms of fishmeals it was probably difficult to put together a bait that mixed well, and boiled, that had a higher protein percentage than 50-60%. I've always felt that the oils in fishmeals were a vital part of the bait. There are times when the roughage content is of extra importance, particularly in cold-water conditions. Their natural needs are so well defined and all we can do is struggle to cater for those needs and hope we are getting it about right.

In the '70s period I'm talking about a lot of people going down the flavour trail, but I think I went into them deeper than anyone else in terms of why a flavour should work; why you wanted a flavour based on a certain concept or line of thought, and knowing what should work. There are two points there. One comes from having a tank and seeing that a carp is very much like a cow and will chew the cud, and they'll eat their own faeces. Really, this is all going back to the Waveney days and how the carp recognise food. Nowadays it's a bit like 'why do carp try to eat plastic'? I think they recognise anything organic as being food and they'll try it out. It goes without

ABOVE
This lovely Johnson's mirror went 27½lb. I spent some time talking baits with Fred Wilton at Johnson's.

saying that they haven't got any hands; if it smells 'right' they can only take it into their mouth, and if they don't like it they can spit it out. I don't know if I've mentioned this in print before, but the thing that really amazed me was at Cassien in 1984 when I landed what was, at the time, my biggest fish of 58lb+, was that its backside opened and out came a full swan mussel, or just like the net shape of it! All the keratin, all the indigestible protein, was still there. All the inside had gone, all the guts of the mussel had been eaten. A carp is like a cow of the water. It digests things several times. It will take it in a second and third time, and I think this is what happens with tiger nuts. It hasn't got enzymes efficient enough to break down a lot of these foods in one go. So going back to the '70s and flavours, I got to thinking about how they find their food and I realised that it was through attraction of some sort. They were being attracted by the faeces of their natural prey, so that was the line of thought behind flavours like Monster Crab, Shellfish Sense Appeal and a few others along those lines which were massively successful baits. There were two lines of thought there on flavour design. One was based on the old fermentation process. What happens in fermentation? In seafood you've got fermented prawns, and shrimps; Monster Crab: if it comes down to it, the true original version was fermented crab. Again, that's breaking down the proteins, so you're at that second stage of making them more digestible, or seem more digestible to the carp, creating that 'partially broken down' message. Scopex is at that same level in fruit and vegetables. That's when the starches are turning to alcohol; that's when they are more digestible to animals. Scopex, Mulberry, and others came from that same line of thought. You're adding something to the bait to give off the message that it is at its easiest to digest, at its most edible from an animal's – i.e. carp's – point of view.

But there is something there that I'm not sure about, which is the most difficult part. Nowadays, when people are catching on foam and plastic and so on there are probably better phrases, but in the old days I used to call it 'novelty value'. I do believe I was one of the first people to use pop-ups and I said at the time that their success might simply be down to novelty value, something different. At the same time I think carp do try out everything for food content. I think plastic is looked upon by fish as being organic: it's got that chemical food basis to it, as Lee Jackson explained in 'Inspirations'. I wasn't that long out of school in those days and I have to say that I considered myself to be a bit of a scientist, and that was the logical way I tended to look at flavours.

A lot of those early baits were down to chance. On the flavour/attraction front there was a trail through the American Loeb Report, through the Lowestoft Institute Research and the Dick Weale and Len Bunn's Black Majic amino acid bait. From there I went into the whole area of attraction to an unparalleled depth, and very scientifically. The Lowestoft Report was based on cod. It all came about from there being a shortage of lugworms for sea anglers; sea angling was very big then. I was a keen shore fisherman as well, but there were problems. Big trenches were being left along beaches from lugworm digs and horses were falling into them, so there had to be some sort of control. One of the big angling companies sponsored research into an artificial lugworm, and it was that research that got people looking at amino acids and the basis of attraction. If you got hold of the papers that were available you found that there was a reference to the Loeb Report. So I read the Loeb Report and there were things in there that made you think, and half the smells in there were associated with rotting, organic things. All this made me think about the basis of attraction from lugworms and set my mind on the track of their faeces. I just couldn't see how there could be attraction from amino acids or whatever unless they were soluble. You give off sweat; you give off bodily odours, all of which betray your presence. So in terms of lugworms I could only think that if they were giving off amino acids then it was via their faeces. In nature, and in the sea, everything is something else's prey; everything tries to hide; shrimps, prawns and crabs hide, and even conger eels hide. In freshwater, bloodworms hide. So how do you betray your presence while you are hiding? Not to put too fine a point on it, by crapping yourself!

Because I had a decent scientific background from school and an ongoing interest in the subject, I went about designing my own flavours scientifically rather than just picking another version of cheese, or maple, or strawberry from a flavourist's list. I discussed baits on a scientific level with Fred Wilton, because he was a bit of science buff. There is something here that people might not know, because only about three people do know, and Kevin Nash is one of them! When I was on Johnson's lakes in Kent, the best conversations I ever had about bait were on the bank with Fred and Barrie Rickards, who was a lecturer at Cambridge University, and Martin Gay, who I think worked in universities as well. It was really enjoyable talking to these guys about bait, and I told them that there were bits that I just couldn't figure out about flavours and attraction, because there were things we didn't know. I'm not so sure we know now, but we know a hell of a lot more now than we did then! In terms of smell I couldn't figure out if things worked in water the same way that they work in air.

ABOVE
*Some of the very
successful flavours
that I developed
working with Peter
Rayners, then of
Barnett and Fosters.*

Anyway, thanks to Barrie Rickards, and possibly Martin Gay, I was able to go and attend lectures at Cambridge University, and this was at the time I was staying with Kevin Nash! Running the business was still part-time then. I could come home at weekends, put the orders together, send them off, and still do two or three days' work. So the business was subsidised by the scaffolding for the first two years. Even when I started fishing Savay I was still scaffolding, then going home and

making Seafood Blend for two nights and sending out the orders. I attended lectures at Cambridge for one year, mainly on the subject of amino acids and pheromones. We were into a new area with the flavour and attraction scene and the thing about carp fishing is that there are always another 10 people as crazy as you are! If you are working on something, there will be another 10 people working on it – at least. Nothing is totally original. As I've said to you before, most carp rigs are derived from really successful sea fishing rigs, even going back to the Hair Rig. You can think that you've come up with a new idea, but it will have been thought of before.

I think it's fair to say that carp baits represented a new science from the early-'70s onwards, so ideas were being brought into carp fishing that hadn't previously been used in relation to carp. Still on the flavour trail, after university I got together with a flavourist, Peter Rayner, then of Barnett and Fosters the big flavour producers, to get to know more about the scientific make-up of flavours. I had two smashing years working with Peter and I learned an enormous amount. Out of my liaison with him came Monster Crab, Shellfish Sense Appeal, Chocolate Malt, Scopex, Maplecream (the 'cream' was Scopex), which was a blend of Maple and Scopex, Enigme, which was based on the geranium smell which Alan Smith used in the essential oil form as one of his favourite attractors, and others. I think Geranium Oil may have come from Fred Wilton originally, although Fred and I always argued the point about the role of what he called 'labels'! As far as I was concerned, they were attractors because that was what caused the fish to pick up the bait in the first place. To me, if an item didn't smell of food then a carp wouldn't sample it, and the more appealing the attractor, the more the carp would want the bait in the first place. I worked with Peter Rayner for two years, and then he went to work for another company, which was researching alternative proteins. At that time people were looking at alternative proteins, the whole food industry; tons and tons of soya were being used in baits. There were four basic proteins for humans: milk, meat, fish and eggs, but the animal feed business was massive. How do you provide livestock and pets with protein all year? There were alternatives becoming available; soya protein alternative, fishmeal protein alternative, and the one I was really interested in, yeast alternative. Peter Rayner became managing director of this new company and we started spraying flavours onto yeast, which we now know is still working to this day. Yeast always did work. We'd been using PYM, and other brewer's yeast health foods like Yestamin, and of course the original Hi-Pro bait was based on PYM. Yeast was a no-brainer – it couldn't not work! The first mix of that type that we came up with was Ultraspice, the base mix, which was a brilliant bait. What we sprayed onto that was Marmite and garlic and... well, I won't say the other item because nowadays I can't! All these items were tested on dogs. Originally, these things were made for the pet food industry but we adapted them for the carp industry as well.

We're going back to the '70s and early-'80s, when all my original bait and attractor research was going on and I was designing those very effective baits. I'll not

labour this point but Richard Williams has recently claimed in print that he helped me design all these original baits and I'm afraid this just isn't true. I've only known Richard in recent years when he became a member at Woldview. Why he said what he said I don't know. He's had no input into the design of any of my baits at any time. I can only presume he was misquoted. His baits are not the original Hutchy baits. They were the property of Catchum Products, which was taken over by Kevin Nash, which is why I can't disclose the full details of those baits.

The '70s were very formative and very influential, and at the end of the '70s some of the leading lights and best minds in carp fishing, and the best technicians, came together on Savay. What happened at Savay, from the outside looking in, is, for many people, the pinnacle of carp-fishing history, although at the time it didn't feel like that! But looking back, even from three or four years on, it did. Even then I wasn't really a young man. I would have been in my mid-30s, but with a young mind, focusing on carp fishing. There were young guys coming through, and some very experienced carp anglers; Lenny Middleton, Geoff Kemp, John Baker, Kevin Maddocks, Andy Kellock, Andy Little, Bob Morris, John Richards, the Waveney Valley guys... I could go on and on. A lot of these guys had cut their teeth on Waveney, and that was a place where people tried everything. It was a real cutting-edge venue. You were on small waters fishing for very pressured fish, and when you took the refined methods that were developed onto the bigger waters, then location became the key issue. If you can find the fish you are going to catch them because they are comparatively naïve. The big

ABOVE
By the time we went to Savay I think we knew what would catch carp.

difference for me was that I moved on from Waveney and had four years on the big gravel pits before Savay came up so I was more in tune with the location aspect than some of the other guys. By the time we went onto Savay I think we knew what would catch carp.

Looking back at Savay it seems unique because to me there was almost a family feel came out of the initial Savay syndicate, which hasn't come across from any of the top waters since. For a water at the pinnacle of carp fishing there was a surprising feeling of camaraderie came out of the fishing there, which I hope comes across in 'The Carp Strikes Back'. That's how it was, it truly was. The greatest thing you can say was that there wasn't a target fish that everyone wanted to catch. It was truly the unknown and we didn't know what was in there. To be fair, Harrow was the same; people didn't know what was in there. There were these gravel pits that had been stocked with a few carp years before. On Savay everyone was learning from each other and gradually word got round that certain swims were producing a few carp. And of course, during the first year we could only fish the Canal Bank, but then the second year, when we could fish the whole lake, well that was a whole different story. It's not just me who has nostalgia for those days; Martin Locke said to me recently that we'll never have anything like that again. It was a great crack and exciting fishing, and most people helped each other.

OPPOSITE PAGE
A lovely mirror from the Pads swim at Savay.

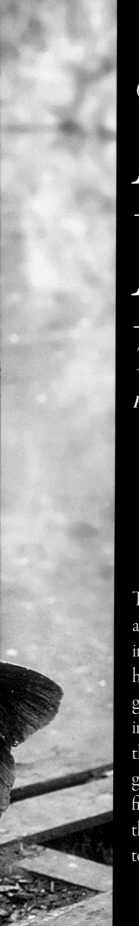

Carpworld's Big Interviews Revisited

Rod

Hutchinson

Talking to Tim Paisley • Part Two

From Carpworld Issue 252

The second part of Rod's interview in which he reminisces about the Colne Valley days and the early Savay syndicate, including some memories of the late Peter Broxup; describes his minor brushes with Kevin Maddocks, and how he later got stitched up by Kevin on the Orient; reveals how his interest in rod design developed over the years, starting with the first carbon rods in the late 70s; recalls the excitement of going to Cassien for the first time and his subsequent love of fishing overseas waters 'where dreams are still alive', and admits that the atmosphere at Rainbow is the nearest he has come to the special Savay syndicate camaraderie of the early 80s.

I 've never known a syndicate like that early Savay one. The closest I've come to it was when we did have that atmosphere for a couple of years on my own water, Woldview, when I was still fishing keenly on there: Coral was still well and all the syndicate members were friends to her. Up to the time of Savay carp fishing had been very secretive and competitive, but at Savay everyone was helping each other, and when I say 'helping each other' one story sticks in my mind. They didn't need to do it for me, but Lenny, through Andy (Little), came to me and said, "We think you should know about this." And that was the Hair Rig! I'm not bulling when I say that at that time I was catching as many as the guys on the Hair, but it was nice that they came to me with it. They asked me questions, and I think I helped a lot of people on bait. I'll mention this point here. I've just read Jim Gibbinson's piece in the 250th issue of Carpworld. Whenever Jim's got an article in the magazine I have to read it. Half of what he says I disagree with! I've had to fight against answering some of his comments hundreds of times, but in the recent issue he wrote about Lenny and Kevin Maddocks with the Hair Rig, and he felt that Kevin should take equal credit for the Hair with Lenny, and I actually agree with him entirely on that point. No matter what you say about whose invention it was, or whose brainchild, one thing you have to admit about Kevin Maddocks is that he is a bloody good carp angler, so it helps to prove a point if you give it to a top angler first to try out. This is no disrespect to Lenny because I know how innovative he was and I spent a lot of time with him, but I think the actual development of the rig moved a lot faster with Kevin involved in it. And the fact that Kevin and Lenny were on Savay meant that the whole Savay syndicate got on it, some of the best anglers I've ever seen my life, and from there it spread so quickly.

I've since been told that there were cliques on Savay, but at the time I didn't realise it. You tend to make friends and, to anyone on the outside looking in, three or four friends can be construed as a clique, particularly if they are high profile! It's like being accused of being aloof when you find yourself in a public situation which

BELOW
I was already catching as many as the guys on the Hair, but using it certainly helped!

you can't quite cope with. Like when a guy I didn't know woke me up on the bank at Savay and asked if he knew me.

I replied, "I don't think so or you wouldn't have woken me up!" I found that quite unbelievable. I would never dream of walking round a lake waking people up, and it can be even worse when you've driven 1,000 miles to a lake in France and someone wants to pick your brains while you're trying to set up! You try to be polite, but sometimes it just isn't on. There was a social element to Savay then, which perhaps tempered the competitiveness.

Well, when you talk about the social element, you're talking about gatherings of more than three anglers, say. On Redmire there was a social aspect, but you're talking about three-man rotas on Redmire, which was a bit limiting socially. There was a coming together in the Colne Valley as a whole at that time, and Savay was just one of the waters. You had the Fisheries, and the Cons, and Harrow, and so on. Those pictures of gatherings in the Horse & Barge weren't just the Savay syndicate; there were carp anglers from all over the valley in those shots. The family atmosphere extended to the Valley. It was exciting. Everyone was learning from each other and it was great. I may have mentioned this already, but I saw Martin Locke at a meeting about four or five years ago for the first time in ages, and we started reminiscing about Savay, and he said then, "There'll never be anything like that again. The closest thing you'll find to that atmosphere is at Rainbow. Get yourself down there!"

Bob Davis ran the Savay syndicate for the first two years. The thing there was

BELOW
Those pictures of gatherings in the Horse & Barge weren't just the Savay syndicate, there were carp anglers from all over the valley in those shots.

that Bob had fished Waveney as well, but I'd never fished with Bob, and a number of the Waveney regulars were in the Savay syndicate, people like Graham Marshall, Derek Cunnington, John Dunne, Dennis Beckett... I first met Lenny (Middleton) on Waveney, and he was experimenting with the Hair then, long before he told me about it. You look at the list in the back of John Harry's book *Savay* and it's amazing the number of top anglers who were in at the start of the Savay syndicate, anglers who were household names then, and many who are still household names today. The following year a number of people got in who I'm still very friendly with today. Mark Lawson got in, as did Kerry Barringer, and Roger Smith...

I'd met Roger once prior the Savay. He wasn't on my rota on Redmire. He'd been part of the Redmire syndicate from the start and he was still in when I joined, although he dropped out at the end of my first year. But I'll just go back to that list in John Harry's book; it's amazed me because the names of almost half the anglers are well known: Andy Little, Lenny Middleton, Kevin Maddocks, Mike Wilson, Paul Bray, John Richards, Geoff Kemp, Albert Romp, Bob Baker, Roger Smith, Keith Selleck, Clive Diedrich, Malcolm Winkworth, and so on. There was quite a line-up of talent there, so however good you thought you were, you couldn't help but learn from what was going on around you. And that list was just from the first year. There were a number of high-profile anglers joined within the next couple of years.

Bob Davis ran the syndicate for the first two years of its existence, and then Peter Broxup took over. In his Carpworld interview Bob made some reference to having to keep me and Kevin Maddocks apart. I should make it clear that this didn't mean physically, just that we tended to rub each other up the wrong way and Bob felt it was better if we were on different rotas. Well, people can say what they want about all that, but I knew Kevin was a very successful angler because of his results, and I think he knew I could catch carp, too. I think we both learnt from each other. We had a couple of incidents, but at the same time I think it should also be known that he took me to Duncan's Mid Northants water to fish. As far as I know we were never enemies, more like friendly rivals, although eventually he stitched me up like a kipper at the Orient, which is another story altogether.

The Savay incidents were blown out of proportion, although perhaps I wasn't as helpful as I might have been. The first one happened when I was fishing the Birches, and to tell the truth I'd had a bit of a hit; I'd had four fish. Early on, the big unknown at Savay was location, so you were trying to piece together every bit of information you could, and get all the help you could. So Kevin turned up and came down the bank and asked me if I'd seen anything, and I said I hadn't, although I was plastered with carp slime at the time, which I think I may have claimed to be bream slime! I think syndicate leader Bob Davis was a bit put out about that! The second occasion wasn't really my fault. I'd found fish behind one of the islands, and to cast to them I had to bivvy up in a swim down from the island and fish the rods at an angle. Kevin turned up, weighed up the situation, and asked me if I could recast my rods straight in front

of me! I don't know if he was having a
laugh or not, but I didn't move them
and he went and fished another swim.

To move on to the Orient
business, fair dos, it was one of the best
stitch-ups I've ever known! When we
first went to the Orient I didn't have
much experience of the big French
reservoirs, and Mally and I were
perhaps a bit wet behind the ears. Our
first two times on there we got chucked
off and nicked, and it cost us a lot of
money! They fined us about 80 euros,
or it may have been francs back then.
There was no night fishing on most
areas of the Orient at that time and we
were done for camping. You weren't
allowed to put up bivvies in the non-

ABOVE
*Kevin Maddocks, an
impressive catcher
of carp. We had
a couple of minor
clashes at Savay, but
he stitched us up big-
style at the Orient.*

night areas, and if you did you were camping. Everyone knew that the Bulldozer – and
I still hate the name to this day (I think she should have been called Angela!) – lived
at Geraudot, but every time I went down there they nicked me. I think John van Eck
got fined an extra 20 euros for making some sort of proposal to a young female garde
de pêche, or gendarme, whichever it was! So next time Mally and I planned to go, we
were going to do it right. I knew Mally had been and recced it a couple of times, and
we both knew where we wanted to be during a certain six-week period. We wanted to
be at Mesnil, on the stretch they call Bivvy City, in October. Fishing was supposed to
finish at the end of October/1st November, and when I'd been on there with Richard
Seal we duly pulled off on 1st November, and Martin Locke and Dave Beacham
jumped straight in after us, and they had a hit! That's what comes of being a good guy
who doesn't pull strokes... Anyway, the following year I told Mally that the only way
we were going to nail it was to get there a week early. Mally had just retired early, and
Alice (Mally's mum) was still in good health, so he was able to do it. So we went out
there for five weeks, and we were prepared to sit there until we got one of the swims
we wanted. We got there on a Wednesday night and sure enough, all the bivvies were
up and all the spots were taken. We passed the time of day with a couple of the guys,
and then put up our own bivvies at the back of the line of bivvies to catch up on sleep
because we were knackered. From there on we were slow to clue up because we didn't
see anyone fishing from the middle bivvies.

In the end Mally went across and asked, "Who's in here?" "He's gone down the
shops, mate!" was the reply. There were just a couple of rods out in front of this bivvy,
and a couple out in front of another bivvy further down the bank. Well, to cut a long

story short, Kevin Maddocks had booked the swim for the Saturday, which was when he turned up. We'd been bivvied up behind the empty bivvies for a couple of days! So Kevin well and truly outdid me in the end, and the best of it was, when he did turn up I just had to hold my hand up – he stitched me up good-style and we just left him to it!

To go back to Savay, one of my last memories of the water was fishing with the late Peter Broxup at the end of the season. Bear in mind I've had a lot of flattery in my life over carp fishing. Every time you pick up a magazine they call you a legend, and that's very flattering; half the time it's bullshit as well, but it's nice to be given credit for something once in a while. Before his untimely death a couple of years back, Peter had started writing one or two pieces for CARPology. Peter was involved with Elite Baits, and I used to supply them with the odd bit of gear. In fact, going back to when I was in Savay, Peter asked me if I wanted to go into the bait business with him and the late Keith Selleck, then of Middlesex Angling Centre, but my business was up and running by then and I decided to stick with what I was doing. Anyway, when I first went to Les Graviers with Frank Warwick I came across these magazines I hadn't seen before, with articles by Pete in them, because, bear in mind that prior to his death Pete was the most successful angler on Savay. Well, over the years Pete had been very flattering to me; he said a couple of things like, 'Rod showed them how to fish Savay,' and he also said that my great edge in the first couple of years wasn't bait or watercraft, but the fact that I was a better caster than most of the others. And many years later he had repeated that comment in one of these magazine articles, which surprised me, for reasons I'll explain.

BELOW
Peter Broxup, firm but fair.

We're still in the early-'80s here, the first year Pete was head bailiff and before he had built the cabin on the island. And of course we are still in the era when there was a three-month close season. So the fishing ended in the middle of March, and I went down for an end-of-season session, thinking there would be a load of anglers doing the same thing. But in fact the only three anglers there were Peter Broxup, Peter Wright (The Brain), and me. When I went down I wasn't sure where the fish would be, but with it getting into spring I felt they would be starting to get up in the shallows, so I was planning to fish the Pads area on the Road Bank. Anyway, I got there

and there was this monster bivvy there, which was Peter Broxup's. I wasn't going to
argue with him because he was leader of the syndicate, and he was a big man from
chucking all that meat around on the market. In fact he always reminded me of one
of my favourite films stars, Dermot Meehan, the sergeant in the Rocky films. Peter
always had this aura of an old American boxing referee: 'Remember me, I'm firm but
I'm fair...' And he was fair. Savay was no different to anywhere else; if you caught fish
you got accused of doing all sorts of different things! The fact is I seem to have been
misunderstood on most of the waters I've fished, and Cuttle Mill was the best on that
front... I wasn't stroke-pulling at Cuttle Mill, that's the daft thing. Cuttle was days only
and we used to sleep in the barn at night. But because I wasn't in the barn at night
there was a rumour that I was actually fishing Cuttle, which I wasn't, I was fishing a
little carp water across the road in the grounds of the Belfry Golf Centre. The problem
was, you weren't supposed to fish that either, and for some odd reason Albert Brewer
(the owner of Cuttle Mill at the time) reported me for fishing it, which I wasn't too
happy about because Albert and I were good friends at the time.

So back in the Pads I was a bit gutted that Peter had nicked my spot. I'd met
up with Pete the Brain in the car park and we knew where we wanted to be, and The
Brain went and set up in the Cottage Bay. I was well up for the Pads, which was a one-
angler spot really, but I had a word with Peter B and asked him where he was casting
his baits. Pete had got what we called the Gap, so he could get through the gap to the
islands; then there's the Pads, then there's another tiny little gap full of snags. Well, to

ABOVE
*The Pads Swim, the
scene of a memorable
end-of-season session
with Peter Broxup
and Pete the Brain.*

91

cut a long story shorter, I went in to the right of Peter to fish this tiny little channel about 12ft wide. He put two in the Gap and we both put two in the Pads; fair enough. Anyway, being the last night of the season this turned into a real social evening. We had a couple of brews, and then agreed that we would go up the pub and then have an Indian. Neither of the Peters was a big drinker, but if you got them in the pub they would have a couple to be sociable. So before we set off Peter B says, "Now there are rumours that some of you guys are leaving your rods out when you go up the pub, and I'm not having that." To be honest I think it did go on but The Brain and I weren't party to that practice, so we all wound in and went off on our end-of-season social event.

When we got back we were as keen as mustard. We all cast out, bearing in mind that it was pitch-black and we'd had a drink. The Brain came round with a couple of bottles of wine, and rustled up some chilli con carne and some of his Marks & Spencer's posh meals, and the social went on all night. And while we were sitting talking, Peter B repeated what he'd said previously: "They all talk about why you are doing so well Rod, but we've been watching you, and your true ability is that you're the best caster on the lake. You can clip the pads; you can hit the bars every time." It wasn't something I'd thought about, although in fairness when I was beach fishing I used to go out on the football field every night when I wasn't fishing to practise my casting, and on Savay this was something that gave me an edge in those early days. Most anglers weren't used to long-range fishing back then. And the fact that I was one of the first on there with carbon fibre rods did help a bit!

Anyway, we sat there all night, and as daylight came Pete the Brain produced

this gorgeous home-cured bacon and a thick crusty loaf. I remember sitting there thinking, 'This is wonderful!' – which it was; memorable. The dawn was breaking and to this day I don't know if we should have been off the water the night before at midnight when the season officially ended, although I think maybe we should have been. The bacon was sizzling in the pan, and Peter Broxup disappeared back to the car park and came back with some field mushrooms. You remember these occasions for the rest of your days, and honestly it was the best meal I've ever had in my life! So we finished the meal and we sat there reminiscing, and commenting that we thought we would have caught during the night, when Peter B says, "What's that in the pads?" because the pads were going up and down. Anyway, we looked up and my left-hand rod had gone up, straight through the trees and down into the pads – and a carp had picked it up. Only three hours before Peter had been saying I was the best caster he'd ever seen in his life! Not only that, but he repeated it in the article I read, which he must have written about 20 years later, which I thought was nice of him. We tried to get the fish out; I even went swimming for it – and the Savay water was cold all year round, never mind in mid-March! – and got all the tackle back, but the fish got off and that was the end of the season.

Talking of long-range casting it was about that time when we brought out the Big Pit Specials. A lot of the anglers of today won't know how much work I did on rods. While I was

Putting a rod through its paces. I have always kept pace with the development of new materials and resins.

at Savay I actually had some 15-footers built; the 15ft Barbusters! To be fair, even with 13ft rods you have got to be able to have a swing in the back cast, and on an awful lot of gravel pits and smaller waters you just haven't got that sort of room because of the trees behind you. As Savay grew up you just didn't have that space. I was with Alan Brown originally, but those rods came about through a hero of mine, Pete Thomas. This was while Dick Walker was still alive, and Peter was a rep for Fibatube (Hardy's), who were building blanks. I met him in Alan Brown's shop. We were in the early days of carbon fibre then, and compared to the backbone you get in today's rods, they felt quite soft – but they made a hell of a difference at the time. The Big Pit Special rod was based on a 10ft salmon blank and I took it and added 2ft of carbon into the butt. That's how I came up with a 12-footer, and that idea came from Jack Hilton's Golden Goddesses, where he put a foot of cane into the butt of a glass rod. I decided that if he could do it with glass, then I could do it with carbon. They were fabulous rods and I wish I'd still got some, but it has to be said that the rods of today have got ten times more backbone than those early carbon fibre-based rods.

Over the years we must have come up with seven or eight new models as I've kept up with the advantages of the new materials that have been developed and have

ABOVE
*One of Tim's
'showcase' Dream
Makers.*

become available. When I met Pete Thomas, who was at Fibatube, they had one product, and it sold well. I wanted a 12ft carp rod, which was why we put 2ft into the butt, which produced a parallel butt. But coming from sea fishing I knew that a rod's casting ability came from its taper, and so much of what I knew about rods to start with came from sea fishing and beach casting. I moved on from the Big Pit Specials to a true 12ft carbon blank, which was the basis of the Spirolite MkI, and from there onwards there was a rapid development of carbon weaves and new improved resins. I always knew the ideal curve I was after; it was a question of maintaining the through-action on the cast but giving the rod greater powers of recovery. I went into all that just as deeply as I did into flavours. Coming up with new models has never been a gimmick, it's been a question of keeping up with technological advances. The whole progression from 1979 onwards has been to arrive at a more powerful rod with a greater amount of feel but in a slimmer blank. We've progressed to this end result through the Spirolites, Sabres, Strikers and IMXs. Looking back, during most of my life in business I've been at the cutting-edge of rod development – while everything was being made in Europe. A lot of that time I was working with Simon at Century, but now all my business is through Frederico in Italy. The rods are still available, including the Dream Makers. When Frederico took over the production of my tackle and baits he told me that it would take time to make the whole range available again, but the baits and flavours are out there now, as are the rods, hooks, and so on.

While I was still fishing Savay my next big challenge came up, which was Cassien. It's not that I get bored with my fishing but I always want new horizons. I may have said this before but I'm always looking for venues where dreams are still alive. I love the mystery of new waters. I love not knowing their potential. I'm fishing Rainbow now, so some might say that I've changed, but does anyone know the potential of Rainbow Lake in the future? But going back to Cassien, there was an even greater element of the unknown there than fishing Redmire. At Redmire there was the so-called big common and one or two other supposed monsters, but when you look back at it all, there were just two big fish that were caught more than once, Pinky and the big 'un, which was Chris's eventual record fish, the 38. By the time we got into Redmire what we didn't know was that Pinky had died during the close season before we started fishing there. To some extent you had a fair idea of what was in there, but Cassien was a very different kettle of fish. I'd fished a couple of times with all-rounder Phil Smith, and out of the blue he sent me a little cutting from the international press saying that a 71lb carp had been caught from a lake in France, and I just thought, 'Why not? Go for it!' There was no picture of the fish and I didn't know anything whatsoever about the place, but I found it on the map and off I went.

Back then 71lb was off the scale, and I was dubious because the first thought that crossed my mind was, 'Who's got 70lb scales?!' But I was ready for a change and decided to give it a go. It was a long, long way, and when I got there it was a bit bigger than I expected it to be. But our approach was ever so basic, because it was basic fishing. We drove very slowly around the road at the top, looking for fish rolling; when we saw a fish roll we stopped there and

BELOW
Cassien: realisticaly there was a greater element of the unknown there than there was at Redmire.

BOTTOM
I always referred to the big Cassien fish as Cottis' fish, because Max was the first one to catch it.

fished the spot next morning. When we went there Cassien was unspoilt. Years later I went to Raduta, which felt very wild, very neglected, but by comparison Cassien was a paradise. But it was unspoilt, and there was this exciting air of the unknown about it. The 58lb+ I caught from there was a very big fish in those days, and the only bigger fish to come out during my time on the water was the 76. I've always referred to that fish as the Max Cottis fish, because he was the first one to catch it, prior to Kevin Ellis catching it at 76lb, and at the time that was seven or eight pounds bigger than anything else that came out of the water. I've got to admit I was absolutely crazy about Cassien from the moment I went there in the June. I went back in August, went back in September; and then went back in October and December. But the following year I went back and it was an entirely different lake, which I suppose was partly my fault because of the publicity we gave it! There were anglers from all over the world there. To be right, you can't expect to write about places without other anglers

TOP
Thirty and forty-pound fish were still big fish back then and we were happy with what we were catching.

ABOVE
I had a special affection for the Mere, and still do to this day.

jumping on the bandwagon and them becoming popular.

The following year was when I went back with Annie, the trip I describe in 'Carp Along the Way' Volume Two, and it was absolutely crazy. People were bivvying up far too close to each other. During '85 and '86 it just became so popular it was untrue. Anyone who's been to Cassien knows that the travelling time makes it a killer of a journey, and because of the pressure on the place I started to think that Cassien couldn't be the only place in France with fish of that size. So we started looking at the lakes round about: St. Croix, which is up in the mountains just above Cassien; Castellain was great because we loved the River Lot region. When you take the family fishing the kids love to catch as well, and on the River Lot you got bags of runs, and it was lovely, peaceful and unspoilt. Salagou was like that, although it was very wild and you could get a camper stuck very easily in those days. They were the untouched places. It's very hard when you've had somewhere practically to yourselves and then you can't get in the swims you want to fish any more, so that was when we went off trying all sorts of different venues.

You just take the chance. You work it out in your head – has this got the potential to produce big fish? The Mere was fantastic. Originally we got invited to Brittany to a water which had done two or three big 40s, Lac de Jurgon they called it. There weren't many French carp anglers in those days, but while we were fishing Jurgon a couple of them came along and starting talking to us about all the carp waters in the area where they had seen good carp. The Mere was one of those waters. We caught a really good stamp of fish out of the Mere. The smallest fish were 20s; you caught lots of 30s, and if you were lucky you'd get a mid- to upper-40, or maybe a scraper-50 even. But the real beauty of the Mere was that you had the lake to yourself, and you had to work it out for yourself, how to approach it, and where the fish were at different times of the year.

I had a special affection for the Mere, as I still do to this day. I was talking to a lad at Rainbow and he'd fished the Mere after we'd been on it, and he said it's still the same lake. The farmer and his family we were friends with still live on the bank, and I'd love to go back and see them all some time. But you move on and there just isn't time to do all the things you want to do. Back then it was above average because there was a big head of fish, but nowadays, since the commercial lakes have started to take over, there are hundreds of lakes holding fish of that size. But back then all we would do was buy a national ticket and go out and fish the lakes that were available to us; 30 and 40lb fish were still big fish and we were happy with what we were catching.

It would be fair to say that we were doing family fishing from the mid-'80s to the early-'90s, but there came a point when I felt I was missing out on the big-fish fishing, that there were waters we couldn't go to as a family that I wanted to fish. Chantecoq and the Orient came up a little bit later, but in the late-'80s the biggest fish were coming from the rivers. Cassien apart, the River Yonne and the Seine were doing the biggest fish and we concentrated on the Montreux area up to Messi, where Kevin Maddocks has now got his lakes. That's where you've got Dream Lakes and a number of other commercial venues. But in those days there were some great gravel pits still connected to the Seine. We spent about three years fishing the rivers there, and some of the lakes, which you could do at that time, although the rivers were a bit more difficult because you still had the 'no night fishing' restrictions. I met up with Mally again on one of the gravel pits; there was me, Albert Romp, Bob Baker, half the Savay lads, all fishing in the same area. For many of us, the Monsieur Rouvière fish from the Yonne was the world record (81lb 3oz), because we all know how difficult big fish are to weigh. But when you see a fish taken into the local post office to be weighed then you know the weight is going to be right! That fish was caught just half a mile away from the waters we were all targeting. We spent a good three years fishing in that area. We're talking about a period when Chantecoq was a new water and the Orient was still being built. I've got a map of the area from the late-'80s and

BELOW
My 58lb 4oz was a real thrill, and one of only a handful of 50lb+ carp to be caught in the world that year.

the Orient isn't even on it! People forget the way things were. There was Cassien, and there were the rivers as big-fish venues. The commercial waters were still a thing of the future and the big open reservoirs were new on the scene, or still being built. I wanted to get on the big reservoirs but they weren't family-friendly, so something had to give, I'm afraid.

I've recently started fishing Rainbow Lake, and I'll have to go back a bit to describe how I feel about Rainbow. I'll start this at the beginning because it was five or six years ago at the NEC Show, which used to be the biggest angling show of the lot, and I suppose I was at a bit of a crossroads in my fishing. Mally and I were still fishing Chantecoq, because that was where we went after fishing the Orient, and to be fair, we did all right there. Not everyone gets a 50 out of Chanty, which we did, but I was talking with Martin Locke and Martin said, "The Savay days will never come back; the only place in the world like it is Rainbow."

At that time Rainbow wasn't big on the radar. There wasn't a lot of publicity about it and it just wasn't in the public eye a lot. Martin went on to say, "The atmosphere there is the best you can ever have; everyone gets on, and there are so many big fish you don't know what's in it!" I thought then that I'd like to fish it, and although it wasn't part of our planning at the time, it seemed to be on everyone else's mind. At that time everything seemed to be through Paul Hunt, and Paul's tours were sold out for two years! We wanted to go but we didn't know how to go about it, which I think is the case with a lot of would-be Rainbow anglers. And to be honest, until Martin started praising Rainbow, the only thing I knew about the water was from watching Big Bill (Cottam) and Cornish Ken's (Townley) video from the early-'90s, when it was first stocked. At that time there were no big fish and a few sturgeon, which I wasn't really bothered about. And I've got to say that over the years a lot of people had told me that I'd hate it there. They all seemed to have all sorts of weird and misinformed ideas of what went on there!

BELOW
With Mally at Rainbow. When you go there you are a novice and you have to learn from the lads who are doing well on there.

Then finally Mally and I got the chance to see the place for ourselves. We jumped at the opportunity. I wouldn't say we were in one of the best swims, but when it comes to Rainbow you take what you can get, and then take it from there, which we did. We went in October, and now I know more about the place, I'd fish in any swim. On that first trip we would have liked a bit of sunshine, but we froze to death, although it was just so exciting that I can't really express how exciting it was. It was like Cassien all

over again, but more so somehow. I'm not sure what our expectations were, but we just loved it. To start with it was very hard because it is so different, and it was raining, and I started the session by falling overboard when I was installing the engine in the boat! It was just a little trip of the foot, but I was quite surprised how deep it was in the margins of the swim we were in! (Swim 6.) That first trip was great.

For three days we couldn't land a fish because Rainbow really does take some coming to terms with in that respect. From there on we worked out ways of landing them, but it's overcoming problems that makes new waters so interesting. No one wants to lose a fish. Martin lands a lot of big fish from Rainbow, and in advance of that first trip I was on the phone to him every night, and we had a lot of help from Martin, and from Alan Taylor, and from Tim, who got us the booking. I mean you don't know little things like where to find 12oz leads, and things like that. And then when we got there the first person we met in the clubhouse was George Csonka, and we picked his brains, too. When you go to Rainbow for the first time you are a novice, no matter how experienced you are, and we accepted that. You learn from the lads who are doing well there. George showed us his gear and we weren't far off. The main difference was that his floats were big polystyrene jobs while ours were big plastic ballcocks, which actually worked very well. I don't know how to describe Rainbow. I just totally love the place. It's just so exciting, and if I could fish there next week I would do so. I think the other thing is that there are so many big fish in there that you aren't thinking about Briggsy's Fish or the Ken Dodd Fish, or whatever other fish, because they are all new to us.

ABOVE
Martin Locke told me: "The Savay days will never come back: the only place like it in the world is Rainbow." Swim One in May 2011.

ABOVE
My biggest Rainbow fish to date weighing in at 62lb+ from the memorable session with Mally in Swim One.

It's exciting; Pascal and his family who run it are lovely people, and there is camaraderie among the anglers, too. But people have to get it into perspective. Everyone who goes there has to go through a learning curve and learn how to get the fish out, and I take my hat off to the guys like Martin and Paul Hunt, and others, who have enjoyed more than their fair share of success there. The only conclusion we came to was that if you can land them from the bank then do so, but if you have to go out in the boat then you just have to make the best of it. Mally and I can't get enough of it and we can't wait to get back, although at this moment we don't know when that will be exactly!

Over the years I think I've done more than my fair share of pioneering different lines of thought on bait. Earlier we talked about my Redmire Mix, and that was made up of items that just weren't looked on as carp baits at the time. As far as I know no one had ever caught a carp on maples before I wrote about them as a carp bait, nor tares, nor hemp. I don't think anyone had ever used those as hookbaits for carp, although hemp had a track record as a barbel bait. But the thing is that once you've proved it works and got confidence in it you can go anywhere in the world with it, knowing that it will work. I don't want to make it over-commercial, but from the beginning my Monster Crab and Super Fish, or Seafoodblend, or Yellow Seed Mix and Chocolate Malt caught carp. Everywhere we went with these baits we just caught.

The methods and baits we developed in England worked wherever we went. A carp's a carp, and they react in a similar way wherever you go in the world.

I'll throw a couple of other little stories in here that I haven't written or talked about before. The first is about pop-ups, which I think I was using as early as anyone else: in fact I may have caught carp on pop-ups before anyone else, but quite by accident, really! We were all impressed by Bob Reynolds' amazing results at Billing Aquadrome; you couldn't help but be. He made it known publicly that he'd caught his fish on bananas after a prebaiting campaign, so of course I had to have a go with bananas – and I found that pieces of banana floated! And I caught a couple of carp on banana hookbaits, which were unintentional pop-ups. Later, when I got the chance to talk to Bob, I learnt that the banana thing was a smokescreen and that he'd never caught a fish on a banana bait in his life!

Moving on, and I don't want to be thought to be name-dropping (!) but many years ago I fished Longfield in the winter with Peter Springate, and Robbo from my village. No one else had anything, but I had two stonking runs, definitely from carp, and I dropped them both. I was using almonds, and the thing about almonds was that they twisted like a propeller on the Hair. We were all disappointed about the losses and Pete suggested that I use fuse wire for the Hair to stop the twisting. So I started using fuse wire for the almonds, and it turned out to be perfect for fishing hemp! Thanks to Pete's tip I use fuse wire for a great many of my rigs now, including lobworms, maggots and seeds. A lot of people might not have heard of that setup, but that's what Pete Springate told me over 30 years ago! It's not through secrecy that I've not gone into print with it, but because sometimes you just forget about things until they jump into your mind at moments like this.

Books apart I suppose that writing-wise my most productive years were during the late '80s and early '90s when I was bringing out 'Carp Scene' as an annual catalogue-cum-magazine. They were productive years, but at the same time I felt that was the hardest writing I've ever had to do in my life. I'm a writer who tends to write when I've really got something to say, when I'm inspired if you like, but during that period I had to have something to say! I was trying to put together a magazine with articles in it, which was why I got other people to write for me during that period, including Frank Warwick, Tim Paisley and other people who just wrote one article for me during that time. But half of 'Carp Scene' was like a catalogue and I had to do every single bit of it – product and bait write-ups, cut, paste, get it to the printers on time... To be honest it wore me down and I think that took the edge off me writing books for a long time. 'Carp Scene' took more out of me than writing any book ever did. I still write longhand. I've never come to terms with machines, and I hate deadlines! If you take 'The Carp Strikes Back' and 'Carp Now and Then', I think that the second part of 'Now and Then' was as good as anything I wrote in 'Carp Strikes Back', although other people might not think so. But at that time there were things in there that I was learning and I wanted to pass them on. Up until going into Savay the whole carp scene was so secretive it was untrue, but that was when it all started to come out. There were so many good carpers in Savay passing the secrets on that they got out that way.

There was a short period there which coincided with the coming of Savay onto the scene when my first book was published, as was Kevin's 'Carp Fever', and The Carp Society and 'Carp Fisher' started, all in 1980 and 1981. I think that was definitively the start of the carp-fishing explosion. I think maybe Kevin's book spilt more beans than my book did ('Rod Hutchinson's Carp Book'), but when I got round to writing 'The Carp Strikes Back' I had far more to say, although I would still only write about ideas that I felt I was responsible for. I've always been reluctant to give away other people's secrets! The thing is that when I've got something to say I really enjoy writing. I may be unusual as a writer in that I don't like to reread things I've written more than twice. I like to write it, go through it once and maybe make the odd alteration or addition, but there are a couple of chapters in 'Carp Now and Then' that I can reread and still laugh at, so I think that's an indication of how much I think of that material. To me writing factual stuff about baits and tackle is a bit like writing textbooks; a bit like being at school. When you're finding out things and pushing the limits further then it can be exciting because you are pushing your own education further. I could go down that particular writing route at one time but nowadays it has to be anecdotes. If I'm not amusing myself, or keeping myself interested, then I can no longer write it. But you know, you look back and just now and then you have to feel a little bit of pride about something. Look at that Redmire Mix we talked about earlier. I came up with that 40 years ago and it still works wherever we take it, and I think more and more people are cottoning on to it, which I love.

In the early days of bait development I was always experimenting. No matter how good something was I could never believe that I'd hit the jackpot first time with that first mix. There always had to be something better. But that's carp anglers all over: 'There's got to be something better!' and you carry on looking for it, sometimes ignoring what you've got. Having a bait company I've been the world's worst for that, particularly after I'd developed the first six baits. There was so much research, work and development went into those baits that it was very, very difficult to come up with anything better. Ingredients have improved over the years but the concepts and the overall make-up of the baits, and the attractors that go into them, haven't. I'm still catching on them, and I'm using baits I used 30 years ago. And rigs haven't changed that much either.

People say a lot of kind things about my books, especially 'The Carp Strikes Back', and I get asked which of my own books is my own favourite. Well people may not believe me but I don't read my own books! By the time you've put a book to bed you've read it that many times that the freshness goes out of what you've written. You finish up at a distance from the book and you don't really know how good it is, or

how good it isn't. Every time I've written a book I've tried to write it as best I could, but looking back, it is probably dependent on what inspiration you had at that time. 'Carp Strikes Back': Savay, right in the middle of it all. It couldn't help but be good. 'Carp Now and Then' included Cassien and the waters in France before people were out there buying lakes. There were two great upsurges and inspirations right there. And now…? I want to write again, make no mistake about that, and I will do so. The Rainbow thing has given me great impetus again, but I still feel I'm a novice and I'd like to get a little bit further there before I start writing about it and do it justice. I'm as inspired as ever to get out and fish for carp but I can no longer fish in England for named fish, or queue for swims, and I don't like pushing a barrow!

The other question I get asked is if I have a favourite fish capture, but there have been thousands, literally thousands. I suppose the first time I had a 50-pounder in my net, when that was probably only one of about three caught anywhere that season, was special. It was memorable not being able to pick up the net when I had that 58-pounder. And then more recently – and I know that to Rainbow regulars these aren't monsters – but on the Thursday night of the last session in half an hour I had a 47lb common and a 48lb mirror. I laid back on the bed but I couldn't get back to sleep, so I went round to Mally, slapped him on the face to wake him up, and said, "Tell me the truth, have I died and gone to heaven?" It was a memorable moment during a memorable session in a special place – and I didn't want to come home!

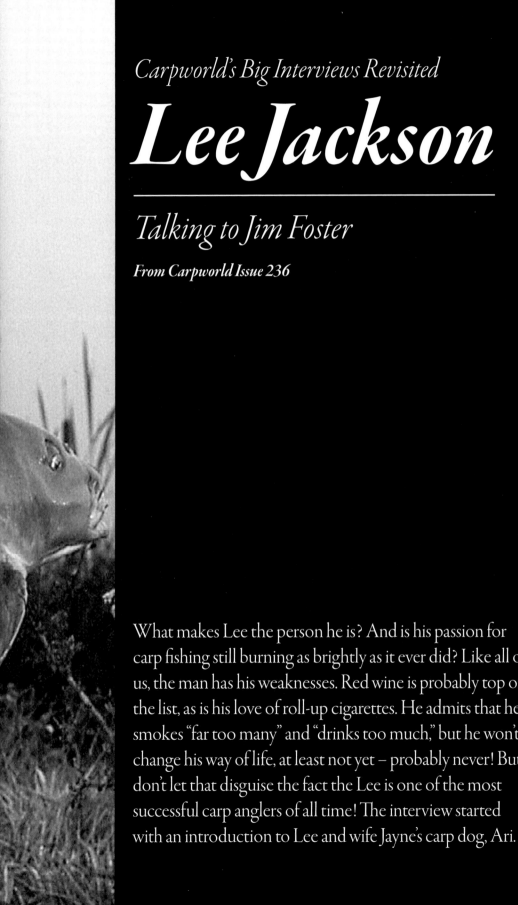

Carpworld's Big Interviews Revisited

Lee Jackson

Talking to Jim Foster

From Carpworld Issue 236

What makes Lee the person he is? And is his passion for carp fishing still burning as brightly as it ever did? Like all of us, the man has his weaknesses. Red wine is probably top of the list, as is his love of roll-up cigarettes. He admits that he smokes "far too many" and "drinks too much," but he won't change his way of life, at least not yet – probably never! But don't let that disguise the fact the Lee is one of the most successful carp anglers of all time! The interview started with an introduction to Lee and wife Jayne's carp dog, Ari.

The dog's a Jack Russell and his name is Ari, spelled A-r-i. It's an abbreviation of Harry, but us true Londoners never pronounce our 'h's! We got him because Jayne has wanted a dog for a while, but the trouble was she wanted a Chihuahua. I wasn't having that. Can you picture me angling with a Chihuahua? So I said a straight no because my street cred would go right down. Imagine what the boys at work would say if I was caught taking one of them for a walk. There have been a few famous carp dogs over the years, and it would be nice if Ari was one day up there with them. Tottenham Bob had one. I'll always remember how that mutt used to drag its arse along the ground. It would always be five paces behind Bob, sliding along on its backside. We'd always tell Bob that it had worms.

"Your dog's got worms, Bob!" we'd say, but he'd never listen.

"My dog ain't got worms, he ain't!" Bob would plead back in a high-pitched voice. "He always does that."

But of course, the dog always did that because it did have worms. I'll always remember my good mate Paul Forward's carp dog. His name was Jim and he was a cracking little fella. Jim hated coots. The funniest thing I remember about him was standing there chatting with Paul, by the side of a lake, when we heard a splash. We turned and saw Jim swimming out into the lake, where he proceeded to take a coot off the surface, a bit like a carp would take a Mixer. Then there was another time when we went to this private club water for a session. As soon as Paul got in his swim, Jim did his usual thing and nestled in the bottom of the sleeping bag. Paul was up in my swim having a cup of tea, then all of a sudden his bite alarm went off, so we both legged it back to his swim. It soon became apparent that it wasn't a carp responsible for the bite, but a coot. As soon as the bird was on the bank, Jim, who had been asleep for an hour, rushed out of the bag, attacked the coot, turned its head on one side and bit into its neck. You could hear the bones crack! I suppose the reason that he turned his head to one side

PREVIOUS PAGES
Lee with Two-Tone from Conningbrook at a record breaking weight of 61lb 7oz.

BELOW
Interviewer Jim Foster and our dog Ari.

BOTTOM
Ari is fascinated by the carp in my pond.

before attacking it was that Paul used to keeps chickens, and it was more than Jim's life was worth to touch one of those, so he was probably checking it out first.

Then there was Bruce at Conningbrook, he was a character alright. We all used to curse him, but he was one of the lads really. When we were having socials, he'd always appear and sit around slobbering until someone gave him some food. He used to love Indian takeaways. His party trick was to grab a can of Fosters in his mouth, clench onto it hard and puncture it with his teeth. He'd then drink the whole can in one mouthful, shaking his head and spraying beer foam everywhere. Bruce used to make some horrendous smells. That was probably because of his diet. I don't think there was anything he didn't eat, which created havoc with his digestive system. Contact lenses, beer, boilies, curry, he'd eat anything. He even ate someone's mobile phone once. Bruce was a character, that's for sure. He had a sidekick called Bonzo, who was an overfed Jack Russell. Bonzo was a fat thing that used to walk around the lake with a sign draped around his neck that said, 'Don't feed me', which was like a red rag to a bull with us mischievous carp anglers. We'd sit there and purposely feed him smelly fishmeal boilies and pellets, and the next day you'd hear Joe (the owner of Bruce and Bonzo, who lived in a house by Conningbrook) complaining that Bonzo had shit everywhere!

I don't think I've ever read anything significant in a carp-fishing magazine about carp dogs before! Bruce and Bonzo were an integral part of the scene at Conningbrook,

after all, but let's move on. I have a carp pond in my back garden and I have to say it's quite an impressive sight. It holds about 4,500 gallons and is 23ft long, 7ft wide and 6ft deep at its deepest. I've got all sorts of carp in there, from koi through to Redmire and Conningbrook strain carp. The trouble with normal carp is you can't appreciate them in a pond really, because to see their beauty you have to see them on their side. That's why I've got the koi in there, to add a bit of colour. I've also got a few Cotton Farm offspring in there, grown on from eggs, and they will go back into their original home once they are big enough. I've got an ongoing stocking policy that I'm very proud of because some of the fish I have brought on from eggs are now topping 30lb. There are orfe in there as well. In fact, all the orfe have got names. There's Bugger, Sod, and Naff… and some ruder names which I'd better not mention here, 'cos I doubt Carpworld would print it! Bugger orfe, geddit? Seriously though, the pond gives me a lot of pleasure. In summer it's nice to sit out in the garden in the morning with a cup

TOP
Jim, Paul Forward's carp dog, and Laney.

ABOVE
Bruce, Conningbrook's King Rat.

of tea, a cigarette or two, and just enjoy chilling out watching the fish. The only thing is, a lot more work goes into maintaining a garden pond than you think.

The pond looks awesome and the water's very clear, but that doesn't mean it's healthy, though. Clear water isn't always good water for fish. When you have a pond, you have to remember you're keeping water first and fish second. You have to keep an eye on the pH levels, the nitrates and ammonia levels, all that kind of thing. You can't let them get out of control or the fish will suffer. If the water's good, your fish will thrive. It's the same philosophy that good fishery owners stick to. You can learn something about carp behaviour from the fish in the pond especially in the winter. We're just coming out of a big freeze at the moment where we have had a lot of ice and snow, real sub-zero temperatures. Despite this, there have been some days when the fish have been really active. You can't explain it. Maybe it's down to air pressures or something, but for some reason they suddenly want to feed, and on those days I reckon it would be worth going fishing. When the pond fish feed it could be a good barometer to indicate when carp in lakes will be feeding, too.

Now-wife Jayne and I went on our first date fishing at St. Ives Lagoon near Cambridge and sometime later it was there that I asked Jayne to marry me. I hatched this elaborate plan where I'd make up an excuse to take a marker rod with me and do some plumbing. I thought I could tie the ring to the float, make a few casts, and then swing the float over to her to look at. She'd see the ring, be amazed, and I'd ask her then! But then I thought, 'What happens if I get snagged?' So I didn't do it.

Jayne: He's very romantic, Lee is. We were going to go away for a week's holiday in a log cabin in Wales and he made up this story about having to go via Cambridge to renew his ticket on St. Ives. I didn't know it at the time, but that was a cock-and-bull story. He had ulterior motives, but I am gullible and believe what he says. Anyway, he managed to persuade me

to walk around the lake with him – bear in mind this was in the middle of February, and when we got to the swim where we'd had our first date, he got down on one knee in the mud and asked me to marry him. I said yes, there were a few tears shed and we were getting married…

Lee again: I caught Jayne at the Lagoon (!) but I never did catch the big mirror from there, although to be fair the Fat Lady wasn't the real reason why I joined that syndicate. I was more interested in a 45lb common I had seen a photo of, which had supposedly been caught from Long Reach, which is another one of the lakes on the complex. So I joined in order to fish that bit of water, because I thought there could possibly be some uncaught monsters to be had. It soon became apparent that there probably weren't any unknown big 'uns because I, and other anglers such as Dave Lane, were giving it a good go and it got to the stage where we were only seeing and recapturing the old same fish, so I started doubting the validity of the 45lb common. I fished Long Reach a few times and lost one on my very first session, it got snagged around a buoy, but that was it, the only bite I had from that lake. On one trip I had a walk around the nearby St. Ives Lagoon, and the first time I walked around it I saw The Fat Lady. So the following week I went up there and did a single night and caught a 22lb common.

The following season I joined again, so I could have a bit more time on the

TOP & ABOVE
Top angling! A rose among the thorns: getting married to Jayne, and my new wife specially dressed for the evening celebrations.

ABOVE
*I cleared the swim,
caught this one,
then never got to
fish it any more!
First night success
on St. Ives Lagoon.*

Lagoon. However, although it's quite a big water, there were really only four main swims worth targeting and they were usually occupied when I turned up on a Wednesday evening after work. I had to keep fishing different swims and as a result I couldn't really get into any kind of rhythm, until one day I found the remnants of an old swim that hadn't been used for years. It was completely overgrown with reeds, but I liked the look of it, so I tossed the marker float out over the top of the reeds and did some plumbing. I soon thought that I'd found somewhere decent. The bottom of the lake felt like it could produce, so I did some 'gardening' and cleared enough space to get three rods out. The ploy worked and I caught a 27-pounder, and I was well made-up. The following week I went up there to find a well-known angler encamped in that swim. I wasn't amused. It was a spot that hadn't been fished for years until I cleared it, and not only that, but he was staying there for three weeks solid. To be honest with you, I was a bit disgusted. This bloke knew I would be fishing on a Wednesday after work, he knew I'd cleared out the swim, yet still he just went in there and sat there for three weeks, all because I'd caught the previous week. I'm not going to say who it was, he'll know who he is if he reads this.

All this was after I'd caught Two-Tone at a then British record weight and it's hard to explain how that capture affected my fishing. For as long as I have been fishing I have wanted to catch the biggest fish, whether that's the biggest stickleback in the canal or the biggest roach in the river. I think that's quite natural with anglers, wanting to catch the biggest, but when your obsession is the biggest carp in the country, Two-Tone, and you eventually catch it, afterwards you feel a little bit lost, you know? You set yourself the target of catching the biggest carp in the country and then you catch it. For someone who always wants to catch the biggest fish that doesn't leave many options. Sure, there are some people out there who are happy to go to the same venue all the time and catch the same fish every weekend, but that's not me. I caught Two-Tone and that was it; I then found it extremely hard to knuckle down and find another target to go for. I used to fish religiously three nights a week, summer and winter. Then I got together with Jayne and suddenly found I would rather sit down in front of the telly and chill out with her and drink a couple of glasses of wine than be down the lake in the freezing cold. I think a lot of people slow down when they get older, other than Tim Paisley, perhaps! To a degree, that's what happened to me, I slowed down. It worries other people more than me that I don't go fishing as much these days.

Don't get me wrong, I still go fishing and still really enjoy it when I do go. It's just that right now I can't see me ever getting back to that obsessive state, the state of mind you have where carp fishing matters more than anything. These days I fish for myself and for pleasure, that's it, though funnily enough I also enjoy fishing international carp matches. I'd dearly love to win one of those (watch this space), maybe partnering Tim Paisley, with a bit of luck, but I can't see me fishing any of the circuit waters again. I've got a mate who has a lake in Kent, in some nice scenery, so I'll take Jayne down there for a couple of nights in the summer, have a barbecue, drink some wine, maybe catch some fish and just have a nice time. The idea of catching another huge, maybe unknown carp, does still appeal. There's one lake in Kent called Larksea that is quite big, but it has all sorts of problems. It almost certainly has one or two surprises lurking in its depths because it's big, but there's public access to it, with a footpath all the way around. You get scuba divers, windsurfers, all sorts of people there, including local hooligans. The fishing problems include an eel population that you can't believe, which means that using boilies is a little tricky, but the carp are in there. It's just extremely hard. Conningbrook was hard, but Larksea is harder. That could be my next major project, I suppose. It's possible.

I should perhaps mention that if readers want to know more about my long quest to catch Two-Tone, they can check out my book *Just for The Record*. I know

BELOW
Conningbrook party time, one of the reasons it was so nice to fish there.

that's a bit of a blatant plug, but I don't really want to be covering anything in here that I've already written about, which is fair enough. There is stuff about my time on Conningbrook that I didn't write about in the book, some of the captures I made, for example. My section of the book is basically a reproduction of a diary piece I did for *Advanced Carp Fishing* magazine, except in the book it's the unedited version. I used to write that diary piece live on the bank while I was fishing. When you're writing an autobiographical story, I don't think it gets any better than writing it live, as you are doing it. I would get home after a session and sit down and type it all up.

One thing that always stands out about the Brook was the social life that went with the fishing down there, and that really came about through the difficulty of the fishing. It reminded me of the early Savay syndicate, which in my mind was the best syndicate there has ever been, because the anglers used to socialise, learn from each other, pull together and help each other out. It wasn't just angler against angler, it was all the anglers against the fish. The thing is, carp fishing is all about enjoying every part of it, not just catching carp. In the evening the Savay lads would reel in, go down the Horse and Barge, have a few beers, then go back fishing again. It was the same with Conningbrook except we used to do our socialising on the bank.

It took a while to catch Two-Tone. Along the way I saw quite a few other anglers catch it before me. That did make me envious, if I am honest, but definitely not jealous. Whenever it was caught, that probably signified the last time it would be out for a while, but because of the social aspect of everything on there, it didn't matter. It wasn't like many syndicates today, where the social scene is sterile and in some instances people are unfriendly. It was the total opposite to that. In my view, the Conningbrook scene was how carp fishing should be: trying to replicate that somewhere else is very difficult.

BELOW
Good old dad with my sister Mandy.

My dad was a Londoner as it happens. He was born in Bermondsey but was never an angler; he never had an ounce of interest in fishing, but he always found time to support me as a kid and drop me off somewhere to go angling, before I could drive. Every year we used to go on holiday to the Isle of Wight. He'd drop me off at the end of the Shanklin pier and I'd spend the family summer holiday sea fishing. Even though he didn't fish himself, he had a big influence on my life. I'm very proud of him, especially of what he did in the war. It should never be forgotten what his generation did for us. He used to fire mortars in the artillery, but he's never really talked of his experiences. The only thing he has briefly mentioned was when he was in a battle at Monte Casino, when the Allies were trying to take a big castle at the top of a hill that the Germans were occupying. He said he'd never been so scared in all his life; he thought he was going to die. He's 89 now and still going strong.

I get asked about anglers I look up to in the field of carp fishing and rate as the best anglers in the business, and that's a tough one. I'll start with the late Alan Smith. His bait application skills were very, very good. He had an understanding about how to get a bait going and where to put it. I'd catch more fish in the short term, but when we concentrated on a lake for the long term, he'd always beat me hands down. I think Tim Paisley next. Tim might disagree, but I think he's mellowed with age, I remember at one time I used to think he seemed like a right self-righteous so and so, but not anymore. He's actually just a normal bloke and a phenomenal carp angler, with an amazing passion and energy. I always call a spade a spade and I think Tim is the same. There will always be a degree of conflict between two people with forceful personalities, like we have, but there's also a mutual respect between us. There aren't many people in carp fishing I respect as much as him, so he would have to be up there. Talking of carp publishers, Rob Maylin is also a superb angler, and Paul Forward is up there. Paul is one of the best instinctive anglers I have fished with. He was one of the first to catch Two-Tone.

Finally, I would have to say Rod Hutchinson. He's unique. He's one of those people who's good at everything he puts his hand to, especially so in his younger days. He used to play professional football for Grimsby Town and he was a handy boxer. I don't know what position he played, but when it came to carp fishing, his catches over the years put him at

the top of the tree. The first time I met him was at the London School of Economics. There was a British Carp Study Group (BCSG) meeting held there one night. I was sitting down, there was an empty seat next to me and Rod came and sat in it. I was a little overwhelmed, star-struck even. He started talking to me and asking questions and I thought, 'Shit, I'm talking to Rod Hutchinson.' After that we hit it off. As gifted anglers go he's right up there, for sure. He's certainly one of the most untidy and clumsy anglers I have seen, but his intuition and instinct are incredible. He just knows what to do and when to do it and has an understanding of everything there is to know about carp and carp fishing.

In my view, there are different types of carp angler. In angling, like any other sport, different people have different strengths and weaknesses. As an analogy, some footballers are strikers, some are defenders, some are dribblers, and some are tacklers. In carp fishing there are anglers who excel at stalking and floater fishing; then there

TOP
*The late, great
Alan Smith.*

ABOVE
*I always call a spade
a spade, and I think
Tim is the same.*

are good, long-stay anglers, whose bait application technique over time is their strength; there are instinctive anglers and mechanically excellent anglers. Rod is definitely one of the best instinctive anglers there's ever been, as is Paul Forward, whereas someone like Kevin Maddocks was very good mechanically. In fact, in his heyday Maddocks was the best mechanical angler I ever saw. By that, I mean that his rigs were always spot-on, in fact nigh on perfect. His casting was metronomic in action and as accurate as you could get. He was a carp-catching machine who used to boast that he would sleep by the rods and could strike a bite quicker than most people could when they were awake. However, while he was strong in these areas, in my view he wasn't as good as Rod at stuff like fish location. People would often tell Kevin where the fish were, simply because he was Kevin Maddocks.

Fishing-wise I keep things simple and it doesn't bother me if things are untidy in my swim, or if the bobbins aren't at the same height, or if the rods aren't aligned! But I understand why people are like that. A lot of the instinct thing comes down to knowing what's happening in the lake. I mean, if you're fishing a weedy lake, then during the day the weed is going to stick up. Cast out in daylight and you may well land your rig on a clear patch, but when the sun goes down the weed can sink down too – and cover your bait, so recasting after dark is a strategy that is often very successful because it gives you a better presentation, which you wouldn't get by leaving your hookbaits out all through the night.

Back there I mentioned my old mate Alan Smith... I want to briefly talk about Alan, because although medicine is better now, someone might read this and recognise the signs of prostate cancer if they have it and get early treatment accordingly. Basically, Alan went to the doctor because there was blood in his urine, but the doctor didn't really do much, he assumed Alan was too young to get that type of cancer because he didn't fit into the right age demographic. So Alan didn't push it. If you ever get blood in your urine you should definitely get yourself properly checked out, Alan's doctor was wrong. Sometime later he was diagnosed with the disease, but by then it was too late; it was terminal. When he told me, we just cried. From there, we watched him slowly deteriorate and it was heartbreaking. Holding conversations was difficult. You couldn't ask him how he was doing, because obviously he wasn't alright. He fought it bravely for two years before finally passing away. It's a cruel world sometimes. Cancer is a very indiscriminate, cruel disease.

I suppose that my drinking and smoking should worry me more, but it doesn't, really. It would more if I had a history of cancer and heart disease in my family, but I don't, my dad has smoked and drunk all his life and I think a lot of these things are genetic.

ABOVE
Rod Hutchinson is unique: he's one of those people who is good at everything.

I am also a great believer in carefully watching what I eat, so I take a lot of dietary supplements such as Omega 3 and 6, zinc, ginseng, spirulina, green tea, etc. and make doubly sure I get all the vitamins and minerals I need. I'm a great believer in all that stuff; I really think it makes a difference in the long term.

I do a lot of writing about carp fishing now, which comes as a surprise to me. At school I was always getting bad grades at English. I left thinking I wasn't a particularly good writer at all. Writing does worry me. Always has done. I guess I don't feel confident with it all the time, I fear criticism in the eventuality of writing something that might not be very good! Also, I don't like it when other people get slagged off for writing in magazines. At least they have had a go. That's what matters, it's not their fault if they are not the most gifted of people at writing, it's not something everyone is good at.

Talking of criticism, that's what really annoys me about a minority of Internet forum users you get on carp-fishing websites. They happily sit on their computers and regularly criticise things they may not have experience of themselves, or people they have never met – all whilst hiding in the safety of anonymity. Another thing that annoys me in carp fishing, both on the forums and on the bank, is when an angler catches a fish only to be told: "So and so had that last week," at whatever weight, and I think, 'Leave that guy alone. He's caught the fish – let him have his moment.' Too often people try to spoil it.

I think most people know that I work at the Tackle Box in Dartford. I've been there well over 20 years now and I've stayed so long because I enjoy it. I'm classed as a carp fishing consultant and work on a self-employed basis, helping customers choose the right kit for their needs and giving advice on all things carp-related. And I might be biased, but I think it's the best carp-fishing tackle shop in the world! I know that's quite a claim to make, but the service we offer is definitely up there. Shop at The Tackle Box and you know you're going to get good advice. Okay, you might not get the discounts, but in my view the service you get more than makes up for this. The subject of discounts in the angling retail industry is something that has always amazed me. Why should you get discounts in tackle shops? What other shops do you go in and ask for discounts? You don't go into Tesco; go to the cashier and say, "Can I have a discount on my weekly shop, please?" But people ask for discounts in tackle shops, all the time and I have to say, for the most part, it's the fault of the shops. The more they offer discounts, the less money they have to renew stock. Then they can't get the stock in, so they lose business. When you buy your kit, what you have to remember is that in real terms, items of fishing tackle have generally got much cheaper over the years. Look how much bedchairs used to cost in the mid 1990s compared to now, despite inflation, as well as bite alarms, rods, reels and bivvies.

I learned my carp catching skills in the late 1970s and '80s on some famous Kent circuit waters, in particular venues like Darenth and the School Pool. We move on and change over the years. Darenth isn't my cup of tea these days. It was a very long time ago that I fished there, and as most people know, it's very different now. School Pool is still going and it still has some nice fish in it, up to upper 30 I think. When I moved onto the School Pool in the early 1980s it contained two 30lb plus carp, one of which was She. The funny thing was that She was one of the most caught carp in the lake, yet try as I might, I couldn't catch her! It was one of those things. You can't pick and choose which fish picks up your bait can you, unless you can see them of course.

In one sense I guess my quest for She was similar to my quest for Two-Tone. I probably fished School Pool for five or six years before I caught She at a weight of 36lb 8oz. Strange as it might seem, I put her back that first time without taking a photo. Usually, once I have caught a target fish, I move on to the next challenge, but I was enjoying my time on School Pool so much that I wanted to give myself the challenge of catching her again for a photo. I went on to catch her three more times as it happens and got my photo. I must admit, it's all very well and good catching the biggest fish in a lake first, but what do you have to look forward to after that? In the case of Conningbrook, it was ever so exciting fishing for the biggest known fish in the country. Every time the bobbin moved it set my heart pounding, because there could have been a record carp on the other end. Wherever I have fished, my strategy has always been to get as many bites as I can and hope the biggest one comes along at some stage. Both She

and Two-Tone became obsessions that, for some reason, took me a long time to achieve.

There were well-known fish in Conningbrook that I never caught. I never caught The Long Common, which is one of the most famous commons in the country, or a mirror known as Tom's Pet. I've been asked if I'm ever tempted to go back and fish Conningbrook, but the answer's 'No'. I did fish the Brook once after catching Two-Tone, but it was eerie, because I think I hooked her again! Former *Carpworld* editor Martin Ford happened to say to me on the phone

ABOVE
*I really don't know
how significant
moon phases are
in carp fishing.*

that I would catch Two-Tone on November 3rd. After speaking to him I looked in the diary and saw that that was a Sunday, when I would be fishing anyway. It also happened to be a new moon phase, which is one of my favourite times for big fish. I really just went for a social with Simon Bater. We bivvied up on Joe's Point and I threw the three rods out, then off one went at 11.40 p.m. Immediately I knew it was a heavy fish; I had a gut feeling while I was playing it that it could have been Two-Tone again. It felt eerie. It soon got weeded up and was totally solid. I could have got in the boat and gone out to free it, but I decided not to. I just pulled on the line to try to get it moving, same as you do on any weeded fish when you don't have access to a boat. Then the hook pulled.

I commented that the new moon is one of my favourites for big fish but I really don't know how significant moon phases are in carp fishing. None of us know the influence of the moon on the feeding patterns of carp. While I have never found a full moon productive for carp fishing in terms of getting lots of bites, you can definitely catch big fish on a full moon. A lot of big English fish have been caught on a full moon, or the lunar phase immediately approaching a full moon. It's the same kind of thing with air pressures and their effect on carp. I studied that a lot, and the theory that a falling pressure was better, but I couldn't come up with any definite conclusions. Besides, it wouldn't really make a lot of difference to me if I could because I can only go fishing on my days off and not pick and choose. When I caught Two-Tone the weather was bizarre. I caught it in thick fog; I could hardly see my hand in front of me. Terry Hearn caught it in similar conditions.

I've been a strong supporter of carp organisations over the years. In fact, a long time ago I was a BCSG regional organiser, as well as a member of The Carp Society. I always support carp-fishing groups like these if I can, because I feel I should support the industry I work in. If a new group started up tomorrow with the aim of supporting carp fishing, I would probably join that, too. Things these days in carp politics are more, how shall I put it, agreeable and less acrimonious. That hasn't always been the case. Years ago there was a lot of political conflict between the BCSG, the CAA and The Carp Society, about all sorts of issues, including fish theft, among other things. Fingers were being pointed, and accusations were made. It got to such an extent that I got a phone call from Peter Mohan of the BCSG with an ultimatum; either I had to resign as a regional organiser of the BCSG, or drop out of The Carp Society. Well, I won't be dictated to and the politics of what was going on was nothing to do with me, so I immediately resigned from being a BCSG regional organiser. They didn't go as far as to chuck me out, but I have always been of the opinion that I should be free to join whatever organisation I want, and I stick with that to this day. I think they gave the same ultimatum to Chris Ball and he made the same decision as me. At the time Peter Mohan was really annoyed at the situation, but as the years have gone by it's all sorted itself out. I see Peter occasionally these days and respect him greatly.

I think The Carp Society has lost its way over the years. I think these days it's more of a fishing club that revolves around Horseshoe than anything else. Politically it doesn't have the clout like ECHO has. It's also lost a lot of its fun. In the early days of the Society, you used to have these massive conferences at Wembley, and then Dunstable. Both were massive venues, The Carp Society Conference was the annual event on the carp fishing calendar. People used to flock there from around the country to see these ultra professional slide shows, some of which were set to music. The entertainment they used to put on was fantastic, first class, while the tackle side of things, although important, was secondary. Now the annual Carp Society Show conference is predominantly a tackle sale, a great big shop floor with a little room at one end where guys sit round while someone hosts a questions and answers panel. It's just not the same.

BELOW
The Carp Society Supergroup.

BOTTOM
Jan Porter, Del Ritchie and me on stage.

I have fond memories of the rock band made up of carp anglers that played at conferences and other events. Clive Gibbins phoned me one day to say he was putting together a band dubbed The Carp Society Supergroup, and that he had heard I was a little musical. He asked me if I would like to play bass. I said of course I would, so each of us in the band learned what we needed to learn from listening to a tape before playing live at Dunstable, and it was brilliant. It went on from there. I think we played at three conferences, including Wembley, which was a big buzz! Andy Bolder was lead guitar and vocalist. Chris Haswell did a bit on vocals as well; he's got a fantastic voice and sounds just like Rod Stewart, but Andy was the star of the band. He came from a musical family, his brother played bass guitar for David Bowie and a group called Wishbone Ash, and then Uriah Heap. It was mainly rock stuff we used to play, with Clive Gibbins on drums, me on bass and Terry Cheeseman on rhythm guitar. Then we used to have guest appearances, Chris Ball guested on bass once, while Mike Kavanagh was good on the drums. Geoff Shaw and his son Brad also played with the band, and we had other guests such as Jan Porter, Kevin Peet from The Tackle Box, and even Del Ritchie, bless him. I used to get so nervous before playing because I was scared of playing a wrong note. One time I forgot to turn up the volume on the guitar and no one could hear me. I don't think anything like that will happen again! There's been talk of us reforming for Madine this year, but I don't know if it will ever be the same again. We played at the first ever Madine World Carp Classic, but French electricity is so bad the whole thing went tits up and we all nearly got electrocuted!

It was from music that I acquired the nickname Python Lee Jackson. In 1972, Rod Stewart provided guest vocals for a band called Python Lee Jackson. They had a No.3 hit in the charts that year and the name just stuck. The nickname is not for the reason that all the ladies might hope it's for!

I have other interests outside carp fishing other than music. I am a great fan of Moto GP. I follow it all the time and think Valentino Rossi is arguably the greatest sportsman in the world, and the best motorcycle racer of all time. I used to have a bike, but not anymore. The last bike I owned was a Suzuki 550GT, quite a long time ago now. It was all raced-up and I used to take it round Brands Hatch, it was quick. I spent quite a lot of money on that hobby. I accidentally knocked someone over on it once though, which although it wasn't my fault, it did put an end to my motorbike career. I had fished the June 16th start of the season on Darenth and was going back to work in the afternoon, on the bike, to collect my wages. I was pulling away from a set of lights when all of a sudden this guy just steps in front of me. I couldn't stop or swerve out of the way, so ran into him. It turned out he was a bit of a down-and-out,

TOP
With Robin MacMillan and a young Paul Forward after we had won the Carp Society Inter-Regional event at Horseshoe many moons ago!

ABOVE
I love playing the guitar and get up on stage whenever I get the chance.

ABOVE
*A fish from Savay,
the best syndicate
water in the world
in its heyday.*

probably a methylated spirit drinker, and he died from a double fracture of the skull. All I remember is, I got off the bike 200 yards down the road with blood running down my face from underneath my full face crash helmet; the impact had pretty much knocked me out and I'd just slumped down on the tank and was going along the road with the bike still upright. Another thing I remember about this incident is, whilst all this was going on, there was a lad riding a motorbike in the opposite direction that must have been 'rubber necking', the result of which, he drove into the back of an AA van and we both got carted off to hospital in the same ambulance, me to have stitches in my forehead and him with two dislocated shoulders. When it went to the coroner's court a few weeks later, there were a lot of witnesses to say it wasn't my fault, but it still affected me an awful lot. It put me right off riding a bike again because it made me realise how dangerous it can be. I still think about it now, his name, the fact that the local newspaper said that he was of no fixed abode, about how once he must have been a family man. Unfortunately something went wrong with his head, or in his life, and society didn't help him. I don't blame myself, I'm over it now, but it had a big affect on me at the time. Fortunately not long after this I had the bike stolen and bought my first car, a MK4 Ford Cortina, the very same car that through inexperience, I knocked the gates down with at the entrance to the Darenth complex, two days after passing my driving test as it happens! Don't think Leisure Sport were that impressed at the time, luckily they didn't find out who did it!

Going back to something a bit more cheerful, carp fishing! One aspect that has always interested me is bait, as for me, after fish location, bait is the second most important aspect. Having said that, if you can get a bait going to the extent that the carp are searching for it, bait can be more important than location as they will locate you! Going back quite a few years, Alan Smith and I had a little bait company called Ultima Baits, and although we didn't produce readymade boilies, as they were very much in their infancy at this time, we produced what I would still rate as the best quality milk protein base mix of all time, The Ultima Mix. Trouble was, it got to the point where we were becoming so busy that one or both of us would have to pack up our proper jobs, something neither of us was really prepared to do as we both had young families and steady jobs, albeit Alan's as a forwarding and shipping clerk, and mine as a dustman! In the end though, the main ingredient that made up the bulk of our base mix was discontinued by the Dutch Milk Marketing Board, so rather use what we considered inferior alternatives, we decided to fold the bait company altogether, which was a bit of a shame. I often wonder, other than Alan's untimely death, where Ultima Baits would have been now had we have continued with it? I've got a little feeling that it would've been massive and that I would be a lot richer than I am now! Nevermind though, the stress of running my own company might not have been quite so good for my health, especially so when you consider how competitive the bait industry now is. Alan went on to start up another bait company, Sensible Baits, a top-quality range that was based on pet food products, products that were initially developed by experts in pet nutrition, which is a world of difference from a carp angler producing a bait through a bit of guesswork! As for me, I still have quite an involvement with bait and have had a hand in helping produce bait products for companies such as Solar, The Tackle Box and even Nutrabaits with their Complete Food Oil. Within the Tackle Box range there is what I consider to be the best (warm water) attractor of all time, Ming Oil. I honestly think that this stuff is like 'drugs for carp', and not only carp; it works extremely well for all sorts of species of fish. Also, taking a leaf out of Alan's book, our Minger range is based on pet food products, that nutritionally, have been formulated by experts in this field. By and large though, I enjoy the freedom to use absolutely what I like bait wise and wouldn't really want to tie myself down to any one bait company as most of them produce absolutely stunning products. So whether it be Scopex Squid, Cell, Trigga, Club Mix, Essential B5, Richworth Tutti's, Quest Rahja Spice, Sniper MC1, plastic, Dynamite, Sticky or Scattered Baits and a few that I've probably forgotten to mention, I'd be happy, and have the freedom to use absolutely what I like and so will it continue with something that is as important as bait.

Carp tackle, wow, same as really. You know sometimes, although people might think that all we do is sit around all day and drink coffee, working in a carp 'empire' like The Tackle Box is what I can only imagine is like working in the stock exchange! Sometimes, and for years, there have been lots of times when I've driven away from the place with my head spinning, phones forever ringing, ordering to be done, mail orders to be picked, serving customers (the most important people), topping up the shelves, it's far more difficult than emptying a few dustbins and the going carp fishing afterwards. Then there's the catalogue time of year when we all get very stressed and hate and want to kill each other, well not quite that severe although it feels that way sometimes. I've worked for The Tackle Box for something like 25 years now, and in that time have seen it grow from a small business run from a little shop in the village of Sutton-at-Hone, to the massive business it is now in our much bigger premises in Dartford. Even now though we have outgrown this shop, and I'm sure we would all like to move on to even bigger premises, a carp fishing superstore, where we had room to display all of the big items that we stock such as bivvies. In reality though, I'm not sure if this will ever happen, because although there are premises available, none is positioned anywhere near as perfectly as our present shop. As for tackle, it absolutely amazes me what is now available to carp anglers, a far cry from years ago when we had to make do or make things ourselves. It's good to have a vast choice however, but I'm sure that all of us, me included, now carry far too much tackle than is absolutely necessary. A few years ago we just loaded it onto our backs and got on our toes, nowadays a lot of anglers struggle to fit it all on a purpose-made carp barrow.

As well as The Tackle Box, I'm a sponsored consultant for Free Spirit Fishing and have been ever since the company first started up, and hand on heart, I truly believe that they produce the best performing and best quality carp fishing rods in the world. Perhaps that might seem like a bit of a bold statement, but when you see the research, testing and work is put into producing every single rod within the range, I very much doubt if any other company go to as much trouble. It's not that the other companies producing fishing rods don't produce good quality carp rods because undoubtedly most of them do; it's just that with Free Spirit, I think they go that extra mile. A lot more recently than Free Spirit, I'm also part of the Ultima UK Carp Team of consultants, which is quite good, because not only have they already got a lot of top quality main lines and hooklink materials etc within their range, it's nice to be working with them to produce even more for the future.

I said earlier that I've always had to have a few ambitions and goals in carp fishing to keep me interested in going. Since the very start of the competition, it was always my aim to win the British Carp Angling Championships, which I did along with partner Gary Peet in 2001. Ever since I very first started fishing at a very young age, and especially so when I started carp fishing, it was always my yearning to catch the biggest that swam, well in the UK anyway, and within a year of winning the British Champs I achieved that goal with Two-Tone at a British record weight, which was perhaps my most memorable carp fishing achievement, although something that happened last year (2011) came very close, winning a World title! It all started out with a chance conversation before the start of the World Carp Classic match at Madine in France, where I was partnering Tim Paisley, and Tim asked if I fancied fishing the Carp Angling World Championships on the St Lawrence River in the USA as part of the Mainline/Fox sponsored

BELOW
*Celebrating
our British
Championships
success with partner
Gary Peet.*

Carpworld team, to which I replied with a very big 'YES'! Can't remember how it came about who'd I'd be partnering, but it ended up being Ian 'Chilly' Chillcott, somebody that I'd never actually fished with as a partner, but I'd enjoyed his humour and company every time we had socialised together, plus the fact that it's fair to say that he's more than capable of catching a few carp. I must admit though, before the event I was secretly a little bit worried whether or not a couple of 50 odd year olds like me and Chilly would be able to compete with some of the 'young guns' in the competition, especially so as a few of them had very good past carp match records on productive venues. Thing is, on venues like Madine the fishing is a little bit laid back as the fishing is usually very slow. On the St Lawrence though, it could be absolutely manic if you were in a productive swim. And then there's everything else that you have to put up with, the usually rocky

terrain that is very physically demanding on your body; flying thingies that bite, sting and draw blood; the difficulty of fishing the river itself with its strong currents and drifting weed; the occasional passing container ship, and the extremely hard-fighting St Lawrence carp, which must be some of the most hardest fighting carp in the world that can take anything up to 100 yards of line on the bite! Well our very unfavoured swim was a middle peg in a fairly tightly pegged shipping channel and gave us all of these problems, and more.

The main thing we had to work out was where to bait up in order to keep free bait in front of us, not only because of the current, but because of the huge container ships that were passing by close to our swim at least four or five times a day and night. The affect that these giant ships had to our swim was that the water would retract by at least 10ft every time one passed, and all of our free bait would probably end up somewhere near the Atlantic Ocean and we'd have to start all over again. After a while though we worked out how to use these ships to our advantage, and every time we saw one approaching, one of us would run along upstream and throw a load of maize into

TOP
One of the huge container ships that frequently passed through our swim during the match.

ABOVE
Chilly and I on our way to success on the St. Lawrence, and looking the worst for wear during the hectic five-day event. We were out on out feet by the end of the frantic five days.

the margins. What we then think happened is that, because the water got sucked in, so did the maize, dispersing it in our swim and in the area of our hookbaits. I think we got it right because often we got bites immediately after a ship had passed. Not wishing to be big headed in any way – although I suppose as World Champions we are entitled to be – once we worked everything out, like exactly where to bait-up with the type of bait we were putting in, where to cast and how often to do it, we were like a well oiled machine and went about everything with relentless pressure. Physically, though, it was possibly the most demanding fishing that I'd ever done in my life: our backs ached like you can't believe, our arms ached through constantly using the throwing stick, casting and spodding and playing carp, and our legs and feet hurt from clambering over rocks. In addition, our minds were sometimes in a different place due to the almost complete lack of sleep. Towards the end of the match we both recognised the fact that we could actually win this thing, so we fished even harder, if that sounds possible. Probably my greatest memory was the last few hours of the match, because although Chilly wasn't quite so sure, I was certain we had won, and when the end of the match was signalled, I just burst into tears and couldn't speak properly. Another memory is the 'feeling' of winning and becoming a World Champion. OK, it's only carp fishing, but the 'feeling' is no different from whether it be winning and becoming crowned World Champion in Formula 1 or Moto GP, winning the World Cup in football, a World title at boxing or any World Class event.

Lastly on the World Championship thing, there are a few people that I must thank. Obviously my partner Chilly for his relentless effort, his friendship and still

BELOW
It's only carp fishing but the feeling of winning a World Championship is no different to becoming crowned world champion in Formula 1, or football.

managing to make me laugh even if we didn't feel like it sometimes, Tim Paisley, again for his friendship and making it possible for us all to be there, the rest of the Carpworld Team, John, Paul, George, Ringo, Steve and Tom, our team sponsors Mainline Baits and Fox International, to Jerry and Marcy and all the other lovely people at Carp Fishing Adventures, the event organisers and event sponsor Kevin Nash, and finally, Gary and Kevin Peet for allowing me to have the time off.

For the sake of figures, to win the 2011 Carp Angling World Championships, Chilly and myself weighed in a total of 122 carp for 1,857lb and a few ounces during the 115 hour match, and considering we also caught 10 or so more that we couldn't weigh in as carp under 10lb didn't count, that's more than one an hour, my body aches thinking about it!

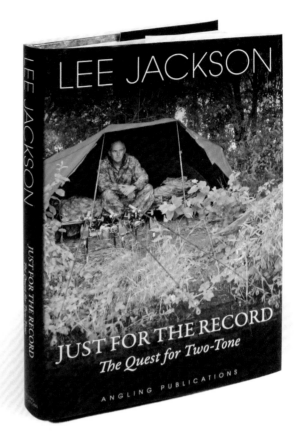

ABOVE
I'm proud of my book chronicling my pursuit and capture of Two-Tone, and the friendships formed along the way.

As for the future of my fishing, I still think I've got it in me to win another major title. I've still got an ambition to catch a 40lb+ English common as I've never ever had one of these. By and large though I enjoy catching carp, enjoy the surroundings of where they live and enjoy the company of the so many good friends that I've met through carp fishing, long may this continue.

You know sometimes I get a bit embarrassed about being high profile, and that tends to spread beyond carp fishing with the added exposure we're getting these days. I've been on holiday before and been recognised. I was in an airport in Egypt and this fella came up to me and asked, "Are you Lee Jackson?" So I said, "Yes, I am." He replied, "I've got your book," before we started talking about the hotels we were going to be staying in. It was a little awkward to be honest. Jayne and I were coming back from a Robert Plant concert once in Kentish Town and were on a packed tube train when this bloke at the other end of the carriage shouted out, "What was better, catching Two-Tone or watching a Robert Plant concert"....What does he think?

Bob Davis

Talking to Tim Paisley

From Carpworld Issue 243

I met Bob at the inaugural meeting of the Carp Society
in May 1981. He was the leader of the then recently-
formed Savay Syndicate, and he became the first chairman
of the Society. Bob lived in Uxbridge when I first met
him, and fished the Colne Valley. He later became a near-
neighbour at Clowne in Derbyshire, and fished with me
at the Mangrove. We have fished a number of venues
together since, both at home and abroad, and he and his
wife Sheila now run their stunning two-lake complex
at Serrerie near Coussac Bonneval in France, which was
where Bob and I put the following interview together.

I've always been an angler from the early age of six when my cousin was taking me fishing to a tench lake. While I caught silly little perch, he was catching decent tench. From there my angling has been a natural progression, starting with pleasure fishing for roach with a little rod, gradually moving up through the species till we came onto tench, then onto barbel, and eventually carp. That seemed to be the natural progression for me as an angler. I used to work in a tackle shop at about the time I left school: that was Young's of Harrow, and I worked there for three or four years. Clive Young was a very, very good angler and took me under his wing, barbel fishing.

I was a member of The Fisheries Angling Club at around the time I was 18 or 19 years of age, and they had a new lake, which they were stocking with fish from here, there and everywhere. The Fisheries was a club in Rickmansworth and the lakes were owned by a hospital and rented by The Fisheries Club. They had one lake, which was an old established tench and bream lake, but they also had a new lake that was being dug at the time when I first went there. It was being stocked from all over with virtually anything they could lay their hands on. The Fisheries as a club used to have two matches each year at night, which at the time was the extent of the night fishing allowed there, but they had stocked the new lake with some fish from the Chichester Canal, brought back from matches, which included lots and lots of small carp. They didn't actually know what they were creating at the time, but as it turned out they were creating a very good carp fishery. I was there one day practising with a fly rod, because I'd recently taken up fly fishing, and I saw a shoal of carp swimming round close to the bank: so from the start of that season there I was fishing for carp, and my carp fishing career had started. At that time you had to fill in the book as you left the fishery. On one side of the page was the Old Lake, and on the other side of the page was the New Lake. My entry into there was the first carp entry ever recorded for the New Lake, on the first day of the season. This would be in the late-'60s – I think probably 1968, although I can't be certain of that.

Although my carp fishing started at the Fisheries what I look upon as my first significant carp was caught prior to that, and actually came from Harefield. I worked at Kodak for a short period of time, and joined the Kodak Angling Club when they were renting Harefield. Thinking about it now this may have been what set me

BELOW
Bob at Marlborough Pool, Oxford, in 1978.

off on carp. I'd gone there legering for what I hoped would be good tench, not knowing there were carp in the water at the time, and finished up catching a 17½lb carp – my first ever carp! That was in 1967, and that's almost certainly when the carp bug first bit.

I'd started out on the carp trail and at some stage I became friendly with Keith Gillings and Lenny Middleton, although my first encounter with Lenny wasn't in connection with fishing at all! My year was broken into seasons, as Lenny's was. Our seasons went through winter, which was for hawking (falconry) and shooting; spring, fly fishing; summer, tench fishing, and then becoming carp anglers. I first met Lenny through hawking: he was a very, very good falconer in his day. He used what were

ABOVE
Lenny Middleton at Marlbrough Pool, 1978.

looked upon as inferior quality birds to catch prey and quarry that the old-established falconers simply couldn't believe. Where they were using peregrines which could catch quality quarry, Lenny was using imported lanner falcons that had never been heard of in the pursuit of partridge and game. He was just so good at what he did. The hawking season comes about through the leaves being off the trees, so the quarry can be seen, and once spring came we got back to fishing, first fly fishing, and then tench fishing, which became carp fishing in the end. We were very similar in our objectives of what we wanted to do, and we came together as a group.

At the time it was quite a small group consisting of Keith Gillings, Lenny, myself and a man called John Barton, who was with us for quite a while before moving away. At the time of our initial experiments and carp fishing John was part of the group. We worked well together, all giving to the pool of ideas, although Lenny had two worlds, even within fishing! He was with us at weekends, but also spent a fair bit of time with Kevin (Maddocks) on Tuesdays and Wednesdays. So he would go off fishing with Kevin in the week, and they would then go on to do their tank-testing at Kevin's, and then he was with us at weekends. I should explain that Lenny didn't drive at that stage so he relied on others for transport.

Lenny looked to me to find new waters. I spent most of the close season chasing all over the country looking for new carp waters, and I involved lots of different people in the hunt: club waters, day ticket waters, wherever we could find them, because

there weren't many carp waters then. So most of the close season was spent up trees looking for the odd carp in what were mostly coarse fisheries. Through the grapevine you'd hear of the odd carp being caught and off you went. Really, Marlborough Pool was the first water where we worked well together. There were a few waters around which became part of our world. Marlborough first, then Lenny and Keith moved onto a place called Milton, and then we moved onto Waterways, a famous carp water. Dennis MacFetrich was there at the time, although I think we just missed Kevin Clifford, who had been fishing there with Pete Evans.

I think Marlborough Pool has been talked about and written about so much that people have got the impression that it was quite a big water, but to be honest it was a puddle, it was a very small lake. When we arrived at Milton and Marlborough the tackle we were using at the time wasn't really up to carp fishing. The rods we were using were just leger rods. Milton was only about 140 yards across and the fish just sat in the middle of the lake, and we just couldn't reach them! Most of our fishing then was waiting for the nights and fishing in the margins, when they came in closer. But what it did was spur us on to adapt the tackle that was available for our carp fishing. Looking back they were exciting times. Carp rods were starting to evolve through fibreglass, and there were a few new models coming on the market. Lenny knew his financial limitations and settled for what he'd got tackle-wise, concentrating on his terminal tackle, even back then. Marlborough was a 'corn water' for us and we discovered that frozen ice blocks with corn inside could be catapulted to the ranges that we wanted to fish. Back then we were young and we used to swim our baits out to reach the ranges we couldn't cast!

It was at the time when we were fishing Marlborough that Fred Wilton's baits started to be talked about and we tried to make our own version of HP (high-protein) baits. We couldn't find Phillips Yeast Mixture (PYM) so we used a product from a health food shop called Yestamin. Anyway, we produced our first high-protein bait, and we used it. It was very successful, but we always found it to be too soft. The skin

that eggs put onto a protein bait in our opinion wasn't hard enough: we always wanted a bait that was harder, that would catapult well and be more useable. At that stage the hardness wasn't considered a necessity for any rig purpose; that came later. Everyone was still burying their hooks, which leads us onto Lenny's first major, major brainchild. Through tank tests and observation he had come to the conclusion that the biggest no-no in a carp's life was line, and the things that they didn't worry about were hooks. He'd done some tests in a tank, along with Kevin, and they'd put into the bait bits of metal, and nails, and found that a carp would go to a bait with a 2-inch nail sticking out of it, take it on board, chew it up, and spit out the nail! Lenny's conclusion was, "Why are we worried about hooks?" I took that on board and in my later angling I've always used bigger hooks. I never use small hooks; the bigger the better. I've always believed what Lenny found out then; big hooks, no problem. Anyway we're moving on a bit, but we'd made a bait from semolina (which I'll come back to in a moment) and liquidised squid. We could drill a hole in the side of the bait it was that hard, and insert an Aberdeen sea-angling hook, and that became known as side-hooking. The greater part of the hook was visible to the fish, and the runs we obtained from that point onwards were fantastic.

We went a long way round to arrive at semolina for making baits rock hard. To start with we were using ground macaroni, grinding it down with coffee grinders. We were burning out one coffee grinder after another! One day I went into the health

ABOVE
Bob's first 30, and the first 30 from the Cons Club Small Lake, 1981.

food shop for the latest supply of macaroni and the woman in the shop asked me what we were using the macaroni for. When I told her, she asked me why we didn't just use semolina, because that was what macaroni was made from in the first place! I stood there dumbfounded, took home the semolina, and found that it did the job perfectly well without us burning out coffee grinders! We then had baits that were so hard that you could throw them at the floor and they bounced.

Lenny had this big thing about squid. He instilled in all of us, which we all agreed with, that natural products were better than things that were produced by scientists, and for many years he only used foodstuffs that could be eaten by human beings: there was a whole succession of different products that we used in our baits. At that time I think it's fair to say that we were still not convinced about Fred Wilton's theory that carp will select a diet for themselves: I think that belief eventually came about after seeing the results from the Kent boys using Fred's baits. So at that time we were happy to use what the rest of the angling world referred to as crap baits, semolina as the carrier with a natural flavour or food source within it. We bought the squid in frozen blocks, removed the ink sacks, mixed it with semolina and eggs, boiled it, and our results on that bait were fabulous. The downside of that bait was that when we fished long sessions we couldn't keep the squid or the baits fresh, and because of that we made a very interesting discovery.

We'd gone fishing with squid to Waveney Valley and halfway through the week we'd run out of fresh squid, which wasn't obtainable in its natural form anywhere

BELOW
Bob, Ritchie MacDonald and Pete Springate on the Cons Club, 1981.

in the area. We struggled to find an alternative but Lenny came up with the bright idea that in among his food for the week he had some Bird's Eye beefburgers. So we liquidised them, added them to the semolina and eggs, and that was our second major bait in terms of success. It was instant and we used it for years on a number of waters, until a time came when I selected a cheaper brand of beefburger off the shelf because they didn't have the ones from Bird's Eye. We added them to the bait, and they didn't work! We didn't catch a fish on that version. Back next session with the Bird's Eye version and the bait was working again. It took us a long time to figure out what the

ABOVE
Lenny Middleton with his biggest Savay fish, 29½lb from Alcatraz, August 1981.

difference was. The Bird's Eye beefburgers were with onions! So we presumed that it was the onion element that was making the difference, and over the years people have used onion in varying forms in their baits with great success.

Kevin Maddocks was part of the group then. Lenny was seeing Kevin during the early part of the week most weeks, and they were fishing together. Kevin was a huge driving force in that he was a very hard-working carp angler, although he wasn't as inventive as Lenny. I think Kevin would admit that he hated using things that were untried and untested, but Lenny loved that aspect of carp fishing: "That works, what's next?" Lenny wanted the indicator to move: after that he lost interest. But they set up tanks at Kevin's, and they came up with some really good ideas. Lenny's first experiment with the Hair was with barbel, at King's Weir. As I said earlier, part of our season was barbel fishing, and we would go to King's Weir and fish for them there. Lenny's first experiments with the Hair were on barbel, where he proceeded to lasso the barbel with the Hair, because they were only small, and he gave it up as a bad job. He left it alone and went back to it much later with carp.

Lenny was never happier than when he was experimenting and trying out new things. He played with hooks, with different designs, with bent hooks long before they came into use. Lenny never ceased to amaze me with what he would come up with next. His take on the Bristle Rig was an immediate success. My son James tested it for him at the Cracker Factory (Stanborough) and results were stunning. But Lenny thought that made things too easy and he moved away from it. We're talking about the early-'80s here and I see mentions of the Bristle Rig now as though it's something new! Lenny believed that the pricking of a fish, whether it was with the point of the

ABOVE
Lenny with the famous Italian from Savay at 28¼lb.

hook or a bristle, or whatever, was what caused the fish to run. His take on the Hair was very different from the way it is usually used today. We used our Hairs tied off the bend of the hook using a Hair of 2-3lb breaking strain nylon, or whatever we could get away with casting. The length of the Hair was always being experimented with, depending on the size of fish you were fishing for. The use of the Hair changed dramatically once it reached the marketplace, and it's changed beyond all recognition now, to the point that you've got people using materials for the Hair that are actually thicker than the hooklink material. But in our minds, Lenny's original concept that they were picking up something which they didn't know was attached to line worked; we thought that was the way to go. Pricking of the fish was what he was trying to achieve.

My first use of the Hair was at Darenth. I was the last person in our little group to hear of the Hair! I had such a big circle of friends in carp fishing that Lenny and Kevin were worried that I wouldn't be able to keep the secret to myself. What then happened was that Lenny had fished a long session with Andy (Little) the week before and he'd told Andy about it, then realised that one of his best friends was still in the dark over it. So we were at Darenth for the weekend and he called me to his swim on the Friday evening and told me about it. I was fishing next to Derek Stritton that weekend and I went back to my swim and had four or five fish on that first evening, whereas one a weekend was normal! This definitely caused some consternation at Darenth regarding what was happening at that time. Lenny, Keith, Kevin – Paul Bray was around at that time, too – the catches that we had were stunning. In fact there's a little story there. When we originally went to Waveney we asked the Norfolk boys, who became close friends in later years, what we could expect to catch in a weekend's fishing, and their reply to us was that if we caught two fish a season we'd be doing well! Well, between us we had 12 fish during that first weekend using the Hair! It was devastating when it was first used, especially on pressured waters like Darenth and Waveney.

The story came out that one of our team cast into the big oak and Pete Regan later swam out, to retrieve it, which wasn't quite true; he didn't swim. What happened was that accidentally Lenny cast from Swim One into the big oak, and snapped off.

Later on Pete Regan was walking round to the caravans at the back of the lake, saw the rig hanging in the tree, and climbed up to retrieve it. He brought it back to Lenny and showed it to him. Lenny, in his naivety, didn't take the rig from Pete; he let him keep it. Pete immediately took that rig to Dick Weale and Len Bunn and the cat was out of the bag as far as Waveney was concerned. They'd fished there the previous season and had an unbelievable season on their Black Majic bait. It did help us, with the secrecy surrounding the Hair, to throw the success onto the bait, and when we were being successful we always pretended that the success was down to the bait. At that time we were using peanuts at Darenth: we were using single peanuts against the island with no prebaits, and the success rate was phenomenal. These were very, very competitive times. The world and his wife were on Darenth then. I left my landing net behind at the end of one session and had to go back to the swim for it. When I got back there I found three very high-profile figures of that era, in the water, trying to retrieve baits to find out what we were doing!

What readers may not realise is that Lenny was a very talented bloke, not just in connection with falconry and fishing. At one time he ran a successful taxidermy business from our kitchen! Lenny wasn't just the most influential angler of his time; he created the group around him, made us thinking anglers, made us think about what we were doing and where we were going. Lenny wasn't just a carp angler, he was a trout angler too, and even in his trout fishing he designed flies that the normal trout fisherman had never seen before, and they were very successful. He came to us one day and said, "Why do I want all these different flies when I can tie the same pattern in different colours, and call it a fuzzy – a black fuzzy, a red fuzzy, a green fuzzy and so on, all in the same pattern, but all in different colours." Everything he ever did was good fun. He was fabulous, fabulous company. For a long time he was like part of the family. My son James looked up to him. He could do some bizarre things. Once, at a party at his cottage in Barkway, he announced that we were going to play hide and seek and we were to go and look for him. Well, to be honest there was nowhere to hide, and after 20 minutes we gave up. Eventually he emerged from his garden pond where he had been lying underwater and breathing through a drinking straw. And this was in December! He loved being in the water, Lenny, and whenever anyone hooked a fish he would strip off ready to go into the water if the need should arise.

Physically Lenny was very hard. He didn't even use a bivvy on his long sessions. He didn't have a car so he was on the water until someone picked him up. We collected him for Christmas after one long winter session on Savay. He came off the water in a one piece suit with half a leg missing, with a moon boot on one foot and a wellington on the other, with a beard full of ice, and didn't want to come away. We dragged him away. Lenny was driven. I didn't understand the expression 'thinking outside the box' until I realised how precisely it described Lenny. He thought outside the box. His bent hook rigs and knicker elastic rigs (which fired the hookbait into the carp's mouth!) were ahead of their time, and still are in the case of his version of the elastic rig. Some of his ideas were far-fetched, but he had a very moral approach to his fishing. He discarded the Bristle Rig because it made things too easy, although for some reason he didn't see the Hair as making things too easy, I think because it was just a hook and a bait. The addition of the bristle was taking things too far. In later years he felt that carp fishing was too easy and went back to tench fishing!

For a final word on Lenny, because he is really a subject that deserves a whole interview, ultimately his crowning glory was his work with computers. When he left us he met Rose and they were married within six months. Before he lived with us I don't know that he'd ever had a girlfriend. After he got married and moved to Royston he spent the next few years not fishing and playing with computers, on which he was self-taught. Eventually he got a job with the gold company Johnson Matthey, a huge worldwide company, and invented some software that separated gold from plastic. He had three computers standing side by side, working in conjunction with each other, and it revolutionised what they were doing. By then he was in his early-50s and he wanted to retire to get back to fishing, so on the strength of his invention they gave him enough money to retire and he went back to fishing! He never had a computer lesson in his life, but what he was able to do with computers just left us speechless. Back in 1981 I took Tim (Paisley) across to Finsbury Park to meet Lenny and to pick up his original Coarse Angler article about the Hair, which has now been published in Rod Hutchinson's 'Carp Inspirations' book. I think that is a fitting tribute to a quite extraordinary man, who had an extraordinary impact on carp fishing – and angling as a whole, come to that. Sadly Lenny was lost to us through a brain haemorrhage some years back.

Then Savay came along... One of the things that had happened during that period was that a small syndicate was formed by Keith, Kevin and the rest of our little group in Hertfordshire, and we'd obtained our own carp fishery. We'd had some work done on the water by a fisheries management consultant by the name of Graham Rowles. Well during the next few years Graham obtained a post with Redlands Aggregates and became their fisheries manager. I answered an advert in the Angling Times – I can't remember whether it was the Times or the Mail, it was one or the other. It was a very small ad in the classified section along the lines of 'Syndicate to be formed in the Colne Valley'. I picked up the phone to

respond to the advert and recognised
the voice at the other end of the line –
it was Graham Rowles. I told him who
I was and immediately he said, "You're
the man for me! Would you like to run
a syndicate on Savay?" I answered that
I thought that was Ruislip Angling
Club's water and his reply was that
Ruislip AC weren't going to be there
much longer (sic), and we formed the
syndicate from friends that I'd made
during my angling years. Boys from
Norfolk came and joined; boys from

Kent came and joined; in fact the world's 'Who's Who?' of carp angling at that time
came and joined what turned out to be our first two syndicates! Forming the Savay
syndicate turned out to be quite difficult simply because I put one syndicate together
and put the names forward, working on as few members as possible so as not to upset
Ruislip, but when I submitted the arrangement to Graham he turned it down. They
wanted double that amount of money! The syndicate fee was already high so there
was no question of doubling that, so the only way we could do it was to double the
membership. That meant having two rotas on a week on/week off basis, with the rotas
merging in the autumn to fish the winter. We went back to Redlands on that basis,
they accepted the revised offer, and the syndicate was formed.

I didn't have to advertise for members. Word got out and I was inundated
with people wanting to join. I knew most of the people who joined initially so I
had no worries about problems arising through the fishing of the water. The first
syndicate was made up of first-class thinking anglers, which was what we wanted.
After that first year I had a waiting list like you wouldn't believe from all over the
country. Rod (Hutchinson) was in the first syndicate. I'd met him once at Waveney.
Rod's name was put forward by the Crafty Cockney (the late Derek Cunnington),
who guaranteed his behaviour, shall we say. I was very worried about having Rod in
the syndicate at the time because I'd heard that he was a loose cannon, but in Rod's
defence he was brilliant. At that time he was the best thinking angler that we'd come
across and he showed us how to catch fish that were constantly on the move. He was
a guiding light to us there, actually. Some of the guys rebelled against his inclusion
for one reason or another, but for those of use who wanted to catch fish Rod was the
way home: he was brilliant.

The only problem I did have with Rod was that he and Kevin Maddocks didn't
get on at all and we had to separate them onto different rotas. There's one incident
with Rod that always sticks in my mind. We were fishing next to each other and we
spent half the night sitting up talking about Marlborough, what we'd been up to, the

development of rigs and so on, and by the time we turned in it was 3.00 or 4.00 in the morning. I got up a couple of hours later only to find that Rod had gone! The wind had changed and he'd upped sticks and moved up to the Canal Bank at the other end of the 70-acre lake! Of course Rod already had a good insight into fishing gravel pits because he'd been fishing in the south for many years by then, whereas many of the guys who joined were only used to estate ponds and small waters and didn't understand gravel pits, bars and so on at all. Gravel pit fishing was a new world to some of them, and of course it is a science in its own right. Didn't Jim Gibbinson have a book, *Gravel Pit Fishing*, devoted to the subject?

I only ran the Savay syndicate for two years. It's funny how things tend to come along at entirely the wrong time in life. At the time that the Savay thing kicked off I'd also obtained membership to the Cons (Conservative Club) which was only a mile or so up the road. Whereas we had two hardened rotas fishing the syndicate at Savay and you struggled to get where you wanted to be to fish at the Cons Keith Gillings and I could fish where we wanted, how we wanted, when we wanted! The fish at the Cons were of a similar size to Savay, and it was a gorgeous place, so it was no contest for us. My attentions started to wander to the Cons and other waters and Savay needed new blood at the helm to run the syndicate. Pete Broxup was already there (as a day ticket angler): he was a very close friend of Graham Rowles, and became more and more involved in the running of the water. As far as I can make out he did a fantastic job of running the syndicate until his untimely death a year or two back.

At about this time I became the first chairman of The Carp Society on 25th May 1981 at a meeting Greg Fletcher and Tim organised at the Kenwood Hotel in Sheffield. I can remember several conversations that changed my life at that time, to be honest. When we arrived at the hotel for the meeting, the things Tim was talking about, and his ideas, were very revolutionary to us down in the south, and it was what carp fishing in England wanted at the time. The carp scene was being strangled by certain people in certain quarters, much to the annoyance of most carp anglers. What we wanted was to share information. We wanted a magazine that was going to get to the people. And when the opportunity came to be the first chairman I grabbed it with both hands and hopefully, during the short time I was in that position, I had some input into it, and some input into its undoubted success.

Because I was still the leader of the Savay syndicate at the time, and known to be a friend of Kevin Maddocks, who was heavily involved with the BCSG and the CAA, my involvement was probably a big influence on many anglers who might otherwise have viewed the new organisation with suspicion. It was the right thing to do; there wasn't any choice. And to go round the country for the initial regional meetings was exciting. We were getting to people who thought they were at the back of beyond, Norfolk being a prime example. We went to Norfolk and had one of the most successful meetings imaginable at Waveney. It was brilliant, despite the fact that a couple of roughnecks broke a caravan window in the early hours! Rod and I got to wrestling in the caravan where we were all billeted. We only leant against the window but it popped out and broke, which caused a bit of gossip in the carp scene; and of course it also meant that the caravan was bloody freezing for the rest of the night! They were fabulous days, and in my carp-fishing career I look back at the early days of The Carp Society with some pride. And to be honest, even today, when people come to our fishery here, out of all the things I've been involved in, and all the things I've done, it's the early days of The Carp Society that they want to talk about. The newer generation doesn't understand

TOP
A lovely linear from the Cons Club Big Lake.

ABOVE
A good common for Bob from the Cons Club Big Lake.

the stranglehold that the BCSG and CAA had on carp fishing at that time, and what was achieved through the formation of the Society was great for carp fishing, and for carp anglers.

The next time I encountered Tim was as a near-neighbour at Clowne in Derbyshire in the late-'80s, where Sheila and I had a successful kennels. I fished the Mangrove with Tim at that time and almost joined the inaugural Mangrove syndicate when it was formed in 1989. We had a very successful business at Clowne, but the Coal Board decided there was coal under our land and we were made subject to a compulsory purchase order, which leads us to a rather lovely story, albeit one that has nothing to do with carp fishing! We had negotiations with the Coal Board for them to purchase the farm where we lived and ran the kennels. The negotiations went on for several months and we couldn't come to an amicable agreement as to how much they were going to pay us. We didn't want to go. We had our first really successful business, which was doing very well, and they were insistent that they were going to buy the place. It got to the stage where it made me very ill, and I had a heart attack at the age of 42: Sheila was getting very worried, too. We didn't know what to do because we thought we were going to have to let them have it at their price, which we felt was way out of line to what the place represented to us as a home and a business.

BELOW
57½lb from Passion in the '90s.

Anyway, we were at home one Sunday and one of our customers knocked on the door and asked if he could come in for a chat. He proceeded to tell us that the following day, on the Monday morning, we were to phone our solicitors and the Coal Board and insist that the Coal Board be served with a Blight Order. We didn't even know what a Blight Order was. Our visitor said that although we wouldn't know what we were doing, that was the way to go, and we'd got to trust him. We did as he directed, made the phone calls the following morning and the solicitors served the Coal Board with a Blight Order that afternoon. Within 24 hours we had an offer for our property at the asking figure we were looking for, which, I might add, was some £300,000 higher than the offer we already had! The man concerned remained anonymous, but bless him, whoever he was!

After we'd been compulsorily purchased we bought another kennels down in Dorset, a very successful business, which was about the time I started fishing abroad. In fact, two things were happening at that time. I was fishing the local Dorset waters, the Roach Pit and Milton Abbas, which was another little syndicate started by a friend. I really enjoyed my fishing down south, doing reasonably well and catching some good fish, but the buzz of France had bitten. Paul Bray had been back in touch with me and we started to make the occasional trip to France. I knew Paul from way back, of course, and he'd been in the original Savay syndicate. He was a very good angler and he started taking me to France. We got a good angling partnership going together, and he whetted my appetite for France. We started fishing obscure waters, not waters that were well known by people in England; club waters and local town waters. We didn't catch massive fish but back then, thirties, to us, were good fish. One of the little waters I fished was Passion, in the Paris region. I made two or three trips to Passion and had big fish from there, including a massive hit of fish with loads of carp over 40lb in one session. I had my first really big fish from Passion, including one of 57lb and another of over 60lb: it was an easy water, and a pleasure to fish. Paul and

TOP
Acton Burnell 40lb+ common from the '90s when Bob starting fishing with Frank Warwick.

ABOVE
Cassien again, this time with Tim Paisley, Simon Crow and Frank Warwick, the trip on which Crowy earned his nickname of Wolfgang.

I took the Method there, and it was fantastic! The water hadn't seen the Method before and it really lifted off.

Frank Warwick and I had been fishing the Method up at Rob Hales' water, Acton Burnell, and doing very well with it. Frank and I used to fish opposite each other, both using the Method, which didn't go down well with the other members, but it worked well for us and we came to terms with the tactic. Then Keith (Gillings) said to me "Why don't you go and see Kevin?" Kevin was fishing Chantecoq at the time and my first trip to the water with Kevin really got me going and I spent the next two or three years targeting Chanty. Chantecoq was a dream that I wanted to pursue. I wanted to be part of the big fish/big water scene. It took me a while to get myself geared up and ready to go, but in the end we went off there. I found it really hard work because it wasn't a type of carp fishing I was familiar with at that time. Fishing in mud was hard: getting to places where there were no other people was a necessity. The regime running Chanty wasn't as it is now; then it was much more relaxed and you could virtually go where you wanted. We used to keep out of the view of people and we managed to get away with an awful lot. We found an area in Chanty in September and October where the water levels were dropping and the carp were going to feed on the crayfish among the roots of the trees. Most people who are familiar with Chantecoq know there is a forest under the water, and as the water dropped the crayfish became available to the fish, and the fish were there. For four or five weeks of the season, fishing off our peninsula into that region, results were phenomenal. I had a three-day session in which I caught a dozen fish over 40lb, including my best-ever Chanty fish of 49½lb. The following season it started to produce 50s but when I was there 49½lb was a very good Chanty fish. They were fabulous fish; big-plated mirrors; they were beautiful. The big-water bug had bitten me by this time and I wanted to go on and fish the other big waters in France. In its day I don't think there was anywhere in France to match Chantecoq for its head of big fish.

ABOVE
Looking across the stunning Lac Serrerie to Bob and Sheila's lakeside house.

I was fishing with Frank Warwick. He told me about the Cassien trips, and we started going there together as a group, culminating, of course, in the making of the Cassien video with Frank, Crowy and Steve Briggs. (Sadly this was immediately after Mary had died and Tim couldn't make the trip.) I had a fish of 49½lb on my first trip there but for some reason I didn't think much of the place. I didn't think I would be going back there, but I hadn't seen the best of the place because the Bridge Swim Frank and I fished isn't really representative of what Cassien is about and I had to see more of it. Once I got away from the water I got it into perspective and I was keen to go back. Around that time I'd fished other big waters and I'd done all right. I started to realise that big waters didn't necessarily mean big blanks. I started to believe that big waters can be easier, because the fish are very mobile. As long as you are an observant angler and have got your wits about you, you can stay in touch with the fish. But you must be mobile on some of the big waters. The following year I was fishing the Pylon Swim in the South Arm below Tim on the South Arm and I started catching. Mr Crow moved below me and he stitched me up like a kipper, which earned him the nickname Wolfgang. He was fishing behind my marker! I hope that my days at Cassien aren't over because I would love to go back there some time because it is a wonderful water. But I know what people mean about having all that space in front of you on the big waters. You have that at Chantecoq, and it's lovely.

Through my overseas travels I fell in love with overseas fishing and wanted my own water, which eventually resulted in the purchase of the gorgeous complex we are running now. What happened was that one day I went home to my wife Sheila after a fishing trip and she announced that she'd had enough. She wanted to be finished with the kennels. She was absolutely fed up with having to have a smiling face all the time and dealing with the general public: "We are going to sell up and leave!" And before I knew it she had sold the kennels! That's true. She sold it to a friend, but where that left us was wondering what were we going to do next? We didn't know what to do, or where to go! I was spending an awful lot of time in France fishing and Sheila said to me, "You always wanted to be involved in fishing, and you love France, so why don't we go to France and have a fishery?" And eventually that was what we did. I found this place via a contact when I was fishing with Tim at Goncourt. I travelled down here, saw it, and fell in love with it as soon as I saw it. After some haggling I bought it, without Sheila even having seen it. In fact the first time she saw it was when we moved down here to live! What a wife, which she is! She has always been very supportive in everything I've done, or wanted to do.

When we bought this fishery we didn't expect it to turn into what it's become. We came here to semi-retire. When I first drove down the lane to the lakes I just thought, 'This is paradise!', and that's what drove us to buy it. It all happened a bit

quickly at the time, and with hindsight we might have done one or two things differently, but having been here for eight years now we certainly don't regret coming here. We've had some wonderful times here. It's a gorgeous place.

It has to be said that carp anglers can be difficult, but over the years we have developed a regular clientele so we more or less know everyone who is coming each year. Holiday carp anglers

don't always seem to understand that carp are wild animals and very unpredictable in terms of when they will and won't feed. Whingers can be tiresome and make the lives of water owners and trip-runners difficult. Fortunately we have got the most wonderful clientele base. A lot of them are friends. A lot of them come back year after year after year, twice and three times a year some of them. We look forward to many of the parties coming. Obviously, you will always get the odd awkward customer but on the whole, our clientele base are good friends and very easy to accommodate. We had to choose what sort of venue we were going to be. We are very fortunate in that we have got two lakes. One of them is the small lake, Badger's Sett, which it would have been very easy to turn into a big-fish small lake. I asked our customers, everyone who came, what they want from their fishing when they come on holiday, and almost everyone said that when they come away they want to catch lots of big fish, but not necessarily huge ones. We've got fish to 60lb+ in both waters, which are still pretty big by most people's standards, but the backbone of the fishing in the top (small) lake is for 30-50lb fish, and that's what the anglers come for. If they get a 60 then that's the icing on the cake. A long time ago I said that as commercial waters in France go you will, in time, be fishing for 40lb+ fish, and that is where we are going.

The biggest problem we have had while we've been here was through a fish purchase. Every fish that has been put into these lakes has been from a *bona fide* French fish farmer. In one particular consignment we purchased 12 fish from this fish farm and to my utter amazement, two months later, after publishing a picture of the biggest fish in the big lake, it turned out to be a fish that had previously been captured from a public water in Paris – unbeknown to anyone, apart from the person who sold it to the fish farmer. The farmer buys and sells fish just as we do, and he bought a batch of 20 fish, and this one was one of those fish. The fish was recognised by someone who had caught it while it was in its original water. I was horrified when I was informed and I immediately offered to take the fish back to its original venue, which was declined. Part of the French carp-angling establishment then wanted to pillory me and nothing I could do or say was going to be of any appeasement whatever, which didn't

make any sense on two counts. One was that if I had known that the fish was stolen I wouldn't have accepted it – and I certainly wouldn't have allowed a picture of it to be published: and the second is that I would think that the fish was moved in the first place by a French angler! Many people who own commercial fisheries in France will tell you that you are often being offered big fish by French anglers. I've always stuck to my own rules of only buying fish from one place, and on this occasion it backfired on me. The whole saga left a terrible taste in my mouth.

The irony here is that our son James, who lives with us here in an adjacent cottage, is now a fish dealer and has a highly successful, well-respected, fish farming business. The fish that we have here are bred by Christophe and James and we have stocked some of the best fisheries in France. They are good fish, and they do well. We won't sell fish to places where we feel they shouldn't go, and we don't sell fish to people who don't really know what they are doing. We try to educate them regarding the running of a fishery as well as supplying them with the fish. The important thing to get across is that you can't put 20 dogs in a kennel and not feed them: you cannot overstock a commercial fishery and not feed them, even though you might think that fish don't need feeding. They do. There is far more to creating a fishery than digging a hole in the ground and stocking it with fish. Many people have to discover that the hard way, whatever advice you try to offer them at the outset.

Moving back to my own fishing, over the last few years my serious carp fishing has been in Belgium. Through my fishing connection with Frank Warwick I started my fishing in Belgium by going to the tackle dealer Daconic's private lake, where I caught the biggest fish caught by a non-Belgian ever at 60lb 2oz, and then meeting Theo and Johnny from the lake called the Surf. They invited us to go back there, and subsequently I became a member of the Surf, the only non-Benelux person ever to be invited in as a member. I've really enjoyed my fishing at the Surf. It's a 70-acre lake with only 10 members, and very few fish. Incidentally, since I became a member my son has stocked the Surf with 25 of his fish, which are doing very well. I go up to fish the Surf about six times each year and Theo and I fish together. It's a different style of fishing. It's long-range fishing using a boat, hoping for one of the big fish. My biggest from the water so far is 61½lb, which I've had twice, and I've had probably five or six fish over 50lb from the water. I call my Surf fish my 'proper' fish; they are fish you've really got to work hard for; you've really got to think about what you're doing. Fishing there has given me a great deal of satisfaction: it's probably the summit of my carp-fishing career, fishing in Belgium. I've just been made a member of another water next door to the Surf – Gerard's – which I'm looking forward to fishing in the future. Belgium is a fantastic place to fish, and fabulous people to fish with.

With my regular trips to Belgium and the return trips to England I do a massive mileage each year. From here it's a 10-hour journey to Belgium. That's probably why they let me become a member, because they knew I wouldn't fish there overmuch. If I was going to be there every week I wouldn't have been an ideal member. When I get back to England I'd like to think that I'll fish it more regularly. Having been here nearly eight years and built up this marvellous business and developed the two lakes to the point where they are both really taking off, Sheila and I are getting itchy feet again and are ready to move back to England and retire! It's time to retire. I don't do anywhere near as much fishing as I used to. We miss England terribly. Keith Gillings is still my closest friend and I miss his company. So, without trying to sound like an advert, the business is up for sale (at the time of printing this book) and we are just waiting for the right buyer to come along, then we'll up sticks and head north, hopefully to somewhere in East Anglia.

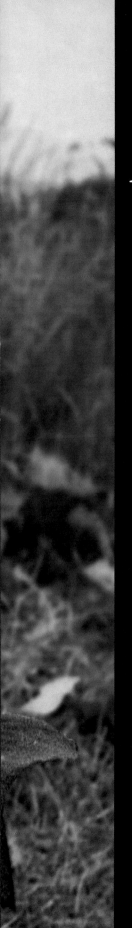

Carpworld's Big Interviews Revisited

Kevin Nash

Talking to Tim Paisley • Part One

From Carpworld Issue 238

Kevin Nash should need no introduction to anyone. He is a successful Essex carper who has been carp fishing for well over 40 years. In the late 70s he started his own carp business which has steadily grown to be the multi-million pound empire Kev controls today incorporating Nash Tackle and Nash Bait. The interview took place on Kev's 14-acre estate on the banks of the prolific Church Pool big fish lake, which was only dug in the 90s. In the pages that follow Kev's talks about the development of his fishing, his thinking, his businesses and the creation of his estate.

The starting point for my fishing, believe it or not, was as a boy scout. I went on a camp and the scoutmaster was the secretary of the local angling club, Rayleigh Angling Club, which had a colossal waiting list of years. To cut a long story short, my parents were going on holiday the day the camp finished, so it was agreed that we'd meet them on the way. Anyway, they got held up and the scoutmaster, in his infinite wisdom, decided to leave me at the roadside to wait for my parents and take all the other scouts back home! Four or five hours later a farmer came along and picked me up; he thought I'd been abandoned and I ended up being put on a train from the New Forest in Hampshire, back to Essex and then home! The upshot was that my parents missed me and my father did his nut. There was a massive row when they got back from holiday and, to appease my father, the scoutmaster let me join Rayleigh Angling Club!

The water was overstocked but it was one of the few waters in Essex that had been stocked with carp – this was at the start of the wave of carp stockings. Rayleigh has a small pool (it still has) which was stocked with the new wave of carp. There were only a handful of carp waters in Essex at that time, which held the old strain of carp – the wildies if you like – including Priory Park where Jim Gibbinson fished, but in the '60s the Kent Water Authority ran this government-backed scheme to rear carp and I guess that was the start of the carp boom, because to fish for carp you need carp to fish for!

PREVIOUS PAGE
Early-'70s syndicate lake.

BELOW
Tim and Kev putting together the two-part interview on the banks of Kev's Church Pool.

I always wanted to catch them because one of the lads at school brought in this picture of a fish he'd caught, a 'huge' carp of about 6lb (it kind of dwarfed the rudd and crucians I had been catching)! So I wanted to catch one from the beginning, but like everyone else at that time I was primarily a pleasure angler, a float angler. I wanted to catch a carp, but I wanted some action, too. But carp always captured my imagination. At the angling club there was this mystical group of three guys who fished for carp. They wore the floppy hats and the camouflage jackets, but they were a fair bit older than me. I'd have been around 12 at that time and they would be in their late-teens. One of them, by the way, was Derek Ritchie, so at one time I was trying to be like Derek Ritchie, heaven forbid! I learnt from these guys and finished up catching all the carp in the water many times over. We're talking different size-scales back in those days. An average fish for the water would be 4lb, while one of 7lb was a monster. The pool only ever produced one double and that was after I'd gone on a baiting campaign with cat food paste and the weights had gone up. I caught that double in a match. In actual fact, I won every cup at the club because I was match fishing as well at the time. When I was fishing the matches I noticed that the skimmers soon went off the feed and I realised that I only had to catch one or two carp to win the match. I worked in a tackle shop and I used to take two gallons of maggots and literally fill them in on one spot, so I started winning the matches with carp, including catching the heaviest weight and the biggest fish. I did so well that I won every cup the club had, except the ladies match cup!

When I was 16 I started work as an apprentice at an engineering company and became friendly with a guy called Bob and his mate Eric. They were keen anglers who mainly fished for bream, but I kept going on about carp and eventually they decided to have a go, so we became a team and that was how I started spreading my wings – because of course at that time I was too young to drive. Now that I had wheels we started to target other carp waters.

We went to Priory Park, where Jim Gibbinson caught the record wildie. Priory used to be a monastery so the monks had introduced carp as a food source. Lake Meadows at Billericay – that was a real carp water at that time with several BCSG members fishing it. Boreham Mere was another water where you could see the mysterious floppy hat brigade; this lake had produced one 20 so was hot! We looked at Layer Pits, but at the time there were only a few fish in there that were rarely caught

TOP
Opening this gate opened up my life of carp fishing.

ABOVE
An early black and white shot of Kevin with a 16lb leather.

so I only dabbled. There were a few waters up towards London that were target carp waters at the time, but you really were talking about just a handful of carp waters to go at back then.

Gradually I became fanatical. The three of us were visiting other carp waters, but I was still float-fishing with one rod and fishing for carp with the other two, but gradually carp took over and eventually I aspired to sitting behind three carp rods. The boredom aspect had gone by the board as I gradually realised there was so much going on under the water that there was nothing to be bored about. As you get into it, thinking about carp can keep your mind occupied full-time. I'm waffling a bit now... There's an Essex County Show every year and in those days the Water Authority used to be at that show and they had a big fish tank on their stand, which had big carp in it, huge carp, weighing up to 20lb or more. I found out that they had been netted from a private estate lake called Braxted and I got on there. I fished it very hard for a season and caught one carp. It was very hard. I now believe that at the time there were only two carp in it. I caught one of these carp on a liver sausage mix and it bottomed my scales at 25lb. At the time I really wanted to get into the BCSG and had previously been interviewed and turned down. Then the regional organiser changed and Derek Stritton interviewed me. I showed him the picture of this fish and Derek kindly let me into the group. Funnily enough, Derek came to one of our trade shows last year and was talking to one of our lads who ironically used to be a pupil of Derek's, and he commented along the lines of, "There was always something about Kevin. He was a cocky little sod, but he had something about him and I knew that he would always catch carp!"

So now I was in the BCSG; manna from heaven. I could now network with proper carp anglers. This would be 1972. I was told that I was the youngest angler ever to get into the BCSG – I would have been 17 at that time.

This would be around the time of the orange copy of the BCSG magazine, *Carp*, which had Fred Wilton's theories on bait in it, so suddenly I was moving from specials onto the PYM baits, and then onto the HNVs. We would bait a water for a week before we fished it. We didn't even bother to carp fish until we'd baited up for at least a week. At the time there was this perception that you couldn't catch a carp unless you'd educated them, and it was incredible because what happened was that you always caught the biggest fish first. They definitely recognised the bait as an exceptional quality food source. In effect, we became the first hit team, at least in the south of Essex. We'd just bait a water, move onto it, catch them, and move on. So I was now meeting other carp anglers; for example that's how I met Zenon (Bojko) when we moved onto Layer. So, not only was I networking through the BCSG membership, but as we moved onto other waters we were meeting the few other carp anglers who were active at that time. Local carp anglers at that time would include Bill Lovett, Geoff Kemp, Tony Howells, Mick Lindsell...

It was a competitive scene back then. It wasn't competitive within the BCSG... It wasn't competitive all the time because I didn't bump into a lot of other carp anglers, but if you did, then it was! It was all very secretive. You didn't tell them anything. An example of how competitive it was is that I started writing to Fred Wilton because we had a nightmare getting hold of proper casein. We didn't fully understand the stuff. There was a vast difference in the grades of edibility. A mate of mine, Eric, turned up with a sack of casein. He'd got it from a factory next door! (We had been searching the country high and low for a good source of casein – then Eric finds it in the factory next door!!)

I said, "You're having a laugh!"

Anyway, we made up a paste using the casein and took it to a water to see the reaction to it – and they were eating it on the drop. So we baited up with it, but when we started to fish we completely blanked. They just wouldn't eat the bait. So I questioned Eric and it turned out that it was a plastics factory next door and the grade of casein was inedible! So I wrote to Fred and he started supplying me with casein – but Derek Stritton stopped that. I have never to this day fished alongside Derek on a water, but we had started looking at some waters nearer London (Derek's patch). So yes, there was that competitive edge if you were on a lake and saw another angler fishing it. Like with Zenon and his mates at Layer, they sat at one side of the pit and we sat at the other. They wouldn't tell us a thing, so we didn't tell them anything either. So, yes, it was competitive because we were all a bunch of secret squirrels! It's understandable. There are a lot of very good carp anglers in Essex and we all want to have our edges. It's a two-edged sword. You don't want to give your edges away, but at the same time you want to use the eyes and ears of the other carp anglers, so you always give the impression that you're telling them all you know, but at the same time you are holding back what you don't want them to know! It's always been like that, carp fishing in Essex, and I guess it always will be, particularly with more and more wannabes coming into the game.

Around that there time it stopped me in my tracks when I heard a voice claim at a BCSG meeting that he was going to make a living out of carp fishing, because of course in the '70s there just weren't enough carp anglers for anyone to make a living out of the sport. Along with everybody else, I was stunned. The room went silent and we all looked around at this new member, Kevin Maddocks. I would suggest Kevin was the first one with the vision to see the future possibilities of actually making a living out of the game. At the time, the number of carp anglers involved wasn't the issue. Fred Wilton decreed that you shouldn't make a profit out of carp fishing. His belief was that we did it for love and that no one shouldn't make a living out of it. Ironically, if you look at the scene now it's gone upside down and become so commercial that maybe Fred was right. You've got to remember that at the time Fred was God, full stop. He was worshipped by the people who fished with him, Derek Stritton, Bob Morris, Robin Monday and so on, and rightly so! The guy was so off the wall with his ideas and he brought so much to carp fishing. People think of Fred in terms of carp fishing in connection with bait, but I remember the idea of a one-piece suit coming out of the Wilton camp. It may have been Robin Monday writing about it, but I think it was Fred. I jumped on that and made myself my first one-piece suit. I think it was Fred who first wrote about, or mentioned, using industrial nylon for carp sacks. There was so much coming out of that mind, or from the people with him, that we all listened when Fred said that it wasn't right to make a living out of carp fishing. It may be that Fred was talking about bait. I remember Rod Hutchinson was nervous of that aspect when he went into business, but certainly at that time the concept of making a living out of carp fishing was frowned on in certain circles. Bait was the starting point for most people going into business so it was probably the selling of bait that was the supposed stumbling block.

The starting point for my own business was sacks and slings. Bait 78 was one of the first companies to sell baits commercially and their premises used to get done (vandalised) every night. That was the way it was then. The attitude was that they were selling secrets really, which went against the grain with the anglers who already knew those secrets! What happened with me was that one night Eric sacked a carp using an industrial nylon sack and it died. At the time I was going out with a girlfriend who had a business making clothing and dresses. I was in the shop one day when I saw this black material, which had a much looser weave than industrial nylon. This turned out to be trouser-pocket material. I put it under the tap and the water just fell through it, and I realised that would make a great sack. So she knocked sacks up for me, Eric and Bob, and of course we were going out and fishing a number of waters where other anglers saw the sacks. They all wanted me to knock some up for them. That's how it started. In the close season I was knocking up sacks for whoever asked and as soon as the season opened I went fishing. Then we hit the recession and work went off, so suddenly the sacks became more important, because I had a big mortgage to keep up. I started advertising in the first Carp Society magazine, or perhaps the second, and started supplying by mail order. Then shops started asking for the sacks and I started supplying a few of them – Jack Simpson, Alan Brown, and Bait 78 spring to mind – but I still looked on it as part-time because when June 16th came around I wanted to go fishing!

At that time I was still part-time. I went full time in 1984, some five years later. By this time demand was increasing and I had expanded my range to include carp additives, side wraps for brollies, and my first big one – the Hooker holdall (the first holdall to take rods tackled up with reels). By this time I was trying to work, run the business, keep a girlfriend happy, and go fishing, and it just reached breaking point. I went to the doctor's because I felt so ill. I was doing a full-time job, getting in at 4.30 in the afternoon, letting schoolboys in to pack (my house was the factory at the time), then I was going out into the garage, cutting up all the fabrics, going round the outdoor machinists delivering the work, collecting what they'd done, get back about 11.00, then pack my parcels to send out and I was getting to bed about 3.00 or 4.00 in the morning!

The outcome wasn't rocket science. I went to the doctor's and he looked at me and asked what I was up to. He said I looked as though I hadn't eaten or slept in about a year! He told me something had to give because I was killing myself. In actual fact, the year before I'd had a really close call at work when I got my overall wrapped up in a lathe. I'd managed to get out of it by bracing my arms against the machine bed just before I had my head ripped off, flexing my back and splitting the overalls right along the back seam. I suffered a really bad back injury and all my ribs were bruised. So I faked the same injury the following year with a view to taking six weeks off work to see how the business went! It was probably my guilty conscience, but I thought my boss sensed I was faking it, so a week into my sick leave I went back to work. I got some black and yellow bait dye and coloured my ribs to make them look as thought they had been badly bruised. My boss was horrified by the extent of my 'injuries'! But within a few weeks I realised there was a living to be made out of the carp business because I was being inundated with orders, so I packed in work and went full-time.

There is an interesting story attached to the setting up of the business. Around 1980 we started having carp meetings at my house, which we called the '10 and 31' parties – they were the numbers on the menu for sweet and sour pork balls and special fried rice that we always ordered – Roger Smith gave the party that name. I started this idea of a meeting on the Friday night at which Roger Smith turned up, Kempy, Zenon, Mick Lindsell and so on. The BCSG meetings had wrapped up so these Friday night meetings were just a gathering of like-minded people. I remember Zenon opening the curtains one night and commenting that it had turned light; we'd been talking all through the night! In the end the odd one carried on through into Sunday. I'd get phone calls from blokes I'd never heard of before, calls from Cornwall, the north of

England, all over, telling me that they'd heard of the 10 and 31 parties and wanted to come along to one! A lot of products were developed from those meetings because we'd got this nucleus of certainly Essex's best minds. It was like a think tank where ideas and opinions could be pooled and without a doubt the development of my business benefited from that pooling of ideas. For example, anti-tangle tube came from there and Roger Smith gave me an idea, which ultimately became the Hooker holdall.

Late-'70s I'd moved onto a water called Barking Reservoir. I was fishing another water and I got talking to a guy from near London who told me about this water near Witham, which was controlled by a club at Barking. He'd been at the stocking seven years before and he said it was stocked with carp, which made me sit up and take notice. Bear in mind that we are still in a period when carp waters containing 20s were comparatively thin on the ground. In fact I recall having an argument with Rick Gibbinson when I commented that there were probably 30 carp waters in Essex with 20s in them. He didn't believe me, but I was able to name 30 (it was a struggle though!), so what I'm saying is that if someone mentioned a carp water you didn't know about, you were immediately interested.

I mentioned the water to Bill and Brendan and they prebaited it. I was fishing the syndicate water at the time but they went up there one afternoon and a guy had caught a 27lb mirror, which is the equivalent of a 40 now. So we all piled in and joined that water, and this is when I got Rod Hutchinson as a lodger – although I think that may have been a bit later. Barking was an eye-opener because it was the first indication we got that rigs were an issue in catching carp. Up to then we'd bait a water and catch the carp and if things slowed up then we'd change the bait. On Barking though it took me three years to catch the big 'un, known as Henry, which was featured on the front of my first little black and white catalogue a few years later. We'd go in with a bait, catch at the start, then all we'd get were twitches. So we were beginning to realise that rigs were an issue. Anyway, I'd just cracked the water with a really good result during opening week when I heard that this other lake had done a massive mirror of upper-30s, which was huge for back then. So I upped sticks at Barking just when I was starting to crack it and moved onto the other water, which was Silver End.

Putting the overall size of fish into perspective I hadn't caught a thirty at that stage. That was what I was after. A good 30, such as the Silver End fish, would be the equivalent of an upper-50 now and that was why I immediately switched to Silver End. From memory, I moved onto Silver

BELOW
Kevin with perm and the Barking Reservoir mirror.

ABOVE
*1985 – Silver End
Pit and the Essex
record – 41lb.*

End in 1980/81 because I was on there four years after that fish. I can only think that for three years I was fishing badly because I have a personal belief that if I haven't caught a fish in a year then I must be doing something wrong! The first season I fished it hard, putting in four nights a week on there, which meant two midweek nights and Friday and Saturday nights. I had an edge at that time because I was on the Hair Rig, but it wasn't an easy water. For instance, Roger Smith and Bob Jones moved on there and I think I'm right in saying that they never had a carp out of it. Ritchie MacDonald hit it hard but he never caught a carp there either. I think the fact that I was catching 90% of the carp was down to the fact that I was first on there and had it to myself, so I learnt the spots they naturally fed on before other anglers moved on and they became pressured and tricky.

After that first season the business was really taking off, but this was before I went full-time making tackle when I still had a full-time job, so at that time I wasn't really fishing it properly. I was just turning up at night, chucking the rods out and sleeping on the rods, so I wasn't getting the chance to observe what the carp were doing, and that's really why it took me four years to catch the big fish. After three years, during the winter prior to me catching it, Phil Harper, a great friend – I've known him since he was 14 – fished Silver End with, I think, Paul Gower, who was treasurer of The Carp Society in the early days. They moved on there, and that was when Ritchie MacDonald moved on there, too. Ritchie's approach back then was

ABOVE
*Saying goodbye to the
Silver End mirror
and watching five
years of effort go
swimming away.*

just to blanket bait. Then, just before Christmas, the phone rang and it was Phil to tell me that he'd caught the fish at just over 40lb. What! A 40? It just blew me away. I think that weight increase was down to Ritchie. It was possibly the first water in Essex to be targeted with that huge blanket baiting and so I think he pushed it up to 40. That made my mind up for me to take the water more seriously again, so the next close season, when I chucked in my job and went full-time making tackle, I really applied a bait. I caught it a few days into the season at a new Essex record weight, just when it was coming up to spawn. In Essex, in those days before global warming, the carp spawned within a week or 10 days of the season starting, which just goes to show what a waste of time the close season was, and I'm sure the big fish was just coming up to spawn when I caught it at 41½lb. As a point of reference, there were just five 40s caught in the UK that year, which shows how big a fish it was.

I caught the Silver End mirror and I've often observed that once you've caught the fish you are after you lose your enthusiasm. I had no real desire to go fishing... Well that's not quite true. I wanted to go to Savay with all my other mates. For example, Zen was there and so was Rod, who'd been a lodger while he was working in Essex, and it was all happening there. I was envious. Savay wasn't just a remarkable water, it was one of those examples of all the biggest names being together on one water, which was amazing. But at that time I was flat out trying to get my business off the ground so I couldn't justify the time. So, to be honest, in fishing terms I just wandered around aimlessly for three years and I wasn't enjoying my fishing. I had the big-fish bug and found it difficult to go back to just fishing for 20s – not that there was a 40 in Savay, but there were certainly 30s in there and that was the big-fish water of that time. So for a while I was just going through the motions when, out of the blue, the Snake Pit Common was caught, by a lad called Richard Westerman, so I went from probably fishing no more than 10 days and nights a year to fishing four nights a week! I just became obsessed with it.

It's always struck me as ironic, particularly for one-man businesses, that the time you most want to be fishing – and that was at the start of the season in the old close season days – is the time when everyone wants products from you and you're just up to your neck in it. It applies to this day. The lads and I have just done a 14-hour day to service the rest of the carp anglers who are all out there catching them and we can't. And then you get some bloke on the phone slagging you off because something's let him down and you think, 'Well, why do I do this?!'

In terms of my fishing, the Snake Pit refocused me really. Now I'd got another fish to go after. It was another 40, and also the second 40 that Essex had produced, and this one was a common. That was the best carp in the country, in my opinion, and what was interesting about the fish was that I'm sure it would almost certainly have gone on to break the record *(which was then 50lb 8oz)* because it had got to 40s

BELOW
Snake Pit – all 10 acres of submerged weed and trees.

without any bait at all. I think that the maximum weight for an English carp is 35lb, based on the natural food items the water provides. You get the odd exception like Redmire, where the original strain grew to big sizes on the basis of the natural food supply of the water, but the descendants of those original fish didn't achieve those weights. You combine those three elements of an exceptional strain of carp, a plentiful natural food supply, and no pressure, and you have the recipe for big carp. I think that's why Essex's track record for big carp is better than that of most counties. A lot of the waters we discovered in the '80s had just a few fish in them. There weren't these big stocks of carp, and clubs weren't managed as they are now, where commercial waters are created. So all the waters had natural biomass stockings, which meant adequate, or even excellent, larders, which I think is why Essex has got such a good track record for big carp.

The Snake Pit is a strange sort of place. It is an old gravel pit, which had actually been larger than it was when I went on there, because it had been back-filled at the far end. When the lake shrank, the level went up. So when we went on there I would say it was about eight acres, but 30-40% of it was submerged trees and the rest was weed, solid to the surface, with maybe seven carp in there (prior to some of them dying). In addition, it was in a rough area of Colchester, and was unmanaged, so you'd got all the local herberts round there using the place as a dump... Next to it was what I think I would describe as a school for wayward kids, but they weren't the problem. For many years I couldn't understand why there seemed to be a disproportionate number of – and it's difficult to put this one politely – nutters and lunatics going round the place. Then I found out that there was a mental hospital in Colchester and near to the Snake

Pit is a halfway house where patients were prepared for a return to society. So many of these people frequenting the Snake Pit did have mental problems and had been released from the hospital in Colchester. The first time I ran into one of them was after I got myself made a bailiff. The lake was run by this club called Maldon, one of those clubs run by match anglers, and in those days match anglers hated carp anglers; they absolutely hated us, and they were sending bailiffs over to check up on us, which always caused a row. So I had the idea of popping down to the club for the monthly meeting and putting myself up as a bailiff with the promise I would check the lake every day, hoping their other bailiffs would thus stay away. Anyway, Phil Harper was over there one day and this bloke turned up who started talking about there being crocodiles in the lake and these big black and white striped fish about 4ft long. Phil told me the story in a bemused way, while I rolled around the floor in hysterics. I turned up one Sunday morning and I couldn't believe it, there was a guy sitting on a box, float-fishing, down the bottom end. There were no fish in it other than a few roach and eels. Well, I thought, I'd better go round and check his ticket in case it got back to the club that I wasn't doing my job. So I went round and checked his ticket

ABOVE
My good friend Phil Harper with the magnificent Snake Pit Common.

and as I was talking to him, this other bloke came along and started talking about the history of the lake. He knew everything and was telling me when it was dug, and how it was dug, when the carp were stocked, so I was all over him like a rash for over an hour. And then he turned round and said, "There are big black and white striped fish in here, and crocodiles…"

I couldn't believe it – I had been done by the same nutter that Phil had met! For an hour he really had me going! That's just an example. And because of the tip at the bottom, all day long there'd be a procession of people pushing shopping trolleys, and they'd spend all day rooting through the tip. On one occasion a builder had tipped a load of breezeblocks, so there were these shopping trolleys going backwards and forwards fully loaded with breezeblocks. I asked one guy what he was using them for and he told me he was building a rabbit hutch! So I thought, 'Well, that must be some rabbit hutch', but then I asked the next guy along what he was building and got the same answer; he was building a rabbit hutch! They were all building rabbit hutches out of breezeblocks!

Initially I did a year on the Snake Pit, but while I was on there Zenon and Rael were the only ones to have it off. What happened was that Bill Lovett was fishing one weekend and while he was packing up he saw a fish roll in the centre of the lake, so like a twit he told Zenon where he'd seen it! Now Zen doesn't need telling twice, he's a really switched-on angler, so he and Rael moved into that swim and basically took it over. Prior to that, Zen had been concentrating in the swim where Dave Westerman, the guy who sadly later committed suicide, had caught the big common and had his big hit where he caught virtually every fish in the lake. Bear in mind this was a time

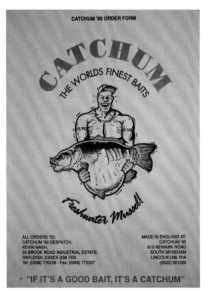

TOP
Harefield – between the partying, Kevin did catch one or two!

ABOVE
The Catchum product list, from the period when Kevin was in partnership with Rod Hutchinson.

when anglers still respected the fact that an angler was baiting a swim and would steer clear of it, and that was the swim Zenon caught the fish from. None of the rest of us caught anything that season.

The following season Phil, Zenon and I got our tickets through for Harefield, but decided to sit on them and stick it out at the Snake Pit. Phil and I shared a point swim. A real nutter was hanging around for three days, after which time we were all rattled by him. This was shortly after that awful massacre at Hungerford and after a few days we'd had enough of this guy. I connected this bloke with the Hungerford thing. We'd got this weird guy in combat gear saying he heard voices in his head, creeping up on us, and finding him behind bushes, so we all decided to pull off and we went to Harefield. There's another mad Snake Pit story here: a week later this creepy guy made the front page of the newspapers – he had murdered his mum. While he had been over the lake creeping around us, his mum was dead under his bed!! Happily I was completely bitten by the Colne Valley water and didn't go back to the Snake Pit that season.

There were three or four 30s in Harefield, which was still a 'wow' factor back then, but the fish I really wanted was the UK's biggest fully-scaled which, if I recall correctly, was around 34lb. I got interested in Harefield when I met a guy at the Snake Pit called Bob the Kraut. He was on Harefield, and he showed us these pictures of all the 20s and 30s. They were bloody awesome fish, so we all got tickets for Harefield. This was the time when Rob Maylin and his four mates were making a name for themselves. It was the Famous Five plus two. You'd got Maylin's lot – although I don't think Rob was there at the start of that season – plus Zenon and me. We were on the periphery of the Famous Five. My mate Phil Harper was one of the Famous Five, of course, so all the information that came out of that group was available to me at the time. It's got to be said, a lot of people don't give Rob Maylin credit for being the thinking angler he was – and still is. He was awesome in his day. Rob's an ex-match angler and you usually find that anglers who have been successful in matches have an angling edge over mere carp anglers! That's why I'm so grateful that I had a grounding in match fishing before I turned my attentions fully to carp. Going back to Harefield, that was a great party and thinking back to that first season at Harefield I still have to smile. When I first went there my name was still shit because of the big fall out I'd had with Rod Hutchinson after our ill-fated partnership in Catchum. Rod was still worshipped by many people in the Colne Valley and I turned up at Harefield and walked into the Horse & Barge, which is next door to Savay. So there were all these Savay anglers in there and the atmosphere was terrible.

Anyway, this guy who was built like a brick shithouse came across and shook my hand and said, "Welcome to the valley, Kev. I take people at face value."

That was Dougal Gray. So because everyone was frightened of Dougal I got accepted. In addition to that, you had a sort of competitive edge between Harefield and Savay. The Harefield anglers were looked on as an outlaw bunch of herberts by the Savay anglers because it was felt they were only fishing Harefield because they couldn't get into Savay because it was a closed shop! I think someone called us the Harefield Rebels and that stuck – we loved it – us against the snobby old-guard at Savay. We even had sweatshirts made up with the Harefield logo of Dougal's fist! You had all these young guys who loved to party and a pub right next to the lake with dozens of scantily clad females in it; it was a very hot summer and basically it was one long party. You'd turn up at the lake and tell yourself you were definitely going to fish that weekend, but it was red hot and by the time you'd walked round to your swim you'd be sweating like mad and a dozen anglers would have already asked you if you were going to the pub that night. You'd tell them no, but by the time you got round to your swim dying of thirst you'd have changed your mind, thought 'sod it', and go for it. We even used to take a change of party clothes with us, so you'd get changed, go to the Horse & Barge, stay there until it shut, then you'd get dragged up to the curry house – the famous curry house in Harefield that Rod mentions in *The Carp Strikes Back*. You'd get back from there about 2.00, just about manage a pub cast, and then in the morning Dougal would come round and say "You are going up the café", and if Dougal told you to do something you just did it! I've always said that unless it was Chris Ladds and Carebear, all the carp caught that summer were caught on a pub cast! So you'd go up the café, then to the pub for lunchtime, get back and have a snooze in the afternoon, then by the time you woke up it was time to get dressed and go up the pub again! Sunday morning we'd go down to Farlows for breakfast because the other café was shut, and then you'd go back to the lake, pack up, and go home. That's how it was. and it wasn't until the winter that I started figuring out that I was wasting my fishing time there, so I started applying myself a bit better.

There were technical problems to fishing the water. On one session I had four takes in a couple of hours and was cut off on the bars every time before I even picked up the rod! That got me thinking about what was happening and that was where the idea of the lead release clips came from, reversing the logic. The bars were just impossible with the gear we had available to us at that time. If you went over the third bar, landing the fish was probably less than a one in ten chance. My idea of going onto the big spool sea reels helped a bit because you could get the required distance with heavier line, but going over the third bar was still a very risky business. The break-off lead clip made all the difference, because once the lead was off, the fish came to the surface. Essex John stayed on there the following year and had terrific success using my idea of a break-off lead. The take rate didn't go up, but the landed-to-take ratio certainly did. I think John landed something like 70 carp the following year. My original rig consisted of a Helicopter Rig, but instead of a lead being attached to a link clip, I cut back the link clip to form a shallow hook, tied 3lb line to the hook and the other end to my lead, which was then attached over the hook. On a take the weak line snapped. Incidentally, I use the same system to fish my Chod Rigs nowadays. So from this came my version of the lead clip, the Safety Bolt Bead, which I was the first to bring out commercially.

I got really friendly with Dougal and then there was a misunderstanding between us, basically because of the actions of John Stent, the guy who then ran Farlows, which was one of a group of waters. The upshot was that it was a wise move for me to stay away from the valley for a while until Dougal calmed down and understood what had really happened. To cut a long story short, Dougal and I are the best of mates again, but the misunderstanding resulted in me giving up on Harefield, so I was back in the wilderness in terms of a carp water to fish. To be honest, I fancied a real change and I'd never caught a river carp, so I spent the summer in pursuit of carp on the Suffolk Stour, trying to locate a river carp. It was ever so interesting. I had a struggle to find them. I looked in all the obvious places, like weir pools and slack water, but I just couldn't locate them. In the end I did find them opposite an old people's home and opposite a private house on the bank. There were no obvious features, but the relevant thing was that it was private on both banks. I think it led me to believe about river carp that they always try to get away from humans.

Because the river was private on both banks fishing it was slightly difficult! There was a bridge below this private stretch and I tried to fish it by casting up river. I'll never forget it because the first time I decided to fish that stretch I saw these electrical wires across the river. I thought they were miles up, but when I cast, the end tackle went straight over them. I just couldn't reach the fish without casting over the wires! So in the end I sneaked up there at night, dropped in the baits and walked back with an open bail arm to the spot from which I was fishing. I caught from there, and then I moved onto Lee Valley and fished a couple of pits along there, before deciding to go back to the Snake Pit, because my dear mate Phil Harper had caught the Snake Pit Common.

I went back to the Snake Pit, but now there were only three carp in there. The lake had really changed and by now it was solid Canadian pondweed. I decided to bait it in the close season, not so much to establish a bait, but to try to keep an area clear of weed before the weedgrowth really got going. The spot I started baiting with boilies and pellets was being kept clear and then the clear spot gradually grew from a foot to about a yard, so I knew it was being visited. By the start of the season that area was about 10ft square; it was amazing. Opening night afternoon the big common rolled over my area so I was really confident, but then another angler (who had scrounged some of my baits, with which I'd been prebaiting all close season!) hooked what I presume was the big common in the snags. It never came back and I really struggled that season because the weed just completely took over.

I was back there the following opening season with the same tactics and, again, the big fish showed in my swim, so again, I was full of confidence. Anyway, I woke up in the morning and looked at my bobbins, which were in exactly the same position they had been in when I went to bed and I just had that sick feeling of 'here we go again'. To cut a long story short, I blanked for five days and never saw a sign of that carp and I had to pull off because I was going to EFTTEX, the European Tackle Show. I'd been fishing a swim near the gate and had to pull off at 4.30 in the morning to catch my plane. At 6.30 in the morning the police turned up and started dragging the lake, looking for a body! They started on the far bank and eventually, after a few days of searching, worked their way round to the swim I'd been fishing, which was where they found the body. I'd been fishing a swim with a corpse in it for five days!! Apparently, what had happened was that a guy had been at a party and had got involved in some kind of punch up. He set off to walk home at about midnight on June 15th, but for some reason walked straight through the gate and into the lake and drowned. This must have happened while I was actually fishing, but I never heard a thing!

After that I had a year off from the place. I was getting my car broken into all the time, which didn't help, so I steered clear of the water for a year – this is when Damian Clarke moved on and really had it to himself. I went back to the old syndicate water for the season, which has no publicity so I can't mention the name of it. There's a story attached to that water, too. I was fishing the syndicate water on and off the season before when I was taking time off from the Snake Pit and I was sure I was getting done on rigs. I'd fish there, get four in a night, then blank for eight sessions, when I knew I had fish in front of me. I was almost sure I was getting done on rigs. That happened at Waterways too, where I was up a tree one day when I saw a fish come up the margins and take my bait. I was sure it was going to run off but I watched it and saw it huffing and puffing, then he just swam off. I thought, 'Blimey, he's done me!' He had definitely been hooked up. I was amazed, and it really fascinated me, and I kept thinking about it and thinking about it, about how they were sucking and blowing, and about the hook. I thought the hook is so tiny, how do they dislodge it and get rid of it? Then I realised it must be the boilie – they were sucking and blowing against the large mass of the boilie to get rid of the hook. This was when I came up with the idea of the ring on the hook blowback setup. So I went back to the syndicate water to test

this rig and have another break from the Snake Pit. I found fish alongside the island and cast out the new rig. Straightaway I started getting bleeps and twitches and within 10 minutes it roared off with the big 'un on the end! This was a mid-30 that only used to come out once a year and I knew from the take that it hadn't known what to do with the rig, so that whole episode was a real eye-opener for me.

So, it was back to the Snake Pit again, and this was about the time that Damian Clarke had the big one from the area I'd been fishing the previous year – where the fish had kept the area clear of weed for me. I found another likely spot where I could watch the carp turn round at the end of their patrol route. It was barely a swim and very uncomfortable to fish. I could just get my bedchair in and had my Oval propped up in the bushes. Anyway, the very first morning I was woken at 4.45 by a single bleep, looked out, and saw a couple of bubbles rise to the surface. 'They're here...' I thought, but I was dying for a leak and had to do something about it. I made a move to get off the bedchair – and it creaked, very loudly in the still, early morning air. I crossed my legs and hung on as long as I could, then tried again and it creaked again. If I moved I'd scared the fish and if I didn't I'd wet myself. So in the end I peed in my lemonade bottle, which only had two or three inches of lemonade left in it, and then dozed off back to sleep. Next thing it was 6.30 and I had a screaming take. I pulled into it and it plodded off, although I felt straightaway that it wasn't the big fish. I'd seen Damien

OPPOSITE PAGE
*The other Snake Pit
Common – minus
the shopping trolley!*

BELOW
*The tight swim
at Snake Pit –
nowhere to pee!*

hook that when he caught it and it had absolutely powered off then, but this one just plodded. To start with it had me weeded solid, but then it slowly started to come, but it was really hard work and I knew something was amiss. In the end I realised that it had swum through a bottomless Sainsbury's shopping trolley! I thought I was going to lose it but there was another guy there who gave me a hand and somehow we managed to land the fish – together with the trolley. It was the smaller of the two Snake Pit commons and weighed in at 31lb 12oz. I felt I'd earned that fish after all the effort I'd put in on the water!

Anyway the reason I've told that episode in detail is that Gary Bayes came down to take the photos and as I was putting the fish back I turned round and he was drinking my lemonade! It was a couple of years before I told him what I'd used the bottle for, but typical Gary, he just said, "Well it tasted all right to me!"

That wasn't the end of the Snake Pit. I continued fishing there, and eventually took control of the water when I paid the builder who owned it £5,000 for a year's fishing. The club had already chucked it in because of the problems attached to fishing the place, and because there were so few fish in there anyway. Because of all the difficulties very few people wanted to fish there. I had one more chance with the big fish when it picked up a margin bait from almost under my feet, but the hook pulled! Then it all started to get a bit complicated. The builder wanted to fill in the Snake

BELOW
Kev with a stunning big mirror from one of his maturing lakes.

Pit to build a golf course, but he was struggling for planning permission. I was running the water, but I couldn't get a lease because the builder was still hoping to get planning permission for his golf course project. By this time the mirror had died, so there were only the two commons left in there, and I was frightened to stock it in case that wiped out the big 'un. So my company paid the rent and if anyone rang up and wanted to fish it then I gave them permission. The following spring I was looking forward to fishing the water hard and ending this saga once and for all, but then I was informed that I'd lost the water! I was gutted, and that's putting it mildly.

Ironically I lost it because something I'd said three years previously came back to haunt me! Back then a bloke came round with a petition asking me if I'd sign it because they wanted to stop the back-

ABOVE
Another monster falls to Kev's tried and trusted rigs and baits.

filling of the lake. I told him he was wasting his time and what he needed to do was tell the council that there were great-crested newts in the lake, and then they would make it an SSSI! They must have gone down this route because some time later my Doberman leapt out of the back of the Oval brolly in the middle of the night and pulled an extraordinary character out of the rushes at the edge of the lake. I thought it was another nutter, because this happened at midnight. He was a small guy, wearing a pith helmet and safari jacket and wielding a torch. Apparently he had been sent by the owner to ascertain if there were any great-crested newts present and seemingly midnight is the best time to locate them! So my suggestion of a great-crested newt ploy had got back to the owner and that was why I lost the water. Again, to cut a long story short, Sudbury Angling Club took over the water, stocked it and the big fish died as a result of the stocking.

So that was the end of my ill-fated pursuit of the big common. That was a magnificent fish and I put a huge amount of effort and time into trying to catch it, but I guess it just wasn't meant to be!

Carpworld's Big Interviews Revisited

Kevin Nash

Talking to Tim Paisley • Part Two

From Carpworld Issue 239

The second part of the Kevin Nash interview in which Kevin recalls some of his Warmwell adventures; how he and Gary Bayes moved on to the Manor, where they both enjoyed big fish success; talks about the development of his business from the Happy Hooker days of the late 70s to the current tackle and bait empires he and Gary now run; touches on the development of his blow-back rigs, and the thinking behind them; discusses the competitiveness that exists in Essex where a number of major tackle and bait companies are based; and talks about the carp lakes which he created from scratch on his estate at the turn of the century, and which are now producing very big fish.

I n terms of what happened next in my fishing, the contrasts between some of the waters I've fished – certainly the Snake Pit – and Warmwell was enormous. They were a universe apart! I just wish there were more waters like the Snake Pit to go at. That is exactly my kind of fishing; wild, very low-stocked waters where, because they are so hard, few anglers will take them on. You have space to fish, and you can fish as you fish best, which in my terms means moving a lot, hunting, finding, and moving onto them; you have to stick at it and work and work to get a result.

There were two major problems in fishing Warmwell, one being the distance involved, and the second, the number of people who were fishing the water most of the time. The distance thing was a good and a bad thing. It was a pig of a journey, but in some ways it was the best thing that happened to me; it committed me because I'd be booked to go for a week. The only way you could get on Warmwell was to book a chalet. If something was going wrong at work, if I'd been more local I would probably not have gone, but as it was they'd have to sort it because when I'd paid £500 for a chalet and driven for 4-5 hours there was no way I was coming back to sort it out! But it was a mad place. I doubt if there's more than an acre and a half of water with 22 swims round it. In fact some banks had got the chalets literally two or three yards away from the water's edge and the anglers would be fishing in front of the chalets. There were parts of the lake where the swims were so tight that your bivvy touched the guy's next door; plus you'd got holidaymakers walking all round you. I remember hooking a carp once and these holidaymakers were stopping to watch – more and more turned up and I must have had 40 or 50 behind me, crammed between the chalet and me all trying to get a look in. I nearly got pushed in the lake! It was like being at a football match. Then there were the drunks who would come out of the clubhouse at night, and several times I had one fall in my swim. Then you had to fight with the bastard to get him out – it could be a real nightmare! It was certainly different to the Snake Pit in many ways, but in other ways it was another madhouse!

I fished it for two seasons until

PREVIOUS PAGE
Warmwell success for Kev in the shape of this lovely common.

BELOW
Warmwell and Kev with a chunky chestnut mirror.

I got banned, although I wouldn't have gone back anyway because Herman the big common had died in the close season. I only went down for the opening week trip because the two guys I had met down there had become good friends and they wanted to fish with me for one last session. The official reason I got banned was that I'd caused a row in the restaurant over baked beans. The actual reason I got banned was because of one John Aplin, which has always me as ironic! When I first got down there I got him the job as fishery manager because some of the carp anglers who fished the place were holidaymakers who hadn't got much of an idea about carp fishing, and certainly about carp welfare, so I was worried about the welfare of the fish. There was a local lad, Tim, who was a bailiff on a part-time basis, working for free. He had probably saved the life of Herman the big common twice, following captures. On one occasion a bloke took the fish back to his chalet – which was 30yds away from the

ABOVE
Gary Bayes at Warmwell – note the chalets in the background.

lake – and photographed it on the decking! Herman jumped out of his hands and rolled down the slope all the way back into the lake! Soon after I moved on there, John Aplin turned up, running a concession of a tackle shop in a wooden shed. I got talking to him and out of the conversation I had the idea to put a plan forward to the management for the proper running of the lake – sponsored by Nash.

As I've mentioned, up until then Tim (and also his brother Nick) were unpaid, so could only keep an eye on the lake after work, and they looked after the lake for the love of it. Tim and Nick were great guys and had been fishing the lake since they were kids: they'd grown up with it and just loved the place. For instance, they showed me a picture of Herman when it weighed 8lb and they'd seen it grow and grow to 40lb+. Tim was a scaffolder who was struggling for work, so part of my plan to the management involved charging a couple of quid a day for the fishing – and I knew everyone would pay, funding Tim and John, enabling them to have the time to look after the lake properly. I think there was a discussion between John and the site manager and as a result Tim never got the job, and there was acrimony between John and me from that point on. He just wanted me off because he didn't like the way I fished – as a 'proper' carp angler. He didn't want carp anglers on there anyway; he just wanted the holidaymaker part-time carpers. The relationship just got worse and worse until I nearly punched his lights out... I won't bore you with the full story, but he wanted me off, and he got me off! He got me banned on the grounds of loutish behaviour, over me arguing with a waiter when I'd paid for baked beans and never got them. I didn't lose my temper but they used the incident as an excuse and I got banned!

Warmwell seems to have dropped off the radar since then. From memory the

majority, if not all of, the original fish died over the next two years after I was banned. There were two lakes at Warmwell and what happened was – well this is my theory anyway – John Aplin stocked the top lake with small fish to try to encourage pleasure anglers. Warmwell was like an aquarium with a spring flowing off the downs into the top lake that was connected by a pipe to the bottom lake (the one we fished). This pipe, six inches or so in diameter, ran flat out winter and summer – and this, I believe, was why Warmwell held such massive carp, and so many. This high-quality fresh water was boring through the lake all the time so there was a constant water change. Apart from the carp, there was huge numbers of goldfish/crucian crosses – I helped net Warmwell and they took two and a half tons of these goldfish/carp crosses out! I think I am right in saying that the maximum natural biomass for a lake is 500lb per acre so there should have only been 750lb of fish in there – total. My theory is, with the stocking of the top lake and pleasure anglers throwing their bait in, the water quality deteriorated and it was this water that then went down the pipe into the bottom lake.

In its prime it was an extraordinary freak of nature with those two very big fish coming through, but it wasn't just the two big fish, Herman (the largest common in the UK) and Bertha, the big mirror. There were all those backup fish there as well, including commons to 30lb, and there was a mirror that I caught several times at just under 30. From memory, I had around 20 different 20lb+ carp from the water! The first season I had over 100 carp, so I was getting repeat captures, wading through them waiting for Herman. It was an amazing place, and I think it was all down to oxygenation through the turnover of fresh water running through the pool all the time.

In terms of my fishing in Essex you've got the syndicate water that we can't mention the name of, and the Manor. The Manor was very competitive! Not only from an angling point of view, but 95% of the syndicate members were from one bait company. I think there were only five anglers who weren't connected with that bait company, and we five were up against it because of the blanket baiting. In fact I was on there the night they had a meeting to decide on their baiting strategy, and as I recall it they all had to buy 60 kilos of bait. Part of the deal was that they had to bait with 30 kilos and use the other 30 kilos for their fishing. So every night someone would turn up to put their 30 kilos in. So what the 'outside' five of us did was spread out to make it difficult for them. It

TOP
Warmwell biggie Herman the ladies' man at 49lb+.

ABOVE
Phil Burke – Kev's apprentice with Bertha at 40lb+.

was quite funny. One of them would come down and there would only be one area he could put bait in, and then the next night the same thing would happen. So the 30kg introductions were all going into one place. It was really competitive!

The year the Snake Pit finished, Gary (Bayes) did his back in. He'd been on the Manor for four or five years and was desperate to get The Annie and that's why I wouldn't join him – because I didn't want to catch it before him. It was just etiquette, or friendship, call it what you will. Two friends after one fish on a water like that isn't a good recipe for long-term friendship. Anyway Gary had done his back in and I was sorry for him because he was desperate to fish, so I volunteered to ghillie for him. I'd carry his tackle and if he needed any help I'd give him a hand. I just took a bedchair over there. It was watching those fish and hearing the bleeps and line pickups he was getting that made me realise that here was another water where there was a rig problem. I'd been on the Snake Pit where rigs just weren't part of the equation. The Snake Pit carp hadn't been caught enough times so it was about location only – find them and get them feeding and you'd hook them. Gary and I had never done a proper campaign on a UK water; for the most part the only time we would fish together was abroad. I think we were enjoying the time together, bouncing ideas between us. Anyway, Gary kept saying, "Why don't you join?" and eventually he convinced me – purely because he had this theory that The Annie stayed in the deeper water on the back of the weed, so I thought I could keep away from The Annie and catch the others. There were some other great fish in the Manor, such as The Gut Bucket, The Fighting Machine and The Big 'Un… At that time The Annie used to just about go 40lb+ if there was a lot of bait going in: I can't remember if The Big 'Un was a 40 or not, but it was certainly a high-30, although it seldom came out.

BELOW
Kevin palm testing the Tube Blowback Rig.

In the winter I went down to Warmwell for a weekend to have a look at it and I decided to take it on. Warmwell had a close season so I couldn't get on there until June 16th. However, for other still waters across the UK the close season had been lifted (at the discretion of the owners) so I decided to do the spring on the Manor until June 16th when Warmwell opened. I had been on the Snake Pit where rigs were not an issue, but now I was taking on the Manor and Warmwell – two high-pressure situations where I believed I could get the edge with my rigs. I went back

to the syndicate lake for the winter to fine-tune the Blowback Rig and experiment with some other ideas I had, such as incorporating elastic into the rig. As it happened, I didn't do much work with the elastic because the fine-tuning I did to the Blowback Rig made it devastating – I caught 20 x 20s in six weeks when no other member was catching. I had learnt so much; I would also add that I was suffering from rig paranoia – I was so into the rig thing. With my confidence sky-high and my obsession with rigs I moved onto the Manor.

I turned up to do my fifth night on a windy, cold evening, and sat in my car, watching the lake and trying to decide where to fish. I saw a fish roll halfway down, seemingly near a swim called The Point. I moved in and was just about to cast my third rod out when a fish rolled further along the bank so I upped sticks and moved.

Two rods out again and a fish rolled further up the bank so I thought, 'Blow this – I have only been here half an hour and now I'm moving again.' I baited along the margin and sat watching, when a fish rolled over one of the baited spots: straightaway I moved again, putting a rod on it. 10-15 minutes later I had a single bleep. This is what I meant by my rig paranoia: I was convinced the fish could have done me and just had to check that rig, so I wound it in – I now know from right under its nose. The rig looked OK but I doctored it anyway, put it back out and minutes later I caught The Big 'Un at 40lb 12oz!

I went back seven nights later and a fish rolled at 5.00 in the morning. I wound in a rod, cast to it, and five minutes later hooked The Annie. So Gary's theory of The Annie only being caught in the deep water on the back of the weed wasn't quite right – but I lost it at the net. On my thirteenth night I had The Big 'Un again at 45lb 6oz – a new Essex record. I went back about six or eight weeks later after they had spawned and walked into one of the swims of a guy whose name I can't remember and he was with a certain other angler who was a big name in some circles – there was obviously some sort of atmosphere. I asked what was going on and was told that The Big 'Un had died and the guy whose name I can't bring to mind said – "Matey

ABOVE
*The Manor's
beautiful Ghost
Linear at 18lb.*

reckons you dropped it." Now the other guy had been there at the time of the capture and I suggested that he put the record straight. His reply was that he had been wetting the weigh sling at the time and didn't know what had happened! I did hear later that he had confirmed that I hadn't dropped that fish, but that's how nasty carp fishing can be sometimes. It was all too silly for words because the whole incident of the weighing and the photographing was videoed, clearly showing that the fish was never dropped!

The fact is that The Big 'Un and The Annie were from the original fish, which were gradually dying off year by year, although I think The Big 'Un died as a result of a pollution that hit the Manor that year. Gary carried on fishing the water and he commented that during one period the carp were acting very strangely on the surface, thrashing around as if they were spawning. I believe there were a number of casualties that year. I've seen that phenomenon in my stock pond when I overfed them one summer. It's an ammonia problem; the ammonia burns their gills so they thrash on the surface in an attempt to gain sufficient oxygen. But the upshot of all that was that I was so disgusted at the politics, and the fact that if you weren't with a certain bait company you were slagged off, that the final straw of being accused of dropping the fish when it had been witnessed by about six people and videoed, made me never go back there again. I could never get on the Grange, but again that's political...

I guess the highs of running a carp business would be being able to make a living out of carp fishing, travelling all over the would, be it fishing or on business, travelling to the Far East, and making great friends all over the world and meeting so many fabulous people along the way. I've always been grateful for being able to work with my hobby. That's definitely the highlight. The company can be proud of its reputation for innovation. It would be an objective statement to say that over the years Nash can be proud of its reputation and its achievements in terms of the carp-care products, rod holdalls, the luggage, the bivvies and terminal tackle. The majority of the designs that I've developed over the years are now standard carp-fishing kit sold by all the other companies. But when you gradually develop something and live with it day in, day out it's just a part of your life. When the company had its humble beginning, in the late-'70s I never envisaged where it would get to today, so from that angle, I suppose I am proud. But the overall feeling each day just centres on coping with the running of the business, which tends to keep your feet on the ground!

In terms of Nash Bait – since the late-'80s Gary Bayes has been a developing that side of the business, and he is now largely responsible for the running of the bait side of things. Gary was the foreman for Catchum, Rod Hutchinson's company. He's been very loyal, and he's a real workaholic. As you know, from Catchum came Nashbait, an amalgamation of all my bait sources and ideas going back to the Wilton days. The younger readers may not know that when I started my company originally I called it Happy Hooker, and within a couple of years I also started selling bait ingredients and additives. Then Rod started on baits, and he started selling tackle, carp sacks and other bits made locally, so we got together and agreed to carve up the market – a bit like the Rolling Stones and the Beatles did when they got together to avoid bringing records out at the same time. So I pulled out of bait and Rod stopped having carp sacks, etc. made locally and bought them from me instead. When I eventually took over Catchum I brought in all my previous bait knowledge and sources and out of this amalgamation of knowledge came Nash Bait. Gary's life 24/7 is bait. There's no compromising with him, it's got to be total quality. We could never bring out a crap bait because Gary just wouldn't wear it and I back him on that one. As far as we are concerend bait quality is paramount to being successful.

Bait is progressing, or changing, all the time. Because of the marketplace we've got to bring out new products, even though we might feel that what we've got is pretty good. The new ideas mainly come from the telephone! Gary's mobile phone bill is bigger than the total of the rest of the staff's put together. All the time Gary is on the

BELOW
Holland in the early-'90s. Kev and Gary Bayes.

phone talking to consultants and fieldtesters, he's getting ideas and getting feedback from the stuff they're trying out for him. From the Nash Bait point of view bait development is 24/7, too. You don't just think, 'Oh, it's time we brought out a new bait!' because that's not how it works. It's ongoing. For instance we are going to bring out a bait next year (Monster Squid) which, to the best of my recollection, has been under fieldtesting for at least six years and in fact contains some ingredients I used in '95 that tore up Warmwell.

BELOW
Monster Squid – six years of field-testing.

BOTTOM
Kev Knight of Mainline Baits (left) and Kevin Nash getting friendly at a carp show in Holland.

We are never struggling to have an idea for a bait and we have too many to bring out: we've got literally dozens and dozens of awesome baits that have been tested and proven. That's where new products are coming from. For instance, Gary is making baits for fieldtesters who want their own unique bait, or they want something adding to an existing bait. Some time back someone came on to him and asked him to do the Scopex/Squid with tiger nut, so we did that and – wow! – we quickly realised what a great bait that was! Having said that, the Squid additive was, you could say, down to me. I picked up on its potential from reading a scientific paper Gary gave me where it was used in the rearing of salmon. Apparently, when they are grading salmon they have huge casualties, presumably from the stress of moving them, and they can't get them to feed again. I don't know how it came about but someone discovered that this extract of squid made a massive difference to the mortality rate. I read that report and suggested to Gary that we try it. He got in touch with the company and they sent him a 10g sample, which is often the way. In other words, you have enough in the sample to make something like a one-egg mix, which meant it wasn't enough to test! The problem is that it is hellishly expensive and the minimum order was half a ton! It really did seem right though and I had a gut feeling that it was a winner. Sometimes you have to take a punt, so I took a gamble because I thought it would be effective, and the rest is history. It's probably the most effective attractor I've been involved with in all the years I've been working with bait. My gamble also paid off because the supplier paid us back by giving us the exclusivity – you can only get the real Squid Extract from Nash Bait. It has often struck me as ironic that squid have the ability to repel by squirting ink, and that stuff is for sure a repellent to carp, but ironically squid also contains, in my opinion, the world's best carp additive.

It's the same with tackle, with regards to the company and its products. I don't feel pride; I use this as a measure – I am proud of the contribution I have made to how my two

ABOVE
Pioneering the carp fishing in Gran Canaria –1988.

boys have turned out, while the tackle innovation is just my job, I just do it with no sense of personal pride. Having said that, yes, we are the most innovative company in carp fishing. The point I was trying to make about the Tube Blowback Rig was that I felt this was my greatest innovation in terms of the hundreds and thousands of carp it has helped anglers put on the bank. The tube version came out of Warmwell, which was incredibly pressured. Class anglers from all over the country were hitting this small, 1½-acre pool after Herman, so the water was seeing every method going and, as I said, there were 22 swims; the pressure was unbelievable. I've often said those Warmwell carp were the riggiest carp I've ever fished for and I learnt more from Warmwell than any other lake. Even with my Ring Blowback Rig, after hammering the lake for a month or two the results dropped off. It was when I started using the tube version – then I really started slaughtering the place. I will give you an example – one week I had over 40 carp: nigh on every swim was taken, but only one other carp was caught; that's how effective the Tube Blowback Rig was when you used it correctly, i.e. the telltale element that told you carp were getting away with it. I was constantly adjusting, playing about with my rig, keeping the takes coming, just like a good matchman does, adjusting his float, his shot, to keep the bites going in a match.

In terms of the big Nash tackle developments my translation of innovation is to come up with something that the market has never seen before: I mean something completely new and fresh – not just a tweak of an existing idea. Take as an example the Cobra Quick Stick. Nina Samson developed the Cobra brand and the innovative curved throwing stick. In fact, it was the pressure of the copies that eventually put her

ABOVE
*Pure innovation
– the Cobra
Quick Stick.*

out of business and this is typical of the fishing industry. Companies claim that they are innovative, but using the throwing stick as an example, all the copiers have done, at best, is change the shape slightly, the material, or the colour – that is not innovation, i.e. you could never protect with a patent a product where you have just changed the shape a bit, the material or colour. When I bought the Cobra name from Nina we reinvented the throwing stick with its innovative loading port, which is patentable. In a stroke, we transformed the throwing stick, dramatically increasing accuracy and you can now load baits 3-4 times quicker than with a conventional stick

This business of patenting throws up some real anomalies in terms of what is patent infringement and what isn't. When you bring out an innovative product it can be very difficult for everyone as to where the line is between imitation, development, or downright copying. It's hugely frustrating for someone who comes up with new ideas which are immediately ripped off. I used to jump up and down about it, but you can go through life being stressed all the time and angry because everyone's ripping you off, or you can take a more pragmatic view and try not to let it affect you. We have always wanted to keep ourselves to ourselves and not tread on anyone's toes. If you look back, our speciality areas of product were a lot narrower than they are now. We have broadened into other product areas because of being ripped off. The pragmatic view I now take is that if company X starts ripping us off and therefore potentially affecting the company's profitability, that could effect the livelihood and families of our staff. We will then have a look at that company's products and it may be that we will bring out a tweaked version. This is not because we really want to; in fact I personally hate it, because my buzz is pure innovation. Rather, it is a case of protecting the livelihoods of our staff. I will give you the company's philosophy – if you found a thief in your house, would you open the front door for him to help him take away all your valuable possessions?

If someone gets a patent it's clear in the claims what the grounds for the innovation are. To obtain a patent it's meant to be truly novel – other than for a certain company that I won't mention which has made a large amount of money by patenting existing, prior ideas... People might ask, "What's he talking about here, because that idea isn't logical, it's not innovative," but believe me, you can take a known idea and if you've got the right lawyers, and the Patent Office is not fully understanding of the background, then you can get that patent through. So that is patenting something that isn't new. And if you've got enough money and can say,

"Well if you take me to court it's going to cost you half a million and you may well lose that money because nothing is clear in law and ultimately it's all down to the mood of the judge on the day", then you can bully people. But really it's a stupid man who knowingly infringes a patent when he knows that company has the clout to stop him.

There are a lot of major players in Essex, both tackle and bait... It's the source of almost all the industry, which is bizarre really, when you think about it. You've got JRC, Nash, Fox, Delkim, Mainline, Korda, ACE, Chub... it's bizarre that it all came out of Essex, and there is rivalry which can get downright nasty at times, but I look on that as their problem, not mine! I have a saying which goes, 'I'll have lunch with any competitor,

because if they're doing a better job than me, then that's my problem not theirs', but fishing tackle is a small, cottage industry with a lot of small, immature minds in it. They all slag each other off and you're the enemy, simply because you're a competitor. Competition is healthy and keeps you on your toes, and we all need competitors. If you didn't have someone pushing you, your products would go downhill. For example, the Titan came about because Fox came up with what I think they called the Superbrolly, which was a revolutionary umbrella, and a large part of my business was based around overwraps and fitting them over Oval brollies. I would have lost a large amount of my business if I hadn't come up with something innovative. My back was against the wall, and I always say I'm at my most dangerous when my back's against the wall. The Titan only came out because of the competition from Fox. Necessity is the mother of invention, as they say. I think it's sad that there are so many small-minded people in the industry, but in many minds it's war; it's us against them; you're not supposed to talk to competitors. I would make the observation that you get this huge loyalty – a distorted loyalty – among the lower echelons, the consultants, fieldtesters and carp anglers. The people at the top are fine with it all; it's the lower echelons who tend to get it distorted.

In terms of growth and our turnover, it's a matter of public record, but instead of our steady growth I think we're going to rocket with all the young guys we've got in here now and all the ideas they've got. The size of the company has got

TOP
A monument to innovation – the legendary Titan.

ABOVE
A new and exciting marketing concept.

to dramatically grow to invest in the people. I've never really wanted that much work: I've wanted balance in my life, balance in my carp fishing, and balance in my business life. To be honest, I was happy in the past to let the turnover sit around the £5,000,000 mark, but you can't ignore the competition, and you can't stand still. There are some really smart people in the industry and they are snapping at my heels, so it's perhaps a good thing that this new generation has come into the business and they can push it up a notch. We also have exciting marketing concepts, one of which is being launched this year – Nash TV.

There are two distinct markets in carp fishing, one based on the price and the other that just wants the right product and for whom the price is less important. We were always quality driven and then what I refer to as the China syndrome appeared in the early 2000s. China opened its doors and it became easy for people to lock into the sourcing over there. As a result, the English market started being flooded with cheap carp gear and that's when I lost my way in terms of design and innovation. For example, we were selling 600 Oval brollies a month and that went down to just 60 because of all the cheap imitations. They were cheap copies: the ribs weren't as strong and they would leak, but people seemed to accept the fact that as it was cheap they didn't expect the quality of Nash – or at least that's what I thought at the time. I couldn't sit there seeing the sales crash when I'd got all these members of staff to keep, so I was trying to compete with the China syndrome, which wasn't a good position to be in, and our quality started dropping. It was strange. If people bought a cheap copy they had no expectations of it, but if we reduced the quality to reduce the price they still expected the quality they associated with Nash and our name suffered. I lost interest because I could see no future in design and innovation and about six years ago I went through a really dark time in my history. For the first time I felt I wasn't enjoying it and that was when I started having thoughts of going to France to semi-retire and just keep an eye on things. The business was going downhill so fast that it dropped 30% in two years and we were headed for serious trouble, so I had to refocus and roll up my sleeves. I made a decision that the only way I could thrive in business and enjoy it again was if I was making quality, innovative gear.

The first project I looked at was our bedchairs. Five years prior to that a bedchair was over £200. At this time they were under £100. I decided that I was going to make bedchairs to my quality and design and we would let the punters decide whether they were what they wanted and were willing to pay for. The reaction was stunning: our bedchairs became market leaders within months. It was strange what happened. I think people woke up to the fact that while gear was costing them much less it was letting them down all the time. But I think there was more to it than that; it became a question of people getting fed up with 'same old, same old'. Most of the gear comes out of a handful of factories; it's all the same with just a different company logo – people just get fed up with that situation. If you look at life there comes a time when you want something new just for the sake of having something new. You might not need

to change your car, but you've got some money in your pocket and you do so simply because there is a new shiny model available, maybe with better extras. I think it's the same with fishing tackle. A guy might have a bivvy, but new trends come, new styles, and he wants to move with the times. Carp tackle is in an era of stagnant innovation: it's all the same, yet Nash is thriving because the anglers can see the difference; our quality and innovation stands out.

One thing leads to another. We now have the leading innovative quality products again, and the new breed of staff members have opened my eyes to the importance of marketing, which is an area I've never been good at, seeing it as hype and bullshit. But now I've got my head around it we have lifted the bar on marketing, but without the bullshit! We've always advertised, and produced catalogues and so on, but looking back, my marketing hasn't always been what it should be. I'm now comfortable with our setup, our products, and our marketing, and it's because of the combination of all these things that we've made such enormous progress in the last few years and are looking to build on that progress in the years ahead.

In terms of our current set-up here in Essex with our HQ and lakes on the same spread I think it goes back to Formula One. I've always admired the McLaren company and now they've got this awesome empire where they've not only got all the manufacturing departments and R&D, but also the test track all on one site. It's

always difficult to fieldtest products and keep them quiet. In fact one instance still hurts where I was seen using a new product on a certain lake and it got back to another company, who have since literally made millions out of that product because they got it out before me! So it's important to have secrecy when you're developing products, especially fieldtesting, but it's difficult to have lakes where you can fieldtest things properly without giving the game away. Bear in mind that sometimes you want to test things over a long period of time. For instance, we once had a prototype Titan bivvy set up on the banks here for three years without taking it down! So for a long time it was in my mind to find somewhere where we could have everything on one site, and the obvious place was a farm, or a smallholding. I saw this property on the market for silly money because it was really run down and derelict. I came round and the owner was away on holiday; the daughter was staying in the house and she was a bit apprehensive about letting me in to look round the house because she was on her own. I told her that really it was the barns I was interested in because I wanted to see what the potential was for offices and manufacturing. I looked at the barns and I just loved it; I knew I would have to come back. Anyway, I came round here three times and had made up my mind that I was going to buy it after just looking at the barns and the land! So I told the missus that we were going to buy it before we'd even seen the house!

Once we'd got the site, the important thing was to get the offices and the manufacturing buildings up and running, which took three years for the planning permission and two years of work – because I did most of it myself in the evenings and at weekends – before we could move in. And then the next stage was the planning permission for the lakes. The development of that side of the estate has really surprised me. I had been looking for over 20 years for my own carp lake. I have managed a few lakes over the years and recognise the dangers in not owning them. I wonder how many fishermen have leased a lake, put all the graft into it, got the fish to huge and valuable size and then lost the lease?! I was so keen to have my own lake that in the '90s I did bid for a couple, but they were serious money. 20 years ago lakes were fetching £10,000 per acre but a couple of years back I saw one that was on the market for £150,000! That was a lake in Kent of 2.2 acres, and the price was for the lake only.

ABOVE & OPPOSITE
It's all hands to the pump as Kevin lands a fish for the cameras during the week of the interviews.

There was no land around it and no fish to speak of in it. That equates to roughly £70,000 an acre. I couldn't believe it. Anyway, I set about exploring the cost of digging and I was stunned at how cheap it worked out! If I'd known how cheap it was to dig a lake I would have done it years before. For example, as a rough guide it works out at £1,000 per foot of depth per acre. Really prime agricultural land costs £3,000 per acre; so let's say you get some rough land for £2,000 and bought eight acres; that's £16,000. If you dug a six-foot deep 6-acre lake on that 8-acre site the digging would cost £36,000, plus the cost of the site, that adds up to £52,000. So compare that with the lake I just mentioned of £70,000 an acre!

It stuns me that just months after the banks virtually bankrupted the country and pushed the UK into recession, I'm getting mail shots through the door from credit card companies offering me loans of £15,000 without wanting any information proving I have the ability to pay the loan back! So basically, four mates could do that off their credit cards, get together and own a six-acre lake with a few quid left over for stocking!

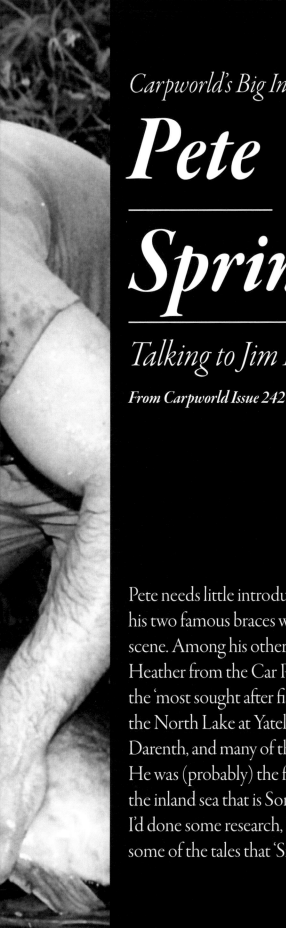

Carpworld's Big Interviews Revisited

Pete

Springate

Talking to Jim Foster

From Carpworld Issue 242

Pete needs little introduction. Most anglers know about his two famous braces which lit up the specimen-angling scene. Among his other numerous successes Pete caught Heather from the Car Park Lake, way before she was on the 'most sought after fish' list. He also had Bazil from the North Lake at Yateley, many of the originals from Darenth, and many of the well-known Redmire fish. He was (probably) the first angler to land The Eye from the inland sea that is Sonning. Prior to the interview I'd done some research, but I wasn't quite prepared for some of the tales that 'Sir Pete' was about to tell me!

I t's true that the guys call me Sir Pete, and it makes me feel... well, how can I say it? It all came about at Horton, when I was fishing with Dave Lane and Keith Jenkins, Frogger, Chilly, and the others. I understand that they did it out of respect for the fish I'd caught. I took it all with a pinch of salt to start with – I certainly never realised it would stick. But it has and now I guess I feel chuffed about it. It's quite nice! And now a book has been published about me, with my name on the cover as 'author', 'Big Carp Legends – Pete Springate'. It's basically a collection of articles previously published in Big Carp magazine, which were taped and then written up by Rob Maylin. I didn't physically write it myself. If I were to do a book one day, it would be a lot different to the one that's just come out. There's so much more that could have been said and written that isn't in the book. For instance, one of my best fishing mates was Johnny Perkins, and I would have liked to include a couple of photos of him in there as a tribute, because he died a couple of years ago. He was like a brother to me, and I'm disappointed there isn't a photo of him in there.

John was a terrific angler. If I had to name one angler to catch a fish to save my life, it would be him. He went out to France a couple of years ago to see his son, who had bought a place out there. He told his wife he was going for a jog along the river as he was into mountain bikes and running, but on this occasion he never came back. He passed away from a heart attack. It was a bit of a shock because he was fit and relatively young, in his 50s. It wasn't long before that he'd run from London to Brighton and we were all there to see him in at the end of the race. I remember it well; all these runners were coming in and they were all exhausted, but then Johnny came running around the corner, and it was then that he saw my daughter. He broke away from the main group, ran up to her, gave her a big hug and carried on to the finishing line. You wouldn't have thought he had just run 50-odd miles. Unbelievable! So it was such a shame when he died. He was a very good angler – he loved his fishing and concocting baits; anything to do with baits fascinated him; he was always changing things! And he was one of the nicest people you could ever meet. I would definitely mention more about him in any book I'd write myself.

Outside of fishing, well, I like my music. I've always been into rock music since the early-1960s. I'm over 65 now and remember the days when The Stones started up. I used to go to Richmond to see them play. God, the pub used to be packed – you could see they were going to be big even back then. I think they played on Eel Pie Island a couple of times, though I could be wrong. I used to live in Battersea and Wandsworth, where I was born and brought up, so getting home after a gig in Richmond was a bit difficult. There wasn't much in the way of trains and buses in those days! I liked the Zeppelin then, and Pink Floyd and Hawkwind. I took my daughter to see Led Zeppelin at the O2 Arena a couple of years ago, and she was really into them. They were absolutely brilliant. But one of my favourite tracks ever is probably Pink Floyd's 'Shine On You Crazy Diamond', which always reminds me of Johnny Perkins – cause that's what he was. My favourite Floyd album is

'Ummagumma' – some great tracks on there.

I have some original LPs on vinyl, but a lot of them got nicked. I have still got some original Stones ones. They might be worth some money, I don't know. I do like my music and would like to have learned to play an instrument when I was younger, but I never got the chance. Education in those days was very different. Battersea in the late-1950s and early-'60s was very different to how it is now – it was rough. It's not as though I had a rough upbringing, it was just the area I lived in. I do remember being rapped across the back of the hand with a ruler by my English teacher a fair few times though, cos I couldn't spell. Couldn't spell nothing! Still can't. Looking back, I think I had dyslexia – I probably still do, so if I do write my own book in the future I would need someone to help me.

I left school when I was 15. My uncle was quite high up in the GPO – British Telecom now – so he tried to get me a job as an apprentice telephone engineer, but I was too young. So instead I became an apprentice electrician. It was alright, but in the end I got fed up with it and left – and finished up working for Hoover, repairing washing machines. The reason I took that job was because they were offering a van with it, which I could drive about. I thought, 'That will be perfect for my fishing', so I used to go fishing out the back of my old Hoover van.

I once fixed the washing machine of that actor out of To The Manor Born. What was his name? Peter Bowles I think. He played a well-to-do bloke, acting alongside Penelope Keith. He used to live in Barnes and was a very, very nice person, just the same as he was in that drama series! He used to live opposite the Barn Elms

Reservoir – his house overlooked it. I think that's become the London Wetlands Centre now – a bird reserve or something. It was strange, because when I went to fix his washing machine it took me back to my childhood when I used to fish at Barn Elms. One of our favourite spots was where the old British record roach was caught, many years before. That's one of the places where I really got into fishing. As a lad I used to fish there with this old boy called Fred – we'd get some lovely roach out of there, but it was slow. One bite a day was a result.

That reminds me of a story; I was working one day in Battersea and I got called out to the 13th floor in this block of flats. There was this Afro-Caribbean woman who had complained that her machine was leaking. The rubber had split, so she thought it was a good idea to try to sew it together with a needle and cotton! She was wondering why the thing still leaked...

One of my earliest waters was this small pond up the end of the road on Wandsworth Common – I used to go there, catching sticklebacks and all that. There was a bigger pond slightly further away and that held bigger fish. Also, my uncle used to take me fishing on the Thames at Hampton Court every Sunday – it was him that really got me into it all. The Thames is very different now. The water's a lot clearer, and I don't think the Thames held the fish in those days that it does now. We used to float fish for roach and dace – whatever came along really. And once in a while we'd borrow a friend's cabin cruiser, which we'd take for a week's holiday. There was also this punt we used to hire. Looking back, I don't know how we did it, but the punt came with a canvas cover, so we'd take it out and sleep in it under the canvas.

Funnily enough, my dad never used to fish, but my uncle and granddad did. Even my aunt used to give it a go! My granddad was a match angler for the Met. Police team, so I assume that's where I got it from. I remember as a young kid how I used to look at the water and wonder what there was in it. I've fished the Thames a little bit in recent times with my good mate Dave Ball. You know, carp have been in the Thames for a lot of years; I fished for them in there back in the early-'80s. Strange to think that was almost 30 years ago! There was one time when I hooked this Thames carp and lost it. It was a big fish – it opened up the bloody great big hook I was using. I was shaking after I lost it. I think I was fishing somewhere upstream of Hampton Court... Not many people fished for Thames carp in the '70s and '80s, but it was done, and there were carp in there. After I'd lost that fish, I called in at Dave Ball's house on the way home and showed him what had happened to the hook. Then about a year later, he asked me: "Do you mind if I go and fish that spot you were fishing?" I said, "Nah, not at all, go for it." And he had a 30-pounder!

Dave probably knows more about the Thames in the Greater London area than anyone. We used to use the same bait, me and him – we sorted it out between the pair of us. I'm amazed how much fishing he does these days, all different sorts of fishing. One day he'll be sea fishing out in the middle of the English Channel for pollack or something, then the next he's tench fishing, or perch fishing, everything except carp. I don't know how he does it – when I swap species, I need time to adjust. I still do some river fishing, the Arun, the Rother and a couple of other rivers. I rate the Arun as one of the best rivers around; it's got everything in it from bass and mullet – which swim right upstream, almost into the fresh water – through to seals, pike and carp.

One story about my recent river angling that sticks in my mind was when I was fishing the Sussex Rother recently, trotting for chub, and I had this funny bite. I struck, and as I was leaning into it, I thought, 'This feels a bit strange...' Then this thing surfaced and I wondered for a moment what it was. It was a terrapin, hooked firmly in the beak! It was probably a couple of pounds in weight, so I unhooked it and slipped it back.

My interest in carp started when I was with Johnny Perkins. We used to go tench and bream fishing together, then one day we came across this little lake that held a few carp. We thought we'd have a go for them – and I remember catching my first carp. I was using a 9ft leger rod. Johnny had given me this green paste, made from garden peas. I can't remember what it was mixed with, only that it was green and had peas in it. So I squeezed it onto the hook and flicked it out to this reedbed. Within 10 minutes I had a screaming run and landed a 9lb carp. I couldn't believe it, I thought, 'Bloody hell!' I couldn't believe the fight it had put up. That was late-1960s, something like that. Maybe 1970. I remember then reading about how Richard Walker used to fish with floating crust off the top at night. I never did catch one like that, even though

BELOW
*Wraysbury No.1.
Pete can't remember
fishing this swim!*

PREVIOUS PAGE
*The 'pet rabbit'
lived at Wraysbury
2. Pete always used
to take it a carrot.*

I was told that was the way to do it. Johnny caught a couple though – and that was the start of my carp fishing. After that we both decided we were going to become carp anglers...

From there to Wraysbury just a decade or so later looks like a hell of a transition, but it wasn't really, and I'll explain why. Remember I said earlier that I used to go fishing with this old boy called Fred at Barn Elms Reservoir? Well, I was going out with his daughter at the time and he said to me, "There's this new fishing club starting up called Hall & Co. Spend five guineas and you can have a ticket to fish a load of gravel pits. What do you think?" So I said I was up for it and we joined. That was in 1967, before I'd even caught that first carp, and guess where the first water we fished was? Yes, Wraysbury! For tench! So when I started fishing for the carp in there, it wasn't too much of a jump, as I'd already got to know it a bit when fishing for the tench. It was a massive great big pit – still is! Because I'd also fished Barn Elms for the roach, and they were both big waters, I was used to it.

That Hall & Co. ticket was the earlier version of what became Leisure Sport, and is now CEMEX Angling. We also used to fish this massive reservoir near Staines, which had roach and big bream in it. It was one of those elevated reservoirs and you'd fish on top of a big bank, in the open, at the mercy of the wind and rain and all the elements. That's the kind of fishing I was brought up on, so when we ended up going to Wraysbury a short time later for the tench, I wasn't daunted by it at all. In 1967 Wraysbury was overgrown and hard to walk round. Then they landscaped it, I think in 1968, so you could get all the way round. There were carp in there then. They decided as an experiment to open Wraysbury up in the close season, so I went along with this girl in a camper van to do a bit of fishing off a point. I remember seeing these carp spawning over a May bank holiday, so there had obviously been carp in there for a while, as some of them were quite big. I had to get me rod out! And have a go with floating crust. Of course, I didn't catch any, but I couldn't believe how powerful these fish looked when they were spawning. They ripped up the weedbeds. It was a good few years later when I remembered seeing the carp that May and thought I'd have a proper go for them.

Just after me and Johnny decided we were going to be carp anglers, we heard about this place called Darenth that was also on the Hall & Co. ticket. So we decided we'd go down there and to begin with we started catching carp, nothing big, maybe 5lb or 6lb – fish that would have been the old Darenth originals. That was where we really learned a lot about carp fishing, and it was a massive learning curve. All the carp anglers who were about then were all fishing at Darenth – Fred Wilton, Bob Morris, and Derek Stritton... When me and Johnny first fished there, everything was freeline. That was the only tactic. We all thought you had to have no resistance at all on the line or the fish would drop the bait. I don't know who thought about it, but then we started using weights on the line. Fred was using a protein mix while we were using cat food and sardines mixed into a paste.

I remember speaking to Fred Wilton, who told me there was this bloke fishing on the other side of the lake who had a list of 100 different smells you could put into a carp bait. I thought, '****ing hell, how can you even get 100 different smells?' I didn't think about artificial flavours and smells at that time. It was just how it was – people were experimenting with everything. We fished Darenth for a few years. Towards the end of my time there, there was a fish called the Pilgrim. Someone caught it at 28lb, then I caught it at 28lb a short while later, but in between the two of us catching it, Andy Little had it at over 30lb! He claimed it as the first 30 to come from Darenth...

I really learned the fundamentals of carp fishing on Darenth. It was a big learning curve. For instance, that was where the idea of the bobbin or indicator came about, with people putting old bottle tops on their lines. We'd started using leads with our rigs and were getting twitches, so the bottle tops helped us see the twitches. We also used to put our rods up high and try to hit the 'twitch' bites. But all the time I was on Darenth, Wraysbury was in the back of my mind. Those fish that I had seen spawning, I couldn't forget them. Then there was Longfield and Yeoveney, they were in the same area, so after I finished on Darenth, it was time to try something new...

Yeoveney was about 12-14 acres, which was pretty small by my standards. Johnny Carver was there, as well as Tom Mintram, and a few of the lads who fished Redmire, as it was a really good 20s water. If you caught one, you were doing well. I can't remember exactly when all this was, but I know that over the road from Yeoveney they were digging this great big lake that was about 70 acres. I remember them landscaping it, and I was told there were no fish in there, so at first I never bothered looking around it, but it was connected to the small Yeoveney by a really tiny stream, too small for carp to swim up. Now, some anglers who I thought were a lot better than me were spending 30 to 40 nights on the 'small' lake without getting a bite. It was a bit hard, so I left it alone for a little bit, for maybe a year or two. It's difficult to remember, it was a long time ago. Then, out of the blue, someone told me that some fish had gone from the small lake into the big one. I thought, 'How the bloody hell are they going to do that? There's no way they could get through the channel.' But I remembered one winter that the whole village of Wraysbury got flooded, so it struck me that carp must have moved into the bigger Yeoveney – the lake they had landscaped – and in there they must have piled on weight because there were no other fish in there. So when I realised that's what had happened, that close season me and my mate Kenny Hodder decided to have a look round it. I soon found a fish that I thought would have gone 30lb, and that was when I decided we were going to fish it. No one knew there were any fish in there because they didn't look!

Well, as many of the readers will know, that detective work led to me catching the biggest brace of carp that had ever been caught at the time. The fish weighed 36lb 8oz and 38lb 8oz. The bigger one might have been even bigger, as I couldn't weigh it. I just couldn't weigh it! I couldn't keep the needle on the scales steady. It was hovering over the 40lb mark and I couldn't hold it steady, just because of the weight of the fish. So I sacked it up and had to wait till the next morning, about 9 o'clock, when Kenny came round to weigh it properly. This was in the days before mobile phones; you couldn't just call someone there and then. We weighed it properly and it went just under 39lb, so to be on the safe side we called it 38lb 8oz. But I reckon that if I'd weighed it exactly straight after capture, it could have been 40lb. That's just the way it is though, and it doesn't really matter.

You won't believe this – I was using a ¼oz running lead attached to a bit of stiff plastic tubing taken from the middle of a biro pen. On one end was the tiny lead, and on the other we'd attached a running ring, which the main line went through, so it could run down the line. The first night I fished it, I had an 18-pounder. Then I went a long time without anything, although Kenny had one or two. Then one day he told me he was going to stay at Johnny Perkins' place for a week. So I told him, "While you're not here, I'm going to fish on the other point on the far side of the lake." It was a right trek, a mile or so with all the gear, but it felt right to me to fish there, because the wind had been blowing in there for weeks.

So Ken went off to Somerset to see Johnny and I walked round to have a look, and at this point, I thought, 'Bloody hell, there's a lot of weed in here,' but I baited it up anyway. I did that a couple of times – once I baited up before going to a BCSG meeting, which we used to hold at the Crooked Billet pub in Staines. The first fish I had from the point was a 24lb mirror, which I had to chase down the bank! I'd forgotten my landing net, so I had to get in the water and scoop it out onto the bank, along with a load of weed! I got a birdwatcher to take a photo – I was well pleased.

It was about then that Kenny ended up in hospital... He was fishing with Johnny while on his Somerset trip and had hooked a fish. Johnny had gone round to help him and noticed that the bottle top indicator on his second rod was signalling a bite too – so he struck it. The bottle top flew off and hit Kenny in the eye! It was quite serious; Ken had to go hospital and was told he couldn't move for a few days and had to relax. So he had to stay in Somerset with Johnny for longer than he was supposed to. That particular weekend, after having the 24-pounder, I saw all these fish crashing out in front of me, and I could tell they were bloody big fish, you know? So I knew I was on the right track. A few days later, Kenny was well enough to come back from Somerset. It was the week before I was due to fish my next session. I phoned him up when he was back and told him what I'd seen (about the fish crashing), so I was expecting to see him at the lake when I arrived for my session, but he wasn't there. He'd gone out to play darts or something. And it was on that trip when I hooked and landed the brace.

When I landed the first one, which was the 36-pounder, I realised I didn't have any scales on me, so I sacked it up and went down the Five Bells pub where I phoned the girl I was living with at the time. Remember, no mobile phones in them days! She phoned my dad and told him to bring some scales along. I also phoned Kenny's house and spoke to Kenny's mum – I asked her to give him a message, to tell him when he got in from the darts that I'd had a 30lb carp, and could he come along and do some photos? I thought, 'I hope he gets that bloody message...' Then I went back to my swim and the fish. My dad turned up with the scales and we weighed it at 36lb 8oz before I sacked it again so Kenny could do the photos. I was sitting there, shaking, thinking of the fish in the sack. I kept checking on it and was prepared to let it go if it looked like it was in any signs of distress, but it was okay. And it was while that one was in the sack that I hooked and landed the 38-pounder. As I parted the net I thought, 'Bloody hell, it's bigger than the last one!'

This was a long time ago – in the days when anglers just didn't know about the possible dangers of sacking fish. You wouldn't sack fish for that long these days.

That brace was kept very quiet. I'd seen a lot of big fish in the lake and didn't want anyone else to try fishing for them. It was winter of that year when we first heard that the government was building the M25 – and that it was going to pass right through the lake. So I went to the council, got all the plans and looked at them with Kenny. We worked out that they were going to build the motorway across the bottom end of the lake, leaving 75% of it in place, but we didn't realise that they were going to pump all the water out first and use the clay to build the embankment of the M25.

Obviously there was nothing we could do about that and the building work started. The pumps pumped away and in the end there was no water left, but the fish were rescued okay and put into Longfield and Wraysbury. Believe it or not, one dinnertime Kenny phoned me and said, "You're not going to believe this – they've just netted your two fish!" They were the first two fish to get netted from the lake. Kenny told me they were sitting in a tank on a lorry outside the Percy pub (the Perseverance), in Wraysbury that dinnertime. So I shot down there, climbed up the back of the lorry, opened up the tank and there they were – my two fish, just sitting there. I asked the bloke with the lorry what was going to happen to the fish and he said, "We're going to put them into Longfield."

I said, "Nah! Put them into Wraysbury!" But apparently the people who owned Yeoveney also owned Longfield, so that's where they wanted the fish to go. They didn't

OPPOSITE PAGE
*Sir Pete's famous
Yeoveney brace from
the 70s weighing
in at 36½lb and
38½lb, huge fish
for the time. These
fish were moved to
Longfield when the
M25 was built.*

own Wraysbury, but they had to put some fish in there because there were too many to put in Longfield. The 36 wasn't seen for 18 months, when it was caught by Colin Swaden – I think at over 40lb. Everyone thought it had died, but it obviously hadn't. The other one went down to 34lb and was caught several times. I'm not sure if I should say this or not, but Kenny caught it off the top and put it in Wraysbury! It was never seen or heard of again…

Kenny and I weren't the first to fish Yeoveney for carp. Keith Roberts spent a whole season on there, fishing for what he thought was a record carp. And I must admit that when I was looking round Wraysbury back then, I saw a fish I thought would go above Walker's record. It was just like Phil Thompson says in his book – it was like Waddle, as it waddled along. I saw it several times. There were one or two other guys dabbling on there when I was fishing; I think one of them had a 40-pounder on floating crust. Kenny has a photo of it.

It's amazing how tackle has developed since those days. Looking back now, there's this island that I couldn't cast to. But now, well, I could cast over the top of it with the modern fishing tackle we have available. When I first fished Wraysbury, fibreglass rods had just come out and were the latest in rod technology. I was tench fishing then, and people used to come over and have a look at my new fibreglass rod, wanting to pick it up, because before then it had all been cane rods. But the tackle we used then was all part of the magic of it – and nobody really knew what was in the lakes, either. We saw them, obviously, but we didn't know exactly what was in there.

It's interesting thinking back to the early Wraysbury fish. Mary wasn't an original. She came from somewhere else, later. The fish I saw from the camper van were the 'original originals'! Where they came from, nobody knows. Mary's Mate was an original original! A guy called Nick West had an original original, too, a fish of around 40lb. That was just like Mary's Mate, too – long, muscular and strong. It was all unknown. There were hardly any other anglers around; I could leave my gear on the lake, go off to work, come back, and fish, and no one would have gone round and found it.

Years later, when I caught Mary and Mary's Mate I think it was the first time they got caught together. They were 37lb and 47lb, Mary being the bigger, of course. It was back in 1992, I think. I am bad with years though, I can't always remember. There's next to no chance of a hat trick of big braces, though, I don't think. I still carp fish but it's different for me now. I'd rather go and get some bites off smaller fish – doubles, 20s and maybe a 30 – than sit it out on a big water and try to catch one or two big 'uns… Unless I find some unnamed, uncaught monsters in a big pit that no one knows about and no one else fishes, of course!

When I caught the Wraysbury big brace I didn't know where the fish were exactly, I fished where I thought they would be, based on an area I'd sussed out the year before. I'd found a spot that I thought would be a very good ambush point, if conditions were right. Through past experience knowing the small number of anglers

who were on there, I had to keep it a bit quiet. I made this little spot where there was this small island, which had a lovely gravel margin, but I couldn't make it obvious that I was preparing the area for when the conditions were right, or I might not have been able to get in there. Then, the season before I caught the brace, it might have been October or November, I was having a go in the spot when this bloke turned up. It was Johnny Holt. I thought to myself, 'Oh no...' because

I thought I'd been sussed. Johnny said to me, "This is a nice little spot," and I said it was, and that I was getting a feel for it for the next year. Then the following June arrived; it was two or three weeks into the season and the right day to fish that spot properly came round. Conditions were perfect for it, there was a strong northwest breeze blowing, and when I arrived at the lake, no one was in the spot – no one had sussed it out! So I put one rod out by the little island and one in a gap between the other two islands. I don't know what time it was – 5 o'clock in the morning maybe – and I had a take. I'd have to have a look back in my diary, but I think I had Mary first at 47lb – the second time I'd caught her. I'd caught her a year or so before at 45lb, and that was the first time she'd been on the bank from Wraysbury – though she'd been caught in her previous home. The time I had the brace, I caught Mary,

sacked her, and thought it was too early to go and wake anyone up for a photo. Then an hour later I had the other one at 37lb, Mary's Mate. It was funny, because at the time they didn't have names. I went round to get Johnny Allen and a couple of other anglers to do a photo – and Johnny Allen said, "Chuffing hell, the amount of times I walked past and didn't know this swim was here!" After that, I never got to fish that swim again; there was always someone in there!

Later I had Mary a third time at 51lb 8oz, which remains my UK PB. You just have to live with the blanks. I've seen over the years that repeated blanks can destroy some people when they're fishing big waters with very small stocks of fish, and there aren't too many carp anglers who can deal with it. It's just something I have always been fine with. When I used to fish Barn Elms Reservoir for roach, you were lucky if you got one bite a day. If you got two bites you were doing bloody well. We were talking 2lb roach and lots of blanks when I was growing up, so I have been used to

OPPOSITE PAGE
The historic Wraysbury brace. Mary's Mate was an original original!

TOP
Getting the congratulatory handshake from Bob Baker of Richworth Baits.

ABOVE
Pete looking understandably pleased following the photographing of his Wraysbury brace.

slow fishing all through my career.

My fishing's changed now, and I'll give you an example. One Monday was the first decent weather we'd had this October, I set myself a little target of catching one off the top in my local lake. I turned up, found the fish and wanted to put the Mixer on as quickly as possible and get one of those carp out. But I missed the first three because I was too eager! My hands were shaking putting the Mixers onto the hook, just like I was a kid again. I thought to myself then, 'These aren't monsters, but this is what it's all about. If I ever lose this feeling, I may as well give it all up.' I think I had four carp that afternoon, all off the top. And I loved it! I just enjoy trying to trick the fish into taking a bait. Years ago, I was always under the impression that you had to spend a lifetime trying to catch a big fish, so the blanks didn't affect me. I just kept going and going. I knew what I was doing – like the rigs and the bait – would work, it was just a case of being in the right place at the right time when it all came together for the big fish I was angling for.

Moving on to Redmire I went there because it was somewhere I had always wanted to fish. I'd enjoyed reading BB's articles on the place, and Walker's – but it was mainly because of Jack Hilton. He used to have a weekly column in the Angling Times. I still have the cuttings now. Getting a Redmire ticket wasn't easy. Funnily enough, Ritchie McDonald came down to see me after I caught the Yeoveney brace. He was into Redmire at the time and I told him I'd like to catch a 30 out of there, so he said he'd have a word with Tom Mintram, who I used to know through the BCSG meetings.

Tom had always said, "Write to me, boy, write to me!" whenever I'd told him I fancied fishing at Redmire.

I remember it clearly – "Write to me, boy, write to me!"
he would say. So Ritchie had a word, then the next thing I
knew I had a phone call and had to go for an interview. The
call was from Tom Mintram, who said, "Do you still want
to fish Redmire, boy?" Of course I said 'Yes'. Kenny Hodder
wanted to fish there too, so Mintram said we'd both better
get over to see him for our interviews. Now that was a thing!
I thought Kenny was going to get in rather than me, because
he'd been going to see Tom and was having cups of tea with
him, all that kind of thing. So I couldn't believe it when I got
a phone call from Johnny Carver that evening, who said that
they had decided I was definitely getting in, but that they
weren't sure about Kenny, and it was a toss-up between him
and a certain Kevin Maddocks! In the end they chose Kevin,
and I thought, 'Bloody hell!' The reason why was because in
the interview, Kenny hadn't seemed that bothered about it.
Afterwards I found out that he wasn't that bothered because
he was buying a house and couldn't afford it. So Maddocks
ended up on my rota.

   I was on the same rota as Kevin and Johnny Carver.
I remember Maddocks calling me and saying, "We should
use the same bait because we're on the same rota." I thought,
'okay', so we came up with this bait and used it together. At the
time there was a rumour that Kevin and I had a confrontation,
but we didn't really argue. He tried racing me to a swim,
which is slightly different, but he wasn't quick enough getting
out of his car. He got to the lake faster than me, but he wasn't
out of his car fast enough. I was in my Hoover van, and he

was in a Grand Prix thing! This was how it happened. There was about a two-hour
gap between one rota ending and the other starting, so we used to meet the anglers
from the week before at a café in Ross-on-Wye, and they would tell us what had been
going on. So on this occasion, I was thinking I wanted to fish the Willow Pitch, based
on what we were being told. Kevin was thinking the same. So when we left the café to
go to the lake, Kevin was straight in his motor and it was, 'Vroooom! Vrooooooom!!!'
And he was gone quicker than you could imagine. But he didn't know the short cuts!
So we arrived at the lake at roughly the same time. I got out of the van quicker and
into the swim quicker. I'll have to admit that Kevin was not happy! Not happy! Ha
ha! I'll give him his dues – he was a good angler. But that season he seemed more into
proofreading his books than anything else. His bedchair would have his rods on one
side, and then there were proofs of his books everywhere else.

   I had three seasons on Redmire and I caught a few of the famous old fish –

TOP
*Rota rival Kevin
Maddocks with
a Redmire 29lb
carp. "Give him his
dues, he was a good
angler," says Pete.*

ABOVE
*The Willow Pitch
at Redmire – scene
of a 'race' between
Pete and Kevin
Maddocks. Pete
was the quickest!*

Raspberry, No Pecs. Chris Yates's record fish, the Old 38, had died by the time I got on the lake. Funnily enough, it has a little gravestone where it's buried. The people who run Redmire now, I don't think they know where the grave is, but I know exactly where it is. It has a little stone, but hardly anyone knows where it's buried. They planted some willows in memory of Richard Walker and BB – I think they're gone now though, them and the plaques.

Les Bamford runs Redmire now and has moved near there, into Davey's Cottage down by the lake. I've been told that he's rejuvenated it – or is going to – so it gets back to something like its former glory. I hope so. The last time I was there, a couple of years ago when someone took me, I fished The Stumps and couldn't cast out because it was so overgrown. Mind you, I did have a couple of commons off the top, which I was really pleased about, because when we were fishing there in the early-'80s you couldn't get anything to look at a surface bait. It always amazes me that carp grow so big in such a small environment. I remember standing on the dam wall and Tom Mintram would say to me, "There's 70 x 20s in here, boy, 70 x 20s!" I don't know how many big fish are in there now.

I fished Horton quite a lot. It was my bogey water, without a shadow of a doubt. I did catch there, mainly tench! ****ing hundreds of tench! I think I had 22 of 'em one January night. That's why they named the swim after me! I struggled with how busy it was; you always felt you were being watched. Mind you, I fished it most in the winter during the first couple of seasons and we had some good socials. I caught some decent fish, like The Peach and Fantail, but it was hard work for the amount of effort I put in.

I've done some stroke pulling, but nothing major, you know... probably using an extra rod, hidden away down the bank somewhere with the alarm turned up louder! I remember one time when I was sitting on one lake, fishing a snide extra rod down

the margin, when the bailiff turned up. So I offered him a cup of tea. He sat with us – like he would every Saturday. My girlfriend would say, "Aren't you worried it will go off when he's here?" And I'd just say that I'd deal with it if it did! It never happened, though. I caught some good fish on that extra rod, from time to time.

There are rumours that my mate Kenny Hodder put the Black Mirror into Colnemere and I think he might have done. I fished there a

ABOVE
*October 2009
and Pete's third
incredible brace; a
22lb pike which was
caught just before a
20lb common from
the River Avon.*

few times. When they were draining Yeoveney, Kenny and I were sticking as many fish in there as we could. We put a load of tench in there and we brought back carp from Redmire and put them in there too – small commons from the natural spawn. I remember seeing someone with a 40lb common out of there and thought it looked like a Redmire common, one of 'ours'. Kenny also put quite a number of fish from Wraysbury 2 in there – the best a 14lb mirror, and I wouldn't be surprised if that was the one that turned out to be the Black Mirror. We were putting them in there in the hope that one day we'd go back and fish there. Some other fish went in from Bedfont, too, but at the time we didn't know any better. I lost a very big common in there, but I never caught anything, I only fished it a couple of times before they stopped the fishing. That was it for me. But it was nice to see the fish we put into Colnemere thrive. That just makes the tragedy that happened on Colnemere when all the fish were wiped out even sadder. What incredible fish they were – irreplaceable in fact – and I suppose link to our angling heritage.

I've moved on. I like my river fishing; I have the Arun and the Rother for chub and barbel – I've got a lake two miles up the road from me that goes back to the Domesday book! There's plenty of carp in there, no big 'uns, but there could be in a few years' time. Some go back to the 1960s – when they stocked them, they put blue spots on them. I've been a member there since I moved down to Worthing, and it's handy; I go up there with one rod and go around stalking. I've had some nice fish out of it. Mind you, these last couple of years I have been fishing a lot for bass and mullet out of the tidal Arun. You can catch the bass and mullet in the same area as carp, though I've never caught a bass and a carp on the same day. But what I did have last

autumn was a brace of a 22lb pike and a 20lb carp within 30 minutes of each other. I was quite surprised really. I put out a couple of rods and noticed something move along the far bank – so I put a bait over there. An hour later, nothing had happened, so I went to pick up the rod, and all of a sudden I was into this fish! It started going down the river and held deep, and kept going. A lot of crap flows down the river and

I thought I'd hooked half a tree along with a fish. Then I managed to stop it, and it moved up river. Eventually I got it to the surface and it was a great big pike, 22lb 8oz, which had taken a boilie fair and square in its mouth. I saw the length of it and thought, 'It looks 30lb – I'm not going to get it in the net' – but I did. And a little later I had a 20lb common! That's my kind of fishing now. I enjoyed the hard fishing for the occasional big fish but I can't see myself going down that that road again.

ABOVE
*Pete thinks this
Korda beauty
weighed in at 33lb.*

Carpworld's Big Interviews Revisited

Danny

Fairbrass

Talking to Jim Foster • Part One

From Carpworld Issue 244

The story of Danny really is a fantastic tale of fishing, of business, of sheer hard work and determination; a story of successes and knock-backs, exploding molten metal, and being in the right place at the right time. And to back it all up, he's a damned-nice bloke, too. As one of his key staffers at Korda told me once, "You couldn't wish for a better boss; he is incredibly generous. I'm a lifer here now. I don't want to work anywhere else, for anyone else."

PREVIOUS PAGE
*Layer Pits 1989.
Check out the gear!
I was so proud of my
Cardinal reels and
Delkim conversions.*

The Korda business started in Romford in the early-1990s, because I needed some money! To understand why I started making leads, you have to look at what was happening on the bank at the time. The most popular leads then were Zipp leads, which were being used on the Helicopter rigs that were in fashion in the early-'90s. Pretty much everyone was using a Helicopter rig of some kind. The original Zipps were perfect for Helicopters because they had nice, rounded brass loops coming out of them, to which a diamond-eye swivel was attached. We used to cut this off and push the loop into one of Terry Eustace's neoprene sleeves. It used to fit beautifully. The rig would be above it, the hooklink swivel sandwiched between two Gold Label Tackle beads. Then the design changed. Specifically, the rounded wire loop coming out of the lead was turned into a huge, oval-shaped loop – like a piece of wire bent round into a Christian-fish shape. So, rather than a nice, round loop, it became huge and didn't look nice under the neoprene sleeve. In fact, it looked horrible. I decided to improve on that. I was up at one of the old Carp Society shows in Dunstable, before the Wembley shows, and I bought a single DCA lead mould from the Middlesex Angling Centre stand. I was in my early-20s, didn't have much comprehension of the big-carp scene, and certainly had no idea of what the angling trade was like. I'd fished the Little Grange in Essex, which is where I caught my first 20-pounder, but was blissfully unaware of anyone else making leads. I just wanted to create something that would be an improvement on the Zipp leads.

I was working at NatWest bank in Plaistow, East London, on a management training programme. I was being fast-tracked, going through all the grades, doing banking exams with a view to being a manager one day. All the lead-making and selling was done in my spare time. At the beginning I bought a stainless steel dog bowl in which to melt the lead. Behind my branch of NatWest there was this scrap metal merchant, so I used to buy my lead there, a few pounds at a time. I'd pick it up in my lunch hour, chuck it in the back of the motor, get all dusty, then go back into the bank to work. I'd make the leads after work, then walk round Walthamstow Reservoirs at the weekend and sell them. To start with, they didn't have coating or swivels on them. They were just plain jobs that I would sell for 50p each.

The turning point came when I went to local tackle shops, such as Specialist Tackle in Romford, and Essex Angling in Elm Park, and showed them the leads. They had swivels on by then and I got orders for 50 of each weight straightaway. That was massive for me because I had to file down every lead so it was smooth as a baby's bum. I used to take a lot of time and trouble over them. I was told that if I could do a good pear lead, they'd have them, because the pear leads already on the market were rubbish and weighed more than they should. I had to try to get some new moulds made so I could give the tackle shops what they wanted. I went to several mould-making companies and showed them the DCA mould I was using. I told them what I needed and asked them if they could make me some new moulds. I had to have six made in total, from 1½oz upwards, in two shapes. The first quote I had was for £300 per mould, which was too much. In the end, I found a bloke who worked for a big mould company who happened to be an angler, and he ended up making the moulds for me in his spare time, with permission from his company, for £30 each. I had no choice because I didn't have £300 to spend. Eventually, I got the moulds I needed and made over 1,000 leads. My dad kitted out the back of my van so I could keep the different weights in different containers, then I took two weeks off work in May (in the days when there was still a close season) and drove round from shop to shop to sell them. I spent those two weeks selling.

The first shop I went to was the Tackle Box in Kent. Lee Jackson was in there. I showed him the leads, which had their weights nicely marked on them and the swivels attached, and they ordered 100 of each. That was a total order of 1,200 leads! I was like, "Oh yes! Here we go! People love 'em as much as I do…" I was chuffed other people liked them. That was as important to me as making money. Business-wise I didn't have a clue. I was a young bloke with no money, so I stood no chance of being able to apply and pay for a patent. All I did was put 'KD' in the moulds so people knew which company was making the leads. I lived in a flat in Elm Park that was owned by the bank. It was in there, in the kitchen, that I started making the leads, using a little gas burner. I didn't use the kitchen's cooker because I didn't want to wreck it!

What I was doing was potentially dangerous. Lead fumes – lead oxide especially – aren't exactly good for you. I'd looked into it; I knew something of the dangers, but to start off with I didn't think about all that. If the weather was nice, I'd melt down the lead outside. If it wasn't, I'd do it in the flat. Liquid lead looks like mercury, and it melts at 325°C. And it is dangerous: I have had a few mishaps. The main enemy when you're pouring any metal is moisture. If there is any moisture in anything when you're making the leads, it can blow up and you'll end up covered in molten metal. I've had burns all over me. If you get bits of lead that have any amount of water trapped inside and start melting them down, you're in trouble – as soon as the water touches the molten lead it's BANG! My kitchen was coated in lead. It was all over the cabinets; everywhere.

ABOVE
The two original shapes of lead, coated and uncoated.

It wasn't all plain sailing! To put it in perspective I have to start back at the Tackle Box, when I delivered that first order. I took the leads in there, pleased as anything, and Jacko said:

"You don't mind if we weigh them, do you?"

Of course, I said no problem, because I had weighed the 4oz job in the distance shape and it was bang-on the money. I thought that if the biggest one was bang-on, the smaller ones must be even more accurate. Jacko weighed them and out of the 12 different sizes, only the 4oz was right! The others were all wrong: so wrong that The Tackle Box couldn't sell them. I was absolutely destroyed. I was behind the counter with my head in my hands, thinking, 'Bloody hell, I have spent all my money. All the money I have in the world I have spent on stock that I can't sell...'

Jacko was very apologetic about it, but he was right – the shop couldn't sell them. I also had two weeks' holiday booked that I couldn't retake. With nothing to sell, I thought, 'What the hell am I going to do?' I collected my thoughts, decided that there was no way this was going to beat me and I went back to the guy who made the moulds. I told him they were all wrong, that they were weighing heavy, so he made them a little smaller. I used my two weeks off to carry on selling. I took orders, then melted down every lead, one at a time. I had to do that, I couldn't afford to buy any more swivels or wire loops.

That was a real chore because we had to melt them down one at a time, holding the swivel with a pair of pliers over the heat, rolling the lead around until it had melted down. When you're making leads, after they are done you chuck them into a bucket of water to cool them down. If there's a little pinhole in any of the leads, water can get in, but you'd never know it until you melt that lead down again. Then the water can boil instantly and the whole thing can blow up. My flatmate Chris and I were making a batch (of leads) and I'd only mentioned to him a bit before then that he should always wear protective glasses, so he put these things on and within 10 minutes of doing so a lead blew up in his face. He had a huge chunk of molten metal stuck to his glasses in front of one of his eyes. If he hadn't been wearing protection, that would have been it – his eye would have been gone. All the undersides of the kitchen cabinets were coated in lead. It was all up the wall, splatters of it everywhere. It had melted the wallpaper into the wall. We virtually ruined the place.

I was still with the NatWest, and we did redecorate the kitchen a couple of times! That incident when the molten lead exploded in Chris' face was probably the biggest accident. I've also had the pot catch alight and had 6ft flames pouring out of it. That's no big drama though – you just stop the air getting to the flames and they go out. The problem is, lead isn't always pure and you can have other flammable substances mixed in with it, such as bitumen, which you get in tar from lead that's been on roofs. Melt that down and it catches fire! But, touch wood, we've never had a bad accident; not a really bad one, and we've made millions of leads now.

I don't worry about the effects on my health. When I first started making leads in large quantities, I was working with another guy, Danny Turley, who now runs Gigantica (Danny's French fishery) for me. We used to make the leads then in my dad's car repair shop, after work, going at it until midnight. Then I'd drop Danny back home, go to bed, get seven hours' sleep, get up and go into the bank for the day. I did that for a year before I left work. It was hard graft – I'd work in NatWest from Monday to Friday, work every evening making the leads in the week, and then sell the leads on the Saturday. On the Sunday we'd make more.

ABOVE
The largest fish of my first brace of 20s from Thorndon Park. I think the year was 1989.

Because we made them in my dad's car repair shop, where he used to spray-paint cars, he had these proper masks to protect him from the fumes – ones that pumped fresh air into a mouthpiece. So I used to wear them when we were making the leads, because I was doing all the pouring. Danny wore a mask too. I used to go to the doctor and request lead checks. Then it would be off to the hospital, queuing up with the old ladies. God I hate blood tests... I used to dread having my blood taken. I virtually fainted on a few occasions, getting massive sweats. I'm getting better now, but I remember times when the needle was in me and I was looking at the little vials, full of my blood, rolling around on the tray. I'd think, "I'm gonna go, I'm gonna go..." It's one of the most horrible feelings. I'm proper squeamish.

I can't remember who first coated their leads. To start with we did a range of powders – five solid colours – that anglers could mix themselves to get a lead that matched the situation they were fishing in. We did a lead coating kit and everything. Back then I wanted the individual angler to benefit from the effort he'd put into creating leads unique to him. I actually used to paint my leads before I coated them, matt varnish over the top, then use the coating powders. I may be wrong, but I think Terry Eustace did lead coating powders then, too. To be fair coating your own leads isn't easy. You need to heat up the surface of your lead evenly before rolling it in the powder. You can overheat it and melt the lead, though... I used to put the powder in a bait box, heat the lead, then sprinkle the powder over the lead before returning it to the flame. Rolling the lead in the powder usually resulted in big, gloopy bits. These days we use special apparatus to coat numerous leads without any risk of melting them, but it's still an art form to get them right. To the credit of our coating team, Sean and Steve, they ruin very few leads.

The leads are still dipped into the powder by hand – just not one at a time. We still coat all our leads in our factory in Basildon. Other manufacturers make some of our leads for us, using our moulds, but we prefer to coat them ourselves, so the finish on each one is the same. We're very protective about our coating powder, because we have a particular type of powder that's very tough. The coating never comes off and extends the life of the lead.

The thing about any kind of camouflage is this – you can coat a lead in whatever you want. You can have a lead in any colour you want. But if it doesn't blend in with the lakebed where you're fishing, it can be totally useless. The vast majority of the carp people catch are *in spite* of what they're doing when they're camouflaging their rigs, not *because* of it. People put on a coated lead and suddenly think the whole rig has disappeared, because they have done that one thing. Drop that rig in the edge... if it doesn't look like the lakebed around it, it stands out. Our brown leads tend to match the clear areas of lakebed; the green ones weed. Years ago, when choosing the coating powder mixtures, I did tests to see which colours blended in best with different lakebeds. Lots of work went into getting them the colour they are now. In fact, Richard Farnan from Trakker has been doing some underwater filming with a diver. I don't know this diver bloke, he's nothing to do with Korda, but he said ours were the best in terms of camouflaging... out of all the different kinds of leads on the market. It's nice for somebody independent to say that. Rob Hughes has said that same thing when he's been diving.

There is a school of thought that says bright coloured leads will attract the fish, but if everyone used orange leads, it wouldn't be long before the fish would be absolutely petrified of them. Believe me! I always think that if the fish don't think you're angling

BELOW
My ponytail period! Another Little Grange fish. This one was a low-20.

for them, they have to be easier to catch. That kind of sums up my view on camouflaging my leads and end tackle, I guess. The underwater films we made show that. What you don't see properly on one of those films is the pattern that emerges in carp behaviour over five or six days. We're cutting down everything to show the highlights, but loads of the bits that we couldn't put in are really revealing. Some fish would come into the swim and kind of 'sieve' the bottom. They would avoid getting caught because they would eat everything by only opening their mouths a tiny amount, a few millimetres. If they took a hookbait, they knew instantly that there was something wrong with it and it would be in and out of their mouths in a split second. The rig might not even go in the mouth at all.

There was one fish at Wellington Country Park, a ghost common that would come in and look around. It would look and look but never pick up the rig. Ever! There are a million

variables, but from what we saw there I can say it's like carp have, for want of a better word, different 'personalities'. Each has its own preferred way of feeding and avoiding getting caught. I've seen some come into the swim and turn on their sides – I think they are feeling for line. In the underwater films there was another Welly fish called Lumpy. He would come into the swim and sit on the bottom, only feeding on what was in front of him. The rig could go in and out of his mouth half a dozen times, but he wouldn't hook himself because he wouldn't straighten the hooklink. I did catch Lumpy a couple of years after the filming – on a two-inch Chod Rig! Lumpy was also caught a couple of days after we filmed him by an angler fishing over chod, as opposed to the clear spot we were filming over. On the clear spot Lumpy was a tough fish to catch. In the chod, fished over a scattering of boilies so he couldn't stay still and feed, and he wasn't as difficult to trick.

We have nine different models of leads. My favourite is the swivel distance, the Arlesey bomb-shape one. They are more stable in the air and less affected by

TOP
Danny at Korda's old premises with Operations Director Damian Clarke – Danny's right-hand man.

ABOVE
Damian with the big La Saussaie common at 88lb in 2011.

crosswinds. Occasionally we get accused of over-commercialisation but I have absolutely no issue with mentioning Korda products all the way through the articles I write, because that's what I use. I am not putting it on for the feature. I am not conjuring up a rig I have never used before. If I am talking about a rig on which I have only caught a couple of fish, then that's what I'll say. But it may have mileage, so I'll talk about it. It's absolutely vital for me to tell it how it is. If I am using an item of kit, then why not talk about it? The person reading it, if they want to emulate you, they have to know. You have to explain that one type of hook from one company is different to another. A Talon Tip from Gardner, for instance, isn't a Korda Wide Gape. To the untrained eye, they might look very similar. Why not explain to a reader exactly how you are doing it? The thing is you get some people who are 'thrown' into the mags simply because they are employed by a particular company. They're not catching a rake of big-fish on a level playing field with everyone else. That's another important point – Korda anglers fish lakes that anyone can fish. Okay, we put our names down on syndicate lists and get into good waters, but anyone can do that. We don't go on waters where catching carp is like clubbing baby seals. We don't put fish into mags that have been caught out of some garden pond, as it were.

I've never been treated preferentially, and I wouldn't want it. I wouldn't want to get treated preferentially. We've been criticised in the past – like the time on our TV show when we fished Walthamstow in the first week of the close season and I had a 40. It snowed and bitterly cold northerlies blew the whole time we were there. I had three bites while Adam (Penning) fished maggots and didn't catch a thing. We moved, we angled well, and I am proud we caught those fish. The fact it was the first week of the close season didn't affect things one jot, in my opinion. We didn't fish into darkness and we didn't get any extensions on the time we were allowed to fish. That session was the culmination of a lot of hard work that had been put in during the winter, and the outcome was that we happened to catch a couple of big 'uns. If it had been two weeks before the start of the season, after the fish had had a good rest and the weather was a bit warmer, then that would be different. That wouldn't be real life. I wouldn't dream of doing that. If you can't catch 'em fair and square, what's the point of catching 'em at all? That's the way I look at it.

In fairness I should add that we do have swims reserved for us when we are filming our TV show. If we get to a lake and there are no decent swims available, we can't make a show. Occasionally this happens for magazine features, too, but not always. In fact, I can't remember the last time I had a swim reserved just for a feature. We all know that some of the stuff that goes into the magazines is from people in very privileged positions, fishing places no one else can fish. This paints an unrealistic picture of how good they are, how good their tackle is, and everything else. The general public aren't always armed with the information to tell the difference – and this can call all articles published into question.

Integrity is important to me. If one of my staff caught a fish on a Kamasan B175 then said it was on a Wide Gape, and I found out about it, they'd be close to the sack. If they caught something on a Snake-Bite hooklink rather than one of our products, they should say that. They should stand up and be counted. What difference does it make? Ideally, I'd like any article to go in on its own merit, because the editor genuinely wants someone like Darrell Peck to be in his magazine; that the editor knows Darrell has something to contribute and not because Korda spends 'x' amount

BELOW
Catching for the cameras is not easy.

of pounds on advertising. I take the emotional side of things out of it. I consider what serves Korda best. I may not like something, or a certain person, but if a magazine were to have a certain level of readership then we would advertise in it anyway. We're interested in the readers and not the person who's in charge of the magazine.

When it comes to tackle reviews, people have criticised my products before in print, so that does happen. I don't mind if criticism is fair and constructive, but I do take offence when it's inaccurate. The classic example of this was when Simon Crow wound in a fish that was dead, tethered to a rig attached to one of our Safe Zone leaders. He didn't actually say it was a Safe Zone leader in print, but the article was published saying the death of that fish was the manufacturer's fault, when it wasn't.

Simon sent me pictures of the leader concerned. I had a look at it. What had happened was that the anglers using it had taken the beads we supplied off the Safe Zone leader and put other beads on it – E-S-P beads, I think. There's nothing wrong with E-S-P beads, but they shouldn't be used on our leaders. In this case, the E-S-P beads wouldn't shift and, as a result, the hooked fish couldn't free itself. The fact that the angler firstly bastardised the rig, making it unsafe, then snapped off on the cast, are the reasons that the fish died. Not because of the tackle. What sort of bloke is that angler? I use an analogy here – if someone were to kill himself in a Ford Focus because he was driving 30mph over the speed limit, then is it Ford's fault that that person died? Of course it isn't.

I've been saying this for a long time, but some anglers will never learn – if a bead moves up a leader, they will Superglue it in place. We had another incident when one angler tied an overhand knot into a Safe Zone leader, to stop the bead moving up it. The line snapped and a fish became tethered to that rig. Those sorts of people – they want banning. There are often knee-jerk reactions to ban leaders, ban leadcore, all that kind of thing, but at the end of the day, don't ban the rig component – ban the person. I run a fishery these days (Gigantica) and if we find someone fishing badly, using tubing incorrectly, we don't ban tubing...

We ban the angler in extreme cases only. If we can show him how to fish correctly and safely, then this is the best solution so it doesn't happen again. If someone's genuinely inexperienced, then fair enough. I remember when I used to fish Maison du Lac Bleu a lot. One tea time I saw a guy using a TFG leader the wrong way round, so the swivel was at the top end. The lead was never going to come off. He was fishing with his brother, so I quietly said to his brother, "Listen, get him to turn his leaders around, he's fishing with them the wrong way round." He genuinely didn't know. He turned the leader round and it was all okay. But if you get someone who Superglues a bead, or ties a leader in an overhand knot, then that person wants talking to.

We never try to dictate to a magazine editor regarding the content of their magazine, but we do say who we would like to be in there – Tom Dove, Jimmy Armstrong, Ali Hamidi, Darrell Peck and so on – based on who we see is suitable for the readership of the magazine concerned. If you can compile the feature for the editor and give him good quality work, then he will often take it. I think we know the readership of the magazine as well as the editor does. But why? We do comprehensive on-the-bank surveys, although I don't want to tell all the other manufacturers what we've found out! But we were the first people in the carp industry to do fully structured surveys on the end-consumer, certainly on the bank, anyway. We know the guys on the bank better than many of the editors know them, because there are 30 of us out there fishing, week in, week out, gathering info. It's the same at exhibitions. We're talking to these people, our customers, all the time. Ali Hamidi has 5,000 people on Facebook who are asking him questions. Darrell (Peck) goes out and does shop open-days twice a week, pretty much every week of the year, talking to anglers. There is no magazine editor in existence who has the time to do that because an editor's job is often more than a full time job.

I have several editors whom I consider friends who I have known for a long time and I understand some of the constraints they have to work under. Sadly some (that I am not as close to) have become institutionalised. Their life becomes all about putting a mag out, on time, that looks nice, at the expense of considering, 'Does this angler derserve to go in, does his fishing represent what my reader is doing?' How many of them are out tonight, angling on a cold November evening? How many of them have the time to do it, because of the constraints of their jobs? It's really important to be out

there doing it on a level playing field with the consumers. I think we have arguably the best website in the industry with a huge number of unique users each month, probably more than any other manufacturer's site. I also think we make the best TV shows and fishing films. And our advertising is second to none. John Hannent designs some of our adverts for us. The man is inspired. Totally insane, but inspired! I think we're leading the way when it comes to marketing. Importantly, I think our passion for carp fishing comes through in all the things we do.

When Korda started, I'd do everything. I'd melt the leads, make the leads, wash the finished leads, sell the leads, distribute them and do the bookkeeping. Then, as the company got bigger, someone else would make the leads and I would do the sales. Then I employed someone to do the accounts, so I didn't have to do that myself. Eventually, I got to the stage where I could employ someone who just did product development, like Adam Penning. And then I could employ someone to help him, which is what Tom Dove does. You know, we even have a guy who only does CAD (computer aided design) drawings. He does 3D technical drawings on products, all day every day. He can tell you where the centre of gravity is on a product! He is a human computer.

The way Korda has grown, in terms of the people we have acquired over the years, has just been a natural progression. We've had a turnover of staff just like any company, but that seems to be at the lower level, where people are just doing a job for some money. The guys at the top of Korda are all head-over-heels in love with carp fishing. If you're not, you don't fit in, simple as that! We have the attitude of 'whatever has to be done, has to be done'. If we have to be up all night to meet a deadline editing the latest film we're putting together, that's what we will do.

Early on I made the decision to expand from leads and manufacture other products. One of the first things we did was create the Konnector Rubbers, which we made to smoothly connect in-line leads to anti-tangle tubing. When we first had them done, the rubber was too soft and we didn't even try to sell them. Then we remanufactured them using tougher rubber. We'd got the product right, but initially used the wrong material. After that, tubing was a natural progression, followed by the lead clips. We weren't the first company to make lead clips but I'd say we were the first to do a dedicated lead-release system. Nashy already sold a safety-bolt bead, but I researched it and found that the original concept came from a French company called Mosella, who'd developed it for swim-feeder fishing. It was designed so you could take the feeder on and off without having to cut the line. There was a tiny lug in the arm of the product to stop the feeder coming off and Nashy was selling the bead as a lead-release system. Everybody was cutting the lug off the arm so the lead would come off. That's what I was doing. But the things took tiny swivels because they were made for bream fishing. So when it came to the Korda clips, we thought about the swivels carp anglers were using and developed the product to suit.

The clips that are out now are second generation. Originally, the arm and the back of the clip didn't have any serrations on it, so the grip the rubber had was minimal and the lead was coming off the clip too often as a result. So we made a different version, giving a circular, cross section to the arm so that the lead could pivot around better. This helped reduce tangles. With the serration, the idea was that the further you pushed the rubber onto the clip, the harder it would be for the lead to come off. If you want the lead to come off easily, you don't need to cut the arm back, just don't push the rubber on a long way. A lot of people cut the arm back, then push the rubber so it's hard against the wider section of the clip.

BELOW
The product development office in the new building.

BOTTOM
My desk – organised chaos!

It does the same job. Personally, I don't push the rubber on as much and leave more of the arm exposed. I'm fishing with a Hybrid Lead Clip at the moment (as we talk) on the left-hand rod and the rubber is only just pushed on the arm. I've cast that rig tight to a weedbed and if I get a take, I want the fish to ditch the lead instantly.

In making the serrated version of the clip I wanted to create a system where you could use a 5oz lead and not lose it on every bite, or at the other end of the spectrum use a 2oz lead and dump it on the bite every single time – basically a system where you can use whatever size lead you like and decide for yourself how easy you want to make it for the lead to come off. You hear comments to the effect that we encourage people to lose leads because it's good for business! That's absolute twaddle. If that were the case I would be in this industry just for the money and nothing else. If I wanted to, if money was my motivation I could go and live on a beach in Thailand for the rest of my life. I could up sticks tomorrow and do that. Yet I still go to work and love every minute of it. I don't need anglers to be losing leads in order to make money!

At the start I really wanted to be finacially secure, not to have to worry about any bill that dropped in my lap. Today I have that so now I have the luxury of going to work solely because I love it. When a throwing stick breaks, people might think, 'That works out good for you.' No, it doesn't. If you have bought one, I want your throwing stick to last forever. The credibility of our brand is massively important. I never, ever

BELOW
Winter, and Gigantica is still a beautiful place.

sell something that we know won't last, just so we sell more. No way on God's green earth would I ever do that! I remember a show called The Big One at Farnborough, which we were at last year. A bloke came up to me and said, "Danny, it's hard times at the moment, I haven't got much money – can't you put your prices down because we're all struggling?"

I said, "Mate, my rent is still the same on the factory. My staff overheads are still the same. The cost of lead is still the same, or more. So I can't put the prices down. That would be crazy." Because the end user has the benefit of meeting and discussing all things fishy with the head of the company it can make some people feel so close to us that we should not make a profit; what I call the 'we are all mates' scenario. I can understand how it happens when we are all so accessable, but you wouldn't make demands of the CEO of Tesco or Apple because you are so totally detached from him. I went on to tell

that guy that I re-use everything I can, from leads through to Sinkers (the tungsten rubbers that get put onto hooklinks to sink them). And Sinkers only cost fractions of pence each. I advised him to do the same thing. I'm not a tight-arse but I just hate wasting things. I'll re-use rig rings, Hair stops – the whole lot. Why throw it away when there's nothing wrong with it? And I don't agree at all with the idea that you have to lose a lead every time you catch a fish. Certainly, if the lead gets caught in something – a snag, or weed – then it's important it comes off. But it doesn't have to come off each time you catch a carp.

With the Helicopter rig, I haven't yet come up with a good system whereby the lead can be dumped when playing a fish. In reality, how many anglers experience an angling situation so severe that they have to lose a lead with every fish?
Not many, really.

I work exceptionally hard. I'm as driven today as I was when we launched Korda, and that's tough on my private life! My fiancée (now Danny's wife) is brilliant though and understands totally that the hard work allows us to go to Ibiza for a month in the summer and allows us to live well. I married a girl before who didn't understand that kind of work ethos. Needless to say, we didn't stay married very long! To be fair to her she was very good about it all. She said she'd never make a claim over Korda, and she didn't: fair play to her for that. We just weren't suited. It was one of those things, a mistake. You live and learn.

Coming back to the whole company and our ethos, we do what we have to do to get things done, no matter how long it takes and how much effort you have to put in. Since I was in my early-20s I have put Korda first in virtually all aspects of my life, and it has cost me relationships. When I started the business, my girlfriend at the time couldn't understand how driven I was. But look at the position I am in now. That was a small price to pay. Lots of people split up from their partners.

ABOVE
This beauty is the mighty Drop Tail at 55lb from Gigantica.

I have paid some quite high prices emotionally. I would guess that we all have. But I don't think you could attribute the break-up of my marriage to Korda. I just married the wrong person. After we split up, I was like a zombie for nine months. I was a broken man; the walking dead. If I wasn't pissing it up the wall, it was because I was so hung over from pissing it up the wall the night before that I couldn't drink anything. It got to the point where I said, "Enough is enough," and I put it behind me and started to get on with life again. If you're a survivor, you can do that, move on and become a wiser and stronger person. That's what I did.

ABOVE
Danny with The Dark One at 39lb.

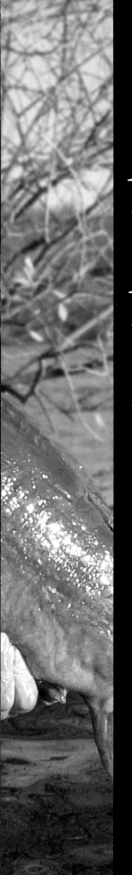

Carpworld's Big Interviews Revisited

Danny

Fairbrass

Talking to Jim Foster • Part Two

From Carpworld Issue 246

The second part of Danny's interview in which he puts his own efforts and abilities into perspective; talks about some of the carp waters he has fished down the years, including his latest loves, Wellington Park and Elstow One; talks about his personal relationships, his love of clubbing and music (another would-be DJ!); the development of the Korda business and the excellent people he has around him; the growth of his Gigantica Lake in France; and finishes with an impassioned plea about the position that angling finds itself in vis-à-vis the current increasing levels of predation, which are now impacting heavily on carp fishing. Danny is a strong supporter of the efforts of the Predation Action Group.

E arlier I suggested that I felt I was in a position to suggest – and I stress **suggest** – what goes in a magazine. I maintain that I feel I am better placed than most to know what anglers want, for the following reasons. There are at least 28 dedicated carp anglers working at Korda UK, and at least 10 in Europe. We all fish waters that the general public can fish. We all speak about what we are experiencing daily, and it really is an amazing melting pot of information and ideas, and this is without the meetings we have with our team of sponsored anglers. I have the utmost respect for many of the editors in our industry and I am sure they ALL know that my reputation is for speaking my mind to the person I have issue with. I was given the opportunity to read the interview before it went to print, but when I read it the potential offence didn't flag up: I knew I hadn't said it in that way so I wasn't looking for it. A lesson learned! I have always written my articles with one aim, to put as many fish-catching tips in them as is humanly possible. I have never added what I do in my personal life because I think, 'Who cares what I do outside fishing? I don't consider myself a celebrity, I am just an angler prepared to share his ideas about fishing and get the opportunity to promote his products at the same time.' I have been brutally honest about my private life in the interview and simply answered the questions, pulling no punches, but having been quoted in a way which I feel was out of context has upset people I consider to be friends, which saddens me. Personal relationships are far more important to me than money or exposure in a magazine, and after this I am certainly going to go back to what I have always done, sharing my knowledge about fishing to try to put some extra fish in your landing net!

Now I've got that off my chest I'll talk about my fishing! I've done quite well at Wellington Country Park in the last few seasons, catching a number of big fish (including several over the 40lb mark). In fact, I've had big fish from just about all the waters I've fished over the last 15 years or so. I consider my strengths as a carp angler to be perseverance, and trying hard... Interestingly, the majority of the fish I've caught this season on Welly have been over very little bait. It's

PREVIOUS PAGE
Split Tail at 43lb from Wellington during the winter of 2007.

BELOW
Wellie, 2010, and a superb 45lb mirror.

been opportunist angling: I've relied on observation, moving onto showing fish, and catching them on singles or a scattering of bait. I think I'm a reasonable angler. Not one of the best. There are people who I fish with who are totally out of my league, yet most of them would never write anything in the magazines. I'm okay at carp fishing, I catch a few, and I'm reasonably consistent. I'm my biggest critic, though. If I have a big hit, I'll go to work and see the boys and say, "Yeah, I had two 40s but I should have had two more!" They usually reply by asking me whether I'll ever be satisfied. Well I'm not. That applies to fishing and business, but I see that as a key strength of mine. I'm always questioning things, always trying harder, always wanting to do and achieve more.

I always do things for a reason – I'm not just doing it for the sake of doing it. You have times in carp fishing where you can do no wrong, where you get to the lake and you know you're going to get a bite. You can have lean periods where you wonder where the next fish is coming from – yet you can't figure out why you're not catching. Those are the times where carp-fishing really kicks you in the nuts! Although I have caught some big fish this year, I have had some lean periods that have got to me; I mean, really got to me. There have been a few times this season where I've been sitting here, by the side of the lake, thinking:

'Where am I going wrong? There is definitely going to be a carp in here, somewhere, that is feeding and could give me a bite, so why are the bobbins hanging motionless. The person doing it bang-on right would have the right bait in the right place in front of that fish and would get a bite.'

That's what I am striving for every single time I go angling. I won't just sit back and think, 'Well, if I don't catch this time it doesn't matter.' It does matter to me if I catch or not. It really does. One of my strengths is consistency, so when my lean spells do come, I feel like I've lost my mojo.

I've got loads of belief in this new bait I'm using, specially made up by Kev Knight at Mainline, and am looking forward to the spring too, so I can really give it a good test. When I started fishing Welly in the late-winter/early-spring of 2010, I think I did 11 nights in total without a bite, watching other people catching fish. I saw other anglers, some who didn't really seem to know what they were doing, catching. I was doing everything right! I was dropping my rig on a sixpence each time, right on my spots. Yet they were catching from bunging a Choddy anywhere and I wasn't! I'm so exact I write down how many turns of the reel it is to each of the main spots I know. All the spots from which I have caught fish, I have that information written down. It means I can turn up in the dark and get back on a fish-producing spot whenever I want. Right now, one of my rods is fishing 93 turns of the reel out in open water, cast towards a specific far-bank landmark. I know exactly where I am fishing and can recast to the spot easily, even though it's dark. I do this on all the lakes I fish. I'll write down what tree I cast at on the far bank, how deep it is, how many turns of the reel it takes to wind back in again, and so on. These days I do it on my Blackberry phone. It's a brilliant bit of kit. All the data I get is backed up at work, just in case I drop the phone in the lake or something! I think most venues are similar from season to season. By this I mean that next spring, there will be a fair number of Welly fish caught in certain spots at certain times, probably using certain rigs. I'm pretty confident about that. Generally, there will always be a convergence of circumstances that will lead to an exceptional capture or two – whether it's wind direction, temperature, all that kind of thing. And if you can recognise that convergence, and you know where to be to take advantage of it, then you will catch fish.

I'm not sure I look on myself as an innovative angler. I think I am capable of developing other people's ideas and making them better. If that's innovative, then yes, I am. What I mean is this: I can take a spod and maybe make it better, or a hook pattern, or a lead clip. So that's a development rather than an original thought. That's why Korda is called Korda Developments. I would say that I am very creative – I get that from my parents, who are both that way, too. My dad worked in the car repair business for many years, but when he was a kid he won a scholarship to an art college in London. He was the only one in Essex to win that scholarship that year; everyone else had to pay. He turned that down though and went hod-carrying, because he could earn 10 times more money, buy sharp suits and get loads of women! So he did that instead, before learning how to respray cars. He was an extremely hard worker. He'd work 14 hours a day, six days a week without batting an eyelid. So I had that kind of influence from him. My mum was such a good seamstress she could buy designer dresses, take them apart, make a pattern from them, then sew them back together again so well that people in the shop wouldn't even know they'd been taken apart and remade. She'd then make the dress herself so she wouldn't have to pay boutique prices. They were workers, and I'm working class all the way. My old man started with nothing. We lived in a normal terraced house in Romford, just like everyone else. I went to a comprehensive, left at 16 because I had to start bringing some money in and got a job in a hospital working in a hospital pharmacy. That didn't last very long, which is why I joined NatWest on the management training programme we talked about.

I did well at school and got nine 'O' Levels. My teachers were begging me to stay on and do my 'A' Levels. But my mum and dad made it very clear that they couldn't support me; that I had to go out and get a job. And thank God I did. I suppose I could have gone to university. Everyone who does go says uni is a great lifestyle – if you can afford it, going out partying, meeting women, carp fishing. Everyone I speak to who went to uni says they were the best years of their life.

My mum's second husband, Charlie, owned a tackle shop in Basildon, not far from where the Korda offices are now. He had to shut it down unfortunately, because they built the Eastgate shopping centre over it. He took me fishing when I was about 13 – we used to go eel fishing, float fishing, that kind of stuff. We'd also visit a number of small ponds and lakes in Essex, catching the usual things – roach, perch and crucians. From there I moved into carp fishing. It was a natural progression to make, with carp-fishing booming in the early- and mid-1980s. In fact, I got more into carp than Charlie and ended up getting him into it, too! I caught my first 20 from Little Grange.

I've never fished the Essex Manor – though I do have a ticket for it now. It was a bomb-hole when I was first carp-fishing: it obviously bloomed but I've never got round to casting a bait in there. I asked at one stage many years ago if they'd be interested in me running the syndicate, but it didn't come to fruition. There are some lovely fish in there now, ones that were born in there. Ali Hamidi got me on the waiting list, and then when my name came up a while back I bought my ticket, but I still haven't fished it, so I guess I'm the ideal member!

The best lake I've ever fished in the UK is Elstow One, without a doubt. Out of the two, it's the lake with more fish in it. I knew I was going to love it before I even went there. It took me five years to get my ticket, and then when I was there I fell in love with it even more than I thought I was going to. That's something to do with the fish themselves, and the precision of the fishing. That made it the perfect water for me. Elstow One – wow! The features are incredible. The depth variations, the topography of the lakebed... it's like an upside-down egg box. In fact, it's worse than that. And when the fish are on you, it's so exciting, because you have big fish – and I mean big

ABOVE
The first 40lb fish of the Elstow brace.

ABOVE
*The second of the two
40s from the brace.*

ones – that really show, one after the other, all over your baited area. I don't think the pictures of the Elstow fish ever do them justice; the detailing of them, the tiny little pin-scales, or their heart-shaped tails. They really are cracking English fish and I loved every minute of my time on there.

The first season I hardly fished it at all. I think I did nine or 10 nights for three fish. In my second year I got to grips with it better and did 25 nights for 36 fish, which I was absolutely over the moon with. The main reason for that was because a particular swim called The Stick did the majority of bites – and over the course of the summer when the lake wasn't so busy I was lucky enough to get in there quite often and have some really good hits. In the third and fourth years, when I fished it again, mainly in the summer, I did about 25 nights again, but my catch rate dropped. I think I had 19 in the third year and 24 in the fourth – but the upside was that I was fishing new swims, finding new spots – so my knowledge of the lake improved dramatically in those years. I had one good year spending almost all my time in one swim. Perhaps I should have appreciated it a bit more, because I thought every year would be the same after that. But my understanding of the lake improved massively through catching fish all around the lake in the latter two years I was angling there.

Captures that stand out include a brace of 40s and two mid-30s in a night. In fact, I've had a few of the 40s out of there, but not the big 'un, Scarface! I will go back to Elstow, but recently I've gotten into fishing at Welly (Wellington Park) so I've had to put Elstow One on the back-burner for a little bit. I like to concentrate on a lake for a period of time before I get bored with it and then I have to go somewhere else. I don't think anyone is capable of fishing two waters properly at the same time, unless they don't have a job! Not if you're going to get the best out of them, anyway. And at Welly the fishing style is utterly different from Elstow, because you're fishing areas rather than specific spots. At Elstow, all my rods would be cast to a single area the size of this bivvy's groundsheet. Or even half the size of it. It would take you days to find three fish-catching spots in one swim! That's how bad the topography of the lakebed is. So as soon as you find a spot that produces, that's where your hookbaits go, even if there's only 2ft between each rig. And when you're spodding, if each cast doesn't scratch the marker float, you're not doing it right. Fishing at Elstow really does hone your skills.

BELOW
One of the two mid-30s that came with the brace of 40s.

The top Elstow boys are among the most talented anglers in the country... I am in awe of some of the guys down there. In total awe – they are in a different class. Their understanding of carp-fishing generally is well beyond that which you and I would comprehend, well beyond it. It's an education to watch them fish. Their understanding of every aspect of carp-fishing is so much better than most – how much bait you put in, when you put it in, where you put the bait in, the rig you use, and the hookbait you attach to it. When I was on Elstow, I didn't go into their swims when they were fishing, so I didn't see their rigs or smell their bait. I was the new boy on there – still am – so I kept myself to myself. But it's humbling

when you watch them fish and see what they catch. On the surface they don't seem to be doing too much differently, but they're doing enough things differently, and perfectly right, to be catching a lot more than me. I've been in a swim there and had a couple of fish in my entire session, only for the bloke after me to catch three 30s within hours, during the day at the weekend, when you're not supposed to be getting bites. We mere mortals bait up and expect a bite that night, or maybe the following morning, but these guys are turning up and catching within hours. Half a dozen 30s in a day is commonplace for some of these anglers. They were doing 30, 40 even 50 x 30s a year, as long ago as 10 or 15 years back. Totally different class, but they'll never put pen to paper, which is a shame... they don't want to let on how they're doing it. Which I guess is fair enough. Elstow One anglers are the ones I have been most impressed with. But then, I haven't fished any of the rock-hard venues, like the Car Park Lake at Yateley, or Conningbrook. I like getting bites too much! As long as the lake I'm fishing has enough big 'uns and can provide a few bites, I'm happy.

I fished Frimley six or seven years ago to try to get my first UK 30+ common. In the end I had three commons in one season over 30lb, including the well-known Charlie's Mate, which was on the front cover of Carp Addict magazine's first issue. Quite an honour, that was. Frimley was a steep learning curve: going from a big and

ABOVE
*Filming Thinking
Tackle 5. It's all
hands on deck when
a fish takes the bait.*

really deep lake where range fishing ruled to a small, feature-filled water was a culture
shock. I adapted, and became pretty successful, ending up with over 50 fish that
summer, and was a better angler as a result. I had fallen into a rut, 'this way is the only
way', and it simply wasn't. Different lakes require different tactics and tackle.

I also did well on 'that' deep sandpit in Surrey. I'm not sure it has a publicity
ban, but I don't want to name it, because it's not very secure and the fish are at risk
from poachers. Most anglers in the know will realise the venue I'm talking about. That
was an incredible lake – it was my first taste of big-fish angling in the UK where you
got loads of bites. There were so many 20s and 30s, even 15 years ago... It was amazing.
Martin Locke told me about it, so I got a ticket. It was days-only to start with, before
going to a night syndicate. I really enjoyed my fishing there. It was certainly deep; at
times I was catching them in 35ft of water.

Fishing at that depth didn't bother me at all. They live there, don't they? They
don't know it's 35ft deep. They just know when they're at the bottom, or where the
food is.

I didn't really try Zig fishing, not back then. I don't like Zig fishing because
I can't get my head round it and can't master it like some anglers I know. I think
primarily it's about confidence, as well as the fine-tuning of your presentation and
getting the depth you're fishing at right. You can get two people fishing in the same
area, both on Zigs, yet one will catch and the other won't because there's a little
something he'll be doing differently. Or one will be more confident than the other. I
do it when I have to. I was fishing in the final of the British Championships at Furzton

Lake a few years back. The competition had been won by Gawthorn and Jarrett the year before and they'd been Zigging, so I wanted to learn how to do it for the following year's contest. I caught an awful lot of fish on Zigs practising for that final – an awful lot. All we were doing was fishing the same as we'd normally fish, but with a longer hooklink and a buoyant bait. We'd just spod over the top and fish on the clip. The hookholds were always in the same place in the mouth. I found that the key to Zig fishing was the visibility of everything. Because the rig is up in the water, you need the smallest hook you can get away with, with a fine mono hooklink. You don't want any dark silicone around the hook or Hair, which would stand out. I just tie on the hook with a Knotless Knot, bending the Hair so the bait is kicking away from the hook's shank, so the two don't touch. It's a short Hair, but it's kicking away from the hook. I seem to get better hookholds that way.

I enjoyed practising up at Furzton and catching fish on Zigs there. It's helped me overcome my phobia of the tactic and I'll be more confident doing it in the future. But as I said, I haven't mastered it when not spodding over the top and still feel I use them as a last resort, which is a weakness, I know!

Darrell Peck is brilliant at fishing them. I saw him catch on 21ft hooklinks and in-line leads at Gigantica. He told me, "Forget your hooklink is 21ft long, just cast them out. If you worry about it something will go wrong." He was catching on them – mind you, he's one of the most naturally talented anglers I know.

I won the British Championships in 2003, I think! The final then was held at Nicholl's Leisure Lake at Hythe in Kent, down on the south coast. That place was teeming with life. All sorts of fish are in there, not just carp! We came 20th out of 28 in the draw. Gawthorn and Jarrett, who were defending their title, came out third and picked what was possibly the favourite swim, because the people who came out first and second chose a bit strangely! Kev Knight and Mick Perry chose a flyer too, and Damian and I ended up in between 'em. It wasn't fancied by anyone, but we went in there and won the match, which made it all feel even sweeter.

I've got mixed feelings about carp matches. I enjoyed it when we were in a good swim catching fish! It's not so much fun when you end up in a poor swim, angling on a lake you don't want to fish, watching other people catch – when you know you're not going through to the next round. And it's frustrating to see people win who have won because they dropped in on the fish. But then, that's match fishing, isn't it?

If I had to name a carp angler to catch a fish to save my life it would be Darrell Peck, or Damian Clarke, because I have fished with them and know them. There are people I don't know who I have seen fishing at Elstow who are of that ilk too, if not better... but Darrell is just a carp-fishing machine. He can do anything and make it look easy, just by dumbing it down and simplifying things. He doesn't disappear up his own arse and make things more complex than they need to be. He uses simple rigs and does all the important things right. Damian, when he has his fishing head on – there's no one to touch him. It's a joy to watch him fish.

The most memorable capture of my carp fishing life was probably my first double. It was a 10lb 4oz common from a place called The Piggeries in Hadleigh, Essex. It was a small place – indeed, I'd find it miniscule now, but you were allowed to night fish it as a junior as long as your parents had been down there and done a night with you first! I'll always remember the sound of the home-made bobbin sliding up the needle waking me up before the spool on the Mitchell 300 reel started spinning. I didn't have any buzzers then. My first 20, from The Little Grange, was memorable too. I can still remember casting the rod round the corner and looping the line over a tree – and catching a 22lb 12oz common later that night. Good memories. I can still remember the swim all these years later – not what it's called, but if I was back on the lake I could take you straight to it!

Most of the original Little Grange fish are gone now, I think, but there are still a few 30s in there. I didn't really see the appeal of the Manor until Ali Hamidi and Darrell Peck went on there. It's well known for being heavily baited – a proper bait war has been waged on that place over the years, so those fish are boilie machines! They have had no choice though: in the past fieldtesters were going down and catapulting kilos of boilies in, then going back a day or two later to fish over them. I joined it to fish days-only because it's not too far away from home. I was going to go down there and fish short sessions, then go home to Sophie at night, because that's important. Sophie is an absolute blinder. She's the girl I always wanted to meet. We're getting married in Ibiza next year – which is awesome! There'll be 40-odd people there. We'll all go out together, spend four or five days doing different things, get married on the Thursday, have a big knees-up, then reminisce on the Friday before all the guests go home on the Saturday. Then Sophie and I will stay out there for another week and maybe have another seven nights somewhere else before coming home. It should be good!

I went to Ibiza for a month in June with the missus. We were looking at wedding venues as much as anything else. I don't go out there solely for the music any more. I've had my mad times in the early-1990s, just after I started Korda. Back then I was massively into house music. The club scene had already been going for four or five years and I fell in love with it all – how mad it was, how many different clubs there were... so I went back time after time for quite a few years. Then I had a lay-off from the Ibiza scene until I met Sophie – and since then we've been going there to enjoy a more adult holiday, a more mature holiday! We'll go clubbing once a week, eating out every night, spending time on the beach during the day. I tell you what though, Ibiza is a lovely place, there are some awesome restaurants there – some expensive, some cheap. Some are tucked away in places most tourists would never find. I know a few people who live there now, so we get inside information. The whole vibe of the place is brilliant. As I said, one night a week we'll go out, Mondays at a club called DC10 are compulsory; it gets its name because it's at the end of the runway! It has two rooms with 700 or so people in each. Circa-Loco is the name of the night we enjoy going to, to, listening to minimal techno. Or you could call it deep house. I couldn't explain the difference between house music and minimal techno. If you were into it, you'd know! The people who go there do so because of the music. The people who go do it for the music, so you get a mixed bag of clubbers. You'll have people there today who were 17 or 18 in the late-1980s, who are in their late-30s and early-40s now. You'll get the usual smattering of 20-year-olds, but also people in their 50s. The majority though are probably 30-somethings. Circa-Loco nights are like the black sheep of the Ibiza music scene; they put up their posters and that's about it. There's no aggressive marketing or anything pushing these nights, but in a way that is what makes them so attractive to me.

I've toyed with the idea of opening my own club a few times. I still might do it one day. But there's a lot of work involved in something like that and Korda takes up too much of my time. It's a dream I hold onto, though. Talking of making music, one of my big regrets in life is that I didn't learn to DJ. I always thought I might be quite good at it... To be brutally honest, I am scared in case I am no good at it. It just goes to show, we all have our own insecurities and faults. Plus it scares me, because if I did do well and got into it, then my entire life would be about the music. And that would be to the detriment of many other things, because I would go into it obsessively, like everything else, and that would mean it would take up a massive amount of time. I know what I would be like, so thinking about it sensibly it's better to just enjoy it and not get into the DJ-ing side. In hindsight, I should have got into it in my 20s and learned how to do it then. I regret not doing that. If I had my time again, superstar DJ would be my career rather than carp angler and tackle manufacturer! A world-class DJ is far more glamorous than a life revolving round carp fishing and carp tackle.

I'd still go carp angling; it's always been in my blood and always will be, but I wouldn't mind trying the superstar DJ lifestyle as well! I've been to Miami and done the body building and beach part of that. I'm going to Miami for my stag do...

BELOW
DC10 is the best club I have ever been to.

I was a bit of a body builder when I was younger. I wasn't very good at it though and didn't have a clue what I was doing. I messed my back up by doing too much weights work, went training with a load of people on steroids, and wondered why they were all getting massive when I was just getting fat. I took it reasonably seriously when I was 19 or 20: I'd eat six meals a day and buy trays of 24 eggs at a time and put three of them raw in a pint of skimmed milk and have it for breakfast. It didn't give me the

muscles I expected, it just made me
fart. I still train now to keep fit and
stay in reasonable condition; after all I
am 40 now.

I'm not into cars, not at all,
despite the rumours about how many
Ferraris I have, which is ridiculous.
They don't do it for me. I have the lake
in France – and to hear about people
catching their personal bests there…
That gives me much more pleasure. I'm
told one of our senior staff members
is thinking about buying a Nissan

ABOVE
*Adam Penning and
me on the DC10
dance floor. In the
background are at
least a dozen reasons
why we go there.*

GTR! What's a GTR? Apparently it's one of the fastest road cars you can get, but it
doesn't interest me in the slightest. I have a six-year-old van which is battered. It's been
Fairbrassed! I ruin vehicles. I have had about 20 cars and have only sold one of them.
They are transport for my fishing gear and that's about it.

I own my own water now, Gigantica in the Champagne region, along with
some land and a small French-style gîte, which we have converted to suit the situation
a little bit better. The French way of doing things is pretty basic – we wanted to up
the standard of facilities, updating the fixtures and fittings, the showers, toilets, all
that kind of thing. It's still a bit of a labour of love right now, rather than a successful
business. When I first took it over, I may as well have been shovelling euro coins
straight into the lake! So the initial outlays have been pretty big, but it's getting better
and better all the time and we're close to getting it right. Anyone can fish it. We film
out there each year, but we make it clear to the customers which week it is that we're
doing the filming – and that some swims will be out of the draw. What we find,
though, is that many people will book to fish that week so they can see us doing the
filming. I'd like to think that the majority of people are pleasantly surprised when
they see what we're like on the bank. People often assume what we must be like, and
usually think we will be full of ourselves and standoffish. How I project myself on the
TV isn't entirely me – it's an exaggeration of me. When you're presenting, that's what
you have to do.

People spend their lives wishing they could change their way of life, then never
get round to doing it. You're never too old. Just do it. I see opportunities all the time. I
see them quite easily. When I'm on holiday in Ibiza I will be writing down ideas I have
for things I can do when I get back to the UK, only to realise when I do get back that
I just don't have the time – like opening my own nightclub. I don't look on myself as
a Branson, or a Lord Sugar! Branson is a massive risk-taker; I'm not. One of his books
is called, *Screw It, Let's Do It*. I'm not like that; I'll take calculated business risks but
that will be about it. Alan Sugar on the other hand seems to be ruthless to the core and

only interested in profit, money and wealth. That doesn't do it for me either. I'm not like that. I do appreciate my success and I never forget what it was like before, when I was working in the bank in the early days. Then, at the end of the month before payday, I'd turn the car off and roll down the hill so I wouldn't use any petrol. I had nothing; nothing at all. Every penny was accounted for before I even earned it. I'm not a tight-arse, but I won't waste anything. It's a lesson I learned when I didn't have anything to waste.

I try to put something back in carp fishing by supporting angling politics, and being involved with the Predation Action Group (PAG). The PAG is trying to do something to redress the balance of fish versus apex predators such as otters and cormorants. It's in its early stages, but the long-term plan is to give anglers more of a voice at government level so these predators aren't left unchecked to eat all our stocks of fish. The PAG is affiliated to the Angling Trust because their sphere of influence is far wider than the PAG can hope to achieve.

Obviously we've all seen the horrific pictures of partially eaten carp, and we know of a number of fisheries that have been wiped out because of predation. If the government is to listen to what PAG is saying, we're going to need some independent scientific advice to fall back on, and I think that will happen. I agree that we need the scientific proof from an independent source. But the first step is to calculate as

ABOVE
A 32lb common from Gigantica caught when filming Korda's free DVD in September 2010.

many incidents as possible where otter predation has affected carp fisheries. The more evidence like this we can get into the public domain, the more support we will get from both the angling trade and anglers themselves. Hopefully, that support will then give us more clout so we can commission more research, get more accurate information, and the ability to present something to the government that is factual.

The environment that otters are being re-introduced back into today is vastly different to what it was pre-Second World War. People who are re-introducing the otter have no concerns about the impact otters are having on the modern-day environment. They just want there to be otters, loads of otters. From what I can see, there has been little research done on the impact the reintroduction of otters will have on other species. Yet it's an apex predator. Top of the chain – nothing kills it and eats it. And they're now back in areas that have changed dramatically since otters were last around. Scores of years of work from anglers is being eroded in one winter by otters that have been re-introduced by man, not otters that have naturally made a comeback. I think that's an important point, because one man's action is now affecting another's livelihood and the sport he loves. It might even affect the entire angling industry if we're not careful. We need more research, more collation of information.

Yes, the man in the street loves the idea of otters, but if you show the non-

angling public a couple of kids who can no longer fish at their local lake because the otters have eaten everything, and they don't have a pastime any more... and you show the general public a 40lb carp with its throat ripped and its guts hanging out, what's the public going to do then? The comparison I draw is that if otters ate dogs and cats, then the public wouldn't stand for their re-introduction. If you came home and your Labrador was lying on the lawn with its throat ripped out, having bled to death, would you still see the otter as the cuddly creature you thought it was?

Because otters are eating something that doesn't affect the public at large, i.e. fish, they're not considered to be an issue. But there is an imbalance that needs to be addressed. So we are formulating our strategy with a team of volunteers, people who are doing this for free. There is a website that will help to log otter and other predation, including cormorants: www.thepredationactingroup.co.uk It's not just carp that are affected, either. Barbel in the Great Ouse and other rivers have been taken: the famous Adams Mill fish have been eaten, the record fish in there has been killed by otters. They've even seen fish being targeted in Elstow One. I see myself now as being in a position of influence, so if I can do something about it then I will. Otherwise more and more fish are going to get eaten, so there will be fewer and fewer for us to fish for. I'm not going to stand by and let that happen.

I would like to finish by saying I have nothing against otters in a balanced ecosystem, but when things are so one-sided in favour of a predator that humans have re-introduced I have to air my views on behalf of all anglers. At least half the reason I go fishing is to be in our stunning countryside and see our stunning wildlife. It almost moves me to tears just being 'out there' seeing what the general public rarely see, our waterways at every time of day and night, and in every season. I hope we can make a difference to the current situation and protect the future of the sport I love so very much.

OPPOSITE PAGE
Filming the return of that stunning 32lb common.

Carpworld's Big Interviews Revisited

Ian Chillcott

(and Lynn!) Talking to Jim Foster

From Carpworld Issue 233

I turn up at Chilly's house to do the interview on a cold day just before Christmas 2009. Sitting in the driveway, is a huge, bright-yellow, imported Dodge pickup truck. Chilly gave 22 years of his life serving his country as a paratrooper, jetting around the world, jumping out of planes and serving in a host of scary places. Chilly has never talked about his army experiences in any sort of depth. Some things in life are best left unsaid and kept private. Perhaps the poppy hanging over his doorbell is an important salute to those who have given their all while fighting for our country.

Nice to see you Jim. I have never felt better; thanks for asking, and have just given up smoking! To explain why, I'll start by saying that I have been fit all my life. I have run lots of marathons, my personal best being 2 hours and 32 minutes. I also did four mega marathons (80 miles each), so I have always been hideously fit. I had my first cigarette at the age of 11, when I picked the remains of a butt out of my grandfather's fire and smoked what was left of it. I liked the idea of smoking in those days and did it to impress this girl, Bryony Tomkins. I'll always remember her! I bought a pack of 10 Embassy No10 and was violently sick – I had to walk to my grandmother's house where I spent the night continually heaving. And ever since then I continued to smoke, like a total idiot. But then whilst I was walking around Wellington Country Park I started feeling out of breath. I thought, f*** this, I can't go on like this! So the following week, at 1905 hours on the 12th October in the year of our Lord 2009, I had my last fag. That was the last one I will ever smoke.

I'm not the type of bloke for nicotine patches; I can't be doing with all that. Lynn's doctors have now become my doctors. I got my first prescription ever the other day, aged 49. It cost £7.50. Seven pounds fifty! Can you believe that? It's a disgrace. I saw this woman at a clinic a while back. She said, "So you want to give up smoking?" I said that I did, so she told me she could sort me out a few patches on prescription or I could go to a group meeting. I told her I couldn't be doing with patches or meetings; that I was in the wrong place, and walked out. If I was going to do it, I'd have to do it on my own, at the right time. I caught a 45lb carp at Wellington soon after I had given up. When I had sacked it and ensured it was safe, I thought, 'I understand why I used to smoke.' I wanted one then, but I didn't have one. So I haven't found it easy; there have been times I have seen why I did smoke. But I haven't succumbed.

I try to help out the local kids with their angling when I can. Angling has the potential to have such a massive impact on society; it keeps them off the streets and out of trouble. There are a few youngsters in the neighbourhood here who enjoy their fishing and it's nice to put something back into the sport. When we moved here, there was a young lad called Tom who lived over the road. He saw me moving in and stood outside our house with some copies of *Carpworld* and *Crafty Carper*. He just stared at me and eventually plucked up the courage to say, "You're Ian Chillcott aren't you? Can you sign my magazines?" I certainly don't think I am famous, though. I'm not sure you could justifiably label me, or any angling 'celebrity' as being 'famous'. I understand fame to be a footballer at Old Trafford playing for Man United, earning £120k a week, the sort of person who's going to be recognised

PREVIOUS PAGE
Chilly holding 38lb of Essex common carp.

BELOW
Lynn Chillcott outside the couple's bungalow in Aldershot.

wherever they go. I don't think fame in fishing can be compared to anything like being a footballer, or something like that. But then again, I write about what I do and carp fishing is a hugely popular participation sport: lots of people read what I write, which is lovely. I am happy with that. I accept I am well known in the carp fishing fraternity and I accept the benefits and occasional drawbacks that that brings.

As sad as it is, there are definitely people in carp fishing for the perceived 'celebrity value' it brings. In fact, I'll be brutally honest with you, there are lots of them: people who think they can get famous through writing about carp fishing: people who are in it for the wrong reasons. And while we're on the subject, let's be honest, a large number of articles published in some carp magazines are ghost-

written by journalists. The anglers concerned won't or can't write their own features, which is a shame. I don't believe you can accurately convey what someone feels about carp fishing, or what they're thinking, through ghost-writing. It loses the soul of the angler. I don't believe anyone can recreate another person's identity, their character, or whatever, by writing for them.

[At this point, Lynn interjects with a very succinct point. She says: "I think the important point here is to emphasise that husband didn't take up carp fishing so that he could write about it. He took it up because he loves carp fishing."]

What Lynn's just said is exactly right. You have people now who are coming into this game – and there are loads of them – who are working within the industry full-time and are writing solely for their own ends and to push the products of the company they work for. They are usually extremely good salesmen. Some of them could sell ice to an Eskimo. There are rakes of them out there who have the ability to sell themselves to the carp world on the strength of achieving sod all. I'm doing it every week, come rain or shine, for two or three days, in snow and ice. Whatever is going on, I am out there doing it, because I absolutely love it. Then I see people writing about how they fished the Car Park Lake, or Conningbrook, yet they caught f*** all while doing so. They have been there once or twice just so they can say they have fished top circuit lakes like that and therefore give themselves some credibility. I remember seeing one so-called carp angling 'celebrity' talking to a group of people on a stand at a recent carp show. He was saying how he'd fished the North Lake at Yateley, moved off there onto the Car Park Lake, before moving on again. He then quickly changed the subject of the conversation. It was clever how he did it as he left the people who were listening to him – and me for that matter – with the impression he'd caught from both venues. In reality he'd done a couple of nights on each lake and hadn't caught at all! Now that's appalling. And we all know that there are anglers like that out there. You have told me in the past during your editor days that you have done features with anglers for commercial reasons – not because they had any real skill. You had to make them look better anglers than they were.

We were on Linear Manor back in the spring of 1998 and you wanted me to pen a few words about fishing in the weed for the old *Catchmore Carp* magazine – you know; how to do it on a technical level, which was fine. That was the first time anyone asked me to write. Since then it's been great. I enjoy writing immensely and have learned a lot from the likes of you and Tim Paisley. A lot of people have said I have a unique ability; that I can convey what it's like to be there, to be on the bank fishing, chasing big carp (or any carp for that matter). How could that be possible through someone else ghost-writing on my behalf? While the praise I get (for writing) is a great compliment to me, I'm not sure that it's true. I mean, I don't think it's a unique ability on my part. It's certainly nothing clever or learned. I just write as I speak. I'm lucky: I find writing relatively easy. I set aside one day a week to get it done; it's as simple as that. I sit down with a cup of tea to get myself in the mood and just do it. It's like anything in life, a bit of discipline helps get things done. It doesn't all come out of my head. I actually keep a diary in one of my holdalls, where I record the pivotal moments the previous month on the bank, as and when they happen. This helps keep my finished diary piece in context, and also in chronological order. I actually write stuff on the bank: I jot down bits and pieces – for instance, if I meet some crazy bloke and spend some time with him in my boxer shorts while loitering in rhododendron bushes, then I'll write about that! Seriously, my 'on the bank' diary contains details of weather conditions, the wildlife I see, what the carp are up to, captures I'm lucky enough to make, the weight of the fish I catch – all that kind of stuff. It helps set the scene when I write later. It jogs the memory. You have to remember that I'm an old sod now and the notes help the old memory. I can't remember everything!

The diary aspect of my writing, I love. In a lot of respects it's the easier of the two formats to write. The hard part can be getting the material to write about. You can have sessions when bugger-all happens. A few years ago I decided to have a go down at Conningbrook for a few months – and as a diarist, on difficult waters like that, it can lead you to not having a great deal to talk about.

Although I caught six fish on the 'Brook, it wasn't easy writing about my experiences there. I didn't catch the big 'un and there were times I didn't have anything to write about. There are some waters where I'd be more likely to grow another leg than catch a carp, and you have to bear that in mind – for how long can a carp angler go on writing about blanking? I find the technical stuff a little boring to write. However, I do it because I realise that technical magazines are popular and people want to learn. I'm in a privileged position to be able to help them to do that. I have a genuine wish to teach newcomers to the sport how to catch and look after the carp they catch – it's just that sometimes I find it hard to write technically about the same subjects one year after another.

My schooling was pretty much non-existent. I went to Brislington Comprehensive in Bristol and played truant a lot. My schooldays were mostly spent walking past the school gates in the morning and buggering off fishing, trying not to go into lessons. At the end of Hungerford Road, where my school was, there was a road that led to the River Avon. It was there that the number 339 bus used to stop, so a guy called Steven Pitfield and I would hide our school uniforms for the day, get changed and just go fishing, either on the Avon or Kennet and Avon Canal. That happened from the age of 12 until I joined the Army when I was 16. If I am a good writer now it's because of the lessons that life has given me, not the lessons I had at school. I don't think you can teach writers how to express themselves in words, they just have that ability. And it has to be said that writing has led, in part, to some neat commercial benefits for me – though you have to catch fish, too, to achieve those!

I can honestly say that I would never recommend or write about something I didn't wholeheartedly believe in, or use. Someone has to make the rods, the line, the reels, the hooks, and your bait. And if it wasn't me helping to publicise my sponsors' gear, someone else would do it. Mainline supply my bait for me and Fox International look after everything else, pretty much. To explain why Fox and Mainline, I need to tell you that after I left the Army, Danny Fairbrass of Korda was supplying me with a few bits and pieces. Something which has given me the utmost respect for Danny and for which I will be eternally grateful. At that stage, that was all I really wanted. I was kind of happy with that, you know? Then the more I did, and with the more time I had, I started catching a few decent fish and, as such, more companies became interested, and eventually I signed up with E-S-P. I have nothing but praise for Peter Drennan (MD of Drennan and E-S-P). He is an absolute legend in angling. My friend Adam Penning was working for E-S-P at the time, so I helped test their bits and pieces as Adam was developing them. I didn't get a penny out of them at that stage; I just got some free kit, which was great. Back in 2002 I didn't have any idea that in the years to come I would be making a full-bore living out of this. I eventually signed a deal with them, tied to a five-year contract. I got out of it after nine months. I got out of it because I don't want people to pay me money simply because I am using their products. And that, primarily, was what was happening with E-S-P. I fail to see how anybody can say something is good if they have no idea about its development and construction.

So I moved from E-S-P to Fox. I went for an interview with Cliff Fox and his directors and told them, that I do use other companies' gear and I would not use any item of Fox tackle until I thought it was as good as, or better, than anything else out there. They knew that, and they accepted it. And I was able to be a part of the development of products, rather then just be given freebies to use. I wanted this; I didn't just want to be testing freebies. That was important to me. So it was more like a proper job than a simple sponsorship agreement.

It was three years ago, maybe four, when I sent an email to Cliff (Fox) and told him that, for the first time in my life, there was only one company's tackle in my tackle box – and that was Fox's. There's no bull with me; I say things as I see them. I love the idea that I fish loads of different places. It means I bump into lots of different people, who can see what it is I am using. And they won't find anyone else's gear there. It can work against you sometimes – in the first book I wrote, *Tackling Carp*, I had people come up to me at shows and say how horrible it was, that it was just a glorified Fox and Mainline advert! My riposte to them was to ask them a question back: would it have been socially more acceptable to lie in a book about the gear I was using? I don't think it would have been. I've shown now that my loyalty is with Fox and Mainline and over the last eight years it's gelled and for a long time I have been making a living out of it. I think people should also look at it this way – because I make a living out of fishing, I don't want to be tying on something I'm not happy with, or using an item of kit I am not 100 percent happy with. If I do, and recommend something which is flawed, it's going to affect my ability to make a living.

Fox has never once – not once – told me or talked to me about how many fish I should be catching, or where I should be fishing. Never! This is because they don't have to. I'm out there fishing three days a week, as well as writing two (or more) features a month, one technical, and one diary-orientated. I absolutely love writing the diary piece as I can put bits of everyday life into it. I don't have to be blasting products in people's faces in either feature. I rarely do that in my diary piece. I might

BELOW
Filming for Fox.

wear a Fox cap when I am holding a fish, or when there's a picture of me playing a fish you can see it's a Fox rod in the photo. But that's it. I don't need to be telling people that, they can see it. The more you're in the game, the less you have to be mentioning the products you use, as people get to associate you with them anyway.

It's a funny thing being successful, and being sponsored! Of everything I have ever done in my life, success in carp fishing is possibly the

most despised commodity I have known! There are a couple of very successful, high-profile anglers whom I hate with every bone in my body! But I don't dislike them because of their success – they're just not my type of people, that's all. I look at their angling and what they have done and think, 'Fair play to them.' I don't want to take anything away from their achievements. Generally speaking, many successful carp anglers are disliked simply because they are successful. I have heard people say, "It's all right for him, he works for Fox." I was at Tesco the other day and bumped into this guy who lives in Aldershot, who I have met a few times. He fishes at this local water, always has done, and will probably keep fishing it forever. He's caught all the fish in there 20 times and doesn't want any more out of it. Fair play to him, you know? I have nothing against that at all, if that's what you want to do and if that's what gives you your excitement in life. Crack on boy! Anyway, he was walking out of Tesco and said, "Alright Chilly, how's it going mate, are you catching?" To which I replied things were OK, yes I was doing all right.

He then said: "Oh, but it's all right for you though, isn't it?"

"Is it?" I asked.

"Yes," he replied. "You get all your gear free, your bait free, you get waters shut down so you can do what you want on them, you get them baited up for you so you can catch, your articles are written for you, all you do is go fishing..."

It's a nice thing that I do. I enjoy it. And though he was right in that I get free

TOP
Meet Dixie – let's ruin the ozone layer!

ABOVE
Putting our beloved Harley Davidson, Gracie, through her paces.

kit and bait, that's it; all the other stuff he mentioned is just made up, bitter nonsense that people assume is true when it isn't. I'm just a simple bloke who's lucky enough to be making a living out of fishing. I am surrounded by people I'm loyal to and they can be loyal to me. Being an army man, that's all I want out of life.

I have fished throughout my life, but I wouldn't say my whole life has revolved around angling. Far from it – I think there is a hell of a lot more to life than fishing. Yes, I earn a living from it, but I have to get away from it every now and then. For instance, I can't wait for tomorrow. Lynn and I are off in the big yellow truck, down to Plymouth, ruining the ozone and having a kick ass time over Christmas. I won't even be thinking about fishing in that time: I won't let it dominate my life. The big yellow machine certainly brings a big smile to my face! It's a Dodge Magnum V8 Pickup, with a 5.9 litre engine and a supercharger, so I suppose I am a bit of a petrol head! It eats an amazing amount of petrol. I remember taking it onto the M25 to go and pick up some bait from Mainline HQ in Essex. The tank was three-quarters full when I left. I caned it and by the time I'd got to Clackett Lane Services, which is 37 miles away, the fuel tank was fast approaching empty and I had to fill up!

You can get roughly 100 litres into the tank, so I wonder what that makes its MPG? Not a lot I suspect! So it won't be a surprise to you that I don't believe in this global warming stuff. Last winter was one of the coldest I remember. Everything froze. It was hideous – the worst winter for 20 years. And everyone blamed it on global warming! Now we're having lots of snow. All this global warming stuff is a load of old bollocks, and my truck gets the blame for it. This planet does what it does every now and then, that's it. I love looking out of the window of the Dodge, peering down on some bloke in a Toyota Prius who thinks he's saving the planet and going, "Hello mate, yeah, wicked..." They try to tax me off the road in the name of green policy. Green policy? They are taxes on fun, that's all there is to it. It is four-wheel drive. It's the full outing, but I don't take it off-road as there are all sorts of little extras on it that are worth rather a large amount of money. The exhaust is very special: it looks like it came from the back end of a fighter jet. So you don't want to take that off-road. The alloys are a few grand each and the tyres £750 a pop, so I like to keep it on the road, and that's where I have my fun with it.

I don't know what it's capable of, but I just know that it's quick. Very quick! A couple of year's back we were in Plymouth, and Lynn came down very ill. Her consultant said she had to be taken to hospital at Frimley Park as soon as possible, so we just got on the road and went hell for leather. We covered the distance from Plymouth to Frimley in about three and a half hours. I have no idea how we managed it without being stopped, or setting a speed camera off. It was the middle of the night though so there was no one on the road, and Lynn got to the hospital in time, which is the important thing.

By the way, have you seen our two-wheeled monster, our Harley Davidson? Her name is Gracie. Dixie is the truck, Gracie is the motorcycle, and Rosie is my Ford Mondeo estate carpmobile. Gracie is Gracie because she's mean, black, and beautiful, like Grace Jones. Dixie was going to be called Buttercup to start with, but I wasn't having that, so we went for Dixie. Rosie is named after the AC/DC song 'A Whole Lot of Rosie'.

At this point Jim asks Chilly's wife Lynn about their relationship, and how they got together, which is a tale worth the retelling!

Lynn: Well there was the incident when you and he were discovered in your underpants, in some rhododendron bushes, by the military police, whilst fishing a lake on army land which you mentioned earlier, and I wasn't surprised. But that wasn't the strangest incident with the Military Police. The strangest was when they found him unconscious on a milk float with no clothes on. I think it was after a Paratroopers' mess do – the police wanted to know who he belonged to. I said, "He's mine. Would you mind dropping him off?" So they did.

When I met Chilly I was on a girls' night out. Towards the end of the night, there was a huge fight and I spotted this fellow rolling around in the gutter outside a wine bar. So I said to the girls, "Look at that paratrooper, do you reckon he's alright?"

They said: "He's fine, he's fine – come on, let's get out of here."

I went over to him anyway and stepped over him. He looked up and as he did so the girls pulled me away, telling me I didn't want anything to do with him. I knew he was a para straightaway because he was wearing his off-duty 'uniform', which was desert boots, a maroon T-shirt and jeans. So you always knew they were paratroopers. The second time I came across him, he had fallen asleep, face down in his curry and I was worried that he couldn't breathe properly. **Then the third time** was when I saw him thrown out of a pub window. It was then that he really started to interest me – I thought, 'I keep meeting this man...' I don't know who came off worse on that occasion, probably the window.

They weren't serious fights. They were good old punch-ups, that's all. The loser would always buy the other chap a drink afterwards. You'd see them fight and fight and fight, then 10 minutes later the two assailants would stop, the loser would buy a couple of pints and they'd sit down and say things like, "Cor, that was a good old knock; how did you manage to throw that punch?" That's what it was like; it was a good way of relieving stress for the lads after they'd been away on tour or something. The lads were acting in the nature of the beast that the army had created. They wanted them to be like that.

Eventually he asked me out. It was quite funny because he was ever so shy. He said something like: "Well I don't suppose, well... no... er... forget it! Well no, erm..." It was obvious what he was trying to say, so I just finished the sentence for him and asked him if he'd like to ask me out. He went, "Well, yeah, but no, but... well never mind, I thought I'd try anyway." I simply said, "Yes, I'll go out with you." My girlfriends took me aside and told me I really shouldn't go out with him. I told them I would and that I liked him. So that was that!

On that first date he took me to Farnborough's Pit 5, fishing! It was a wonderful, beautiful place – and I just saw the man I wanted to marry. No one had ever seen what he was like when he was fishing, around a lake, excitedly looking for carp and respecting the wildlife. I just saw a completely different person and thought, 'You are not the man everyone thinks you are.' He could name every species of bird we saw, what it did, and I was fascinated. I thought, 'He'll do me nicely.'

He's been a remarkable husband. I don't know any man who, within six weeks of getting married, his wife had to have a double mastectomy and he has supported her unconditionally. I don't know any other man who would bathe his wife, take her to the toilet, do all of those things when she's very ill. He totally looked after me when I was ill and still does. I don't know any other man like that – especially with the reputation he had for fighting. I just knew from that time at Pit 5 that he wasn't the sort of man people thought he was. It started with people saying it wouldn't last five minutes, then people saying it wouldn't last a year, then that the engagement wouldn't last, and finally that the marriage wouldn't last. That was 17 years ago!

Chilly again: The fight Lynn referred to was a draw!! Lynn saw my opponent throw me through a closed window, but it was part of a longer fight that lasted three hours and happened in four pubs. We'd just played rugby and the two teams had gone to the mess afterwards. This guy was in the opposing team. We'd been arguing about

ABOVE
*She was massive:
the magnificent Jack
from Horton caught
on a floater during
the opening session
of the 1996 season.*

something, so he had a swing at me and I had a swing back at him. It's hard for you to understand just what a horrible bloke I was in those days. I really didn't give a f*** about most things. Nothing mattered. There were very good reasons why I was like that, but it's not something I really want to talk about. It's like anything in life – until you find a way to express yourself and let the pressure out, then things you have seen and experienced stay inside you. The bad things cause you to blow up occasionally and that's exactly what happened. I'd get into fights: that's what I would do. I'd get back from wherever the army had sent me, put on my jeans and my desert boots, go out into town and start drinking. I'd get very pissed and start as many fights as possible, because it was always a good hoot. You see, that's the era I lived in – after a few scary trips I probably needed a little help. Things have improved today with the recognition of post-traumatic stress and how to deal with it. But one bad thing these days compared to my time is that they're now sending 18-year-old kids into combat who haven't lived, who don't know enough and haven't been trained or equipped properly. It's the Gameboy era – as soon as you're 18 you can go out to Afghanistan and get shot at, or blown up. A lot of them aren't ready for it – they're so underprepared it's frightening. And it's frightening, too, that we have a Government that will allow kids like this to

PREVIOUS PAGE
*Chilly, photographed
by Tim Paisley
during a session
at Rainbow Lake,
France, back in 2008.*

go and defend the country, yet the country isn't prepared to defend the soldier. I find that horrific.

I believe the cause in Afghanistan is a good one and that we can win the campaign there. The route through Afghanistan into Pakistan is the root of all evil and unless we take control of that, then it's game over, because you have allowed the terrorists access to the world. Afghanistan is the departure lounge for terrorism and unless we crush it, it will always be there. But the Government needs to invest in it. If the commanders on the ground decide we need 27 new helicopters, then you give them 27 new helicopters. If they want to stick a bunker bomb in a cave somewhere, you give them the means to do it. There's no point in having an army and then expect it to bow to political whims. You give it a mission and let it get on with the job.

If it hadn't been for carp fishing and Lynn's illness I would have pursued my army career. The thing is, when Lynn got ill in the mid-1990s, it was the time my military career started grinding to a halt. I couldn't get promoted because of my commitments at home so I couldn't go away as often as I had been doing. Had it not been for Lynn I would have gone for more military options. I probably would have specialised in close-protection work in Iraq or Afghanistan: a lot of people I know in the army are doing that. The thing with Lynn is that she eased my transition into Civvy Street. You can't take the army out of the man and I will always be a military person, but if it hadn't been for her... well, I don't know. I don't like to think about it too much. Maybe I wouldn't even be here now. You just can't tell, can you?

There are things I've seen over my 22 years of service that very few people will ever get to hear about, and I don't know that I will ever write about it. Some things just have to stay personal. If you sell your soul to the devil, it is not very often that you can afford to buy it back. It's a hugely personal thing – I have been offered considerable amounts of money to write about it. But I love what I do now and I don't want to compromise that.

On the other hand, some of my most memorable fishing moments came when I was with the army. I caught a 4lb 8oz wild brown trout in the foothills of Mount Kenya – there was a little river and a tiny weir pool, and I caught him on a small Mepps spinner. I don't think fishing gets much better than that. We used to fish in Belize, too – a couple of lads in the troop were into fishing, so we'd bung a couple of cases of beer in a RHIB (inflatable rigid hulled boat) and shoot off down the Belize River, through the estuary and into the Caribbean. We'd find an island and inevitably there would be a drop-off into deeper water, so we'd either fish from the beach while drinking a few beers or troll along the drop-off catching barracuda and other tropical things. Once we'd caught a few fish we'd barbecue them on the island and get very drunk on Jack Daniels and Red Stripe beer.

We were on this island drinking, snorkelling, fishing, and this yacht pulled up – it was like something out of the Bounty advert. Three dollies dived over the side and swam to the island. They got to the beach and started throwing rocks and stuff into a tree to try to dislodge a coconut. This guy Geoff, decided to monkey up a tree to knock the coconuts out for the girls. He'd drunk half a bottle of JD so wasn't in the best state. Still, he managed to get a couple of coconuts before falling back to earth and busting his leg! I wouldn't let him go to hospital. I said, "You can't go anywhere till we've drunk everything and caught some more fish." I wasn't his superior or anything like that. We weren't serving in an environment where that was important. It was just a small fracture, nothing life-threatening. Mind you, I did get a bollocking for not bringing him back sooner!

In terms of the carp fishing scene I just like people who 'get it', anglers who understand the thrill of the chase. For me, it isn't all about the end result. You find people – some of the guys at Yateley for instance, such as Richard Spencer, Lee Picknall, Little John Coxhead – for them the thrill of the chase is as exciting as the actual capture. Look at Mark Walsingham down at the Ashmead Fishery in Somerset: he's a top angler. He wanted to create a natural fishery in a natural environment. We talk about everything surrounding fishing as well as fishing itself, like the wildlife – there are barn owls, kestrels and buzzards at Ashmead. To me, that's all part of the carp fishing experience and some people can't seem to see that. But if I had to name one person as being the most complete carp angler I have fished with, it would have to be Dave Lane. He can turn his hand to any aspect of carp fishing and be good at it. I've met some incredible anglers over the years.

ECHO came about through my concerns regarding the illegal importation of carp *(Chilly stresses the word 'illegal' strongly here)* because that's what ECHO is primarily concerned about. While we have tried to toughen up the legislation concerning the allowable importation of carp, ECHO is not against the legal importation of carp: an important point to make. So where are we now? Well, answering your question, ECHO has achieved everything we ever set out to do, and a whole lot more. I ran the whole thing practically on my own for five years: it was probably one of the loneliest times of my life, as it was hard to make people understand what we were trying to achieve for the welfare of carp and carp fishing. What we were trying to do was hijacked by the 'Keep it Real' brigade. They said that only fish born in this country are the ones that count, which is ironic, as probably 50-60 per cent of the fish the 'Keep it Real' brigade would consider 'proper' carp were imported into the UK as fingerlings and sometimes a whole lot bigger. One of the most iconic fish that ever lived, Bazil, was brought into the UK as a fingerling. That's where our whole history comes from – the importation of carp into this country.

The people we were fighting, and continue to fight, were bringing in fish from the Continent illegally. They were bringing carp in to try to break records, to increase revenue on their fisheries. The side effect of that was that they were bringing new diseases into the country – and a lot of established UK fish, whether they were brought in as fingerlings or born in the UK, had no defence against these diseases. We're being taken down avenues now where these kinds of people are ripping out the pages of carp-fishing history and wiping their backsides with them just for their own personal greed and to massage their egos. The mystery of carp fishing is being taken away.

My reason for living is the journey that life provides me with. I want that feeling of satisfaction that only comes when you earn something. I totally understand that some anglers are pushed for time, with families, jobs, and so on. I had that for 22 years in the army, where sometimes I couldn't go carp fishing for six months, or even a year. What people want to know is what it's like to catch and hold a big carp. There's a fishery I know in England that is illegally importing big carp from France. I know the person who's supplying that fishery, though I can't name either party here. So we fight it by asking people who want to fish for such fish to spare a thought for the number

BELOW
Chiily with one of his captures of the remarkable, big Ashmead mirror Single Scale of 53lb 12oz.

ABOVE
*A 43lb 6oz mirror
from Wellington
Country Park.*

of carp that have to die in the illegal trade of importation. And there are thousands of carp casualties. To hold a carp caught from a water where it has been illegally stocked, you are condoning the death of thousands of other fish that didn't make it.

As much as it grieves me, I think the vast majority of carp anglers don't give a stuff about all this. I will qualify that statement by saying that, initially, ECHO got to over 2,000 members. But we have, over the past six years, hovered between 600 and 800 members. It only costs £20 for a year's membership, which is absolutely nothing when you take into account what we have achieved. We're looking after carp fishing not only today, but also for the future, so our kids can go carp fishing – and their kids. We all tend to think of carp as being the toughest fish, but they're still a fragile wild animal and unless we look after them there may not be any carp fishing in the future. That doesn't just affect our children, but also the economy, as an entire industry goes down the pan.

Ruth Lockwood ran ECHO for many years. I was the ideal man to start it, as I am not particularly PC (politically correct)! My philosophy is that if you have something to say, say it: if you can't be honest, shut your mouth. I can't be doing with all this purple hair-dyed, tree-hugging sh*t, it doesn't work. I ran ECHO for a while on a very direct basis, and it opened doors at government level. People wanted to listen. Steve Maidment at DEFRA became the best ally I had – and because of him and because I wouldn't shut up, the government listened. Now it needs someone with

Cleveley Mere's Hendrix, at a weight of 44lb, which I caught with my first cast at the venue!

a bit more patience and political tact and Ruth is that person; she's just incredible. I am now the president of ECHO – I get it in the public eye and, through articles and features like this, try to put across precisely what it is we are trying to achieve.

I say this quite unashamedly: ECHO has shown everyone the way forward when it comes to lobbying for angling interests at government level. They will act on what you tell them. DEFRA was totally unaware of what fishing was worth to the UK economy. We provided all that information, which was why they started to listen. It was why environment ministers started to listen to us – and why we were mentioned in the House of Commons. First, we showed the government that we were concerned about the fish and the environment – and second, we showed that there were people prepared to do something about it. I was prepared to 'gob-off' and then we had Ruth Lockwood to take things on from there. ECHO opened the gates and led the way for the formation of the Angling Trust, which hopefully is going to look after angling as a whole. Hopefully, we can all help the Angling Trust represent angling at a political level. Without that representation, God knows what could happen to fishing. I believe that everyone has to realise that the time for single species groups is probably over on the political front. I would even go as far as saying that I would give ECHO a sword to fall on. If the most influential political angling organisation folds and encourages its members and others to follow the Trust, then I would hope it sends out a very important message. You cannot moan about what the Trust is doing if you are not part of it and be prepared to change the things you don't like!!

Talking about Ashmead, as we were earlier, it was the place I chose to carry out the next phase of my carp fishing journey. Having caught Charlie's Mate from Frimley at a weight comparable to Walker's record, the next thing I wanted was a mirror to compare with Yates's 1980 record. This is where Ashmead came into the frame. I had been speaking to Mark Walsingham for a while, he had even offered me a ticket, but I had so many other places to fish at the time, I asked him to give it to someone who would get more out of it. However, the following winter he offered me a half price ticket and in January of 2009 after the worst carp-fishing winter we had experienced in 30 years, I landed Single Scale at 53lb 12oz. It sounds so simple just to put it like that, because the story is incredible. I even amazed myself with what I did to catch that fish. Maybe I will tell the complete story in a book one day. I have to admit, it was hugely difficult to motivate myself after that, and I just couldn't find a special fish to fish for. I have no wish to catch every big fish that is available, because the more you catch, surely the less special they become? To that end I have visited many waters, and in the main I have had a great time. Cleveley Mere was great, so great in fact, that with my first cast I ever made in anger there, I landed my target carp, a mirror of 44lb. Mercers Park was brilliant, and not just on the fishing front, the membership was great and I remember my time there just as much for the company as for the fish. The last time I fished there was for the TV cameras, and unbelievably I landed a brace of 40s for the camera, how cool is that!! I did manage to get a very cheap ticket for Wellington Country Park, and have spent my time since I fished there wishing I had never bothered. Maybe I'll write about that one day too. Now that will be interesting! I think the writing was on the wall from day one really, because I bought the ticket from someone else, and when I got the rule book out, rule number one said that the tickets were not transferable... Go figure eh?

Much of my time these days is taken up with the more commercial side of carp fishing, and as much as I always thought I would hate that, it throws up many unique and interesting challenges. So much so that I really enjoy the time I spend doing all the magazine and product related work that I do. And that surprises me a lot, but not as much as my involvement in carp fishing matches. To qualify that statement, I really should explain. To me carp fishing is about me versus the carp. I have never really had a wish to compete against other anglers. However, in 2003 I was asked to be part of

ABOVE
With the Carpworld team checking out the St. Lawrence prior to the 2011 World Cup.

the Angling Publications team that was fishing the World Championships at Lake Raduta in Romania. All I needed to do was sort out a partner and that was that. In the end I fished the match with Keith Jenkins and I have to say, along with coming in a very good fourth, it was one of the most incredible adventures of my carp fishing life. We did it all over again the following year when we fished the World Carp Classic in France, but that experience was at the other end of the scale. I can only describe it as a pitiful waste of time. Sucker for punishment that I am though, Adam Penning and I fished the World Championships on the St Lawrence River in 2005. Again, it was a biblical experience, we didn't do well because the match was probably held a little too early, but I wouldn't have missed it for all the world. And then five years later I was contacted by Tim Paisley who was fishing with Lee Jackson at Madine in France. Did I want to fish the World Championships again in America the following year? I bit his hand off at the shoulder, but I would have to find a partner. Well that really didn't take too much thinking about because the answer was sitting right next to him. Lee and I would be taking on the world, and as we became more and more excited about the prospect we could never have realised what was just about to happen.

And so it was, courtesy of Angling Publications, Fox, and Mainline, we arrived in Upstate New York. When I look back on it all now it's not just the result but the whole trip that will remain with me forever. The team were all very experienced, and we pooled our collective thoughts and came up with a plan of sorts. The trouble is

you are always at the mercy of the draw bag, and I know that Jacko and I weren't that happy with the swim we ended up in. We knew we would catch and decided that all we could do was get the best from it. We went to work, and apart from a poor start on the first night, Jacko had three fish I had none, we never took our foot off the pedal. By day four we knew we were in the lead and there we stayed. It was the most shattering physical and mental thing I had done since leaving the army, but we had won. I am just so glad that I did it with such a special bloke as Jacko, he really is incredible. So my thanks to him and everyone else that helped in the epic journey. I definitely need to write about that one day too...oh hang on a minute, I am! I have started my third book, and that is where most of my efforts are being directed at the moment. 'Fanning the Flames' is beginning to take shape, I can tell people how much I love my fishing and just as importantly, how much fun it has all been...and I just can't tell you how happy I am about that...

ABOVE
Lee Jackson and I roaring our way to success in the St. Lawrence World Cup. Check out Lee's interview for further coverage of this special occasion.

Carpworld's The Big Interviews Revisited: Volume Two

We are so pleased with the end result of our first Big Interview book that we are already planning Volume Two, which we hope to publish early next year. In the next volume our Features Editor Jerry Bridger is included in the list of interviewers, along with Volume One's Jim Foster and Tim Paisley. As in Volume One we are endeavouring to ensure a good spread of carping lives in Volume Two, which will include reprises of the previously published interviews with the following:
Steve Briggs, Terry Hearn, Frank Warwick, Les Bamford, Max Cottis, Derek Ritchie, Chris Ball, Bruce Ashby, Jerry Hammond, Jason Hayward and Terry Dempsey.

Other books published by Angling Publications

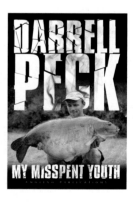